ACTIVE CITIZENSHIP

Active Citizenship

What Could it Achieve and How?

Edited by

Bernard Crick

and

Andrew Lockyer

Edinburgh University Press

© editorial matter and organisation Bernard Crick and Andrew Lockyer, 2010
© the chapters their several authors, 2010

Edinburgh University Press Ltd
22 George Square, Edinburgh
www.euppublishing.com

Typeset in Goudy by
Servis Filmsetting Ltd, Stockport, Cheshire, and
printed and bound in Great Britain by
CPI Antony Rowe, Chippenham and Eastbourne

A CIP record for this book is available from the British Library

ISBN 978 0 7486 3866 6 (hardback)
ISBN 978 0 7486 3867 3 (paperback)

The right of the contributors to be identified as authors of this work has been
asserted in accordance with the Copyright, Designs and Patents Act 1988.

Contents

Contents

Acknowledgements

This publication has seen the light of day only with the support of diverse parties.

Financial assistance came from the Stevenson Citizenship Trust Fund at Glasgow University. The Stevenson Trust Committee are to be thanked for their sustained commitment seeing the project through.

The publication would have been abandoned without the endorsement and encouragement of Bernard Crick's family, Olly and Tom Crick and Una Mclean.

Margaret Murray and Ian Gillan are to be thanked for their sterling work in preparing and checking the text and references.

Edinburgh University Press has been immensely tolerant and understanding. Nicola Ramsey and James Dale, in particular, have afforded help and advice without which the project would not have been completed.

Preface

Party leaders have talked a lot about encouraging both good and active citizenship and about more community and voluntary involvement in the business of good government and a just society. Many academics have written a good deal in recent years (ourselves included) about theories of citizenship, while others produce measures of popular participation (heartening or disheartening according to the base-line of what is counted as involvement). The party debates and proclaimed policies do not always seem clearly connected with actual practice and much or most of the academic debate has not seemed able – or even intended – to reach out beyond seminars and research ratings to a wider public and publicity.

So rather than plunging back into the internal debate we have asked our expert contributors to write relatively short but pointed essays assuming, on top of all that writing and research, that a radically more active citizenship is a worthy aim; but then to speculate and spell out what they each think, in respect to some broad area of concern, could be the social and political consequences of the United Kingdom, as a whole or in its parts, becoming a citizen culture. However, each essay will also indicate how these aims could be achieved, through what institutions, old or new, or through what changing mind-sets or values.

So these are our 'starter's orders' for each of the contributors to consider, no more but no less. We all want to address aims and instrumentalities in terms relevant and readily comprehensible to the intelligent and concerned reader, not specifically the academic or research specialist, although students may like this book for trying speculatively to get to the heart of possible reforms more than their teachers secure in their specialisms. This sense of who we are writing for follows the origins of this book in the Stevenson Lectures on Citizenship for 2006–7 at the University of Glasgow, an evening series specifically aimed at the general public. Not all the original lecturers figure here – lectures are more discursive; new voices and topics have joined us and everything has been rewritten and pointed to this book's title: 'Active citizenship: what could it achieve and how?'

Bernard Crick
Andrew Lockyer

Prolegomenon

The origins and purpose of this book are stated succinctly in its Preface. The need for an introductory prologue might seem superfluous, except for the circumstance that delayed its publication.

Sir Bernard Crick died on 19 December 2008 in St Columba's Hospice, Edinburgh, aged seventy-nine, having lived and worked for over two decades with the knowledge of incurable prostate cancer. The publication of this collection of essays is no more and no less than the fulfilment of an undertaking that Bernard wished to have seen through. It was not the most important academic piece of work that outlived him. (He was working on a political history of the United Kingdom, parts of which may or may not be recoverable from his papers.) However, it has significance beyond the content of the essays in being Bernard Crick's last initiative in an enduring project to advocate for a real improvement in British civic and political life by wholly embracing active and inclusive citizenship into our institutions and culture.

The difficulties for me have been to exert editorial authority without Bernard's clout and to provide an introduction that he would have written, undoubtedly with more insight, style and persuasiveness. It is the harder by this project becoming evidently my inheritance during Bernard's last days: it was something to discuss when there was nothing more to be said about hospice food, ministerial gaffs, the state of Labour, Edinburgh traffic cones, and lesser matters of life and death.

This collection is not to be elevated as a series of essays in honour of Sir Bernard Crick – although most of the contributors were his choice and were influenced by him. There is already such a collection edited by Ian Hampsher-Monk *Defending Politics: Bernard Crick and Pluralism* (1993), which was presented to him at the Oxford Political Thought Conference on his retirement from Birkbeck. Bernard would not have welcomed another *festschrift* – though he graciously tolerated this one. He admitted 'there was some surprisingly good stuff in it': a judgement which his anno-tated copy confirms. (Adrian Oldfield's essay on 'Political Education' gives the best account of Crick's intellectual heritage – a mixture of clas-sical republicanism and moderate socialism.) But as Ian Hampsher-Monk points out, even to do justice only to Bernard's contribution to the study of Politics would require volumes. This leaves aside his contribution to other forms of literature; his role as a commentator on public affairs in all forms of media and his active involvement with agencies responsible for delivering policy on citizenship.

Neither is this a place for another Crick obituary. There are plenty of these – most are informative, some fairer than others. There is good reason to expect, and look forward to, enduring discussion of his work in many forums. Crick was acknowledged in 2000 to be one of the five leading contributors to the study of politics in the second half of the twentieth century by the Political Studies Association, the professional body of uni-versity politics teachers. If the reader wants a short assessment of Bernard Crick's place as a public academic, read Richard Hoggart's brief but acute Foreword to *Political Thoughts and Polemics*, a collection of Crick's essays published by EUP in 1990 – 'a cousin in spirit of Orwell'. But better to read the man himself.

The background to these essays does merit some amplification. As men-tioned in the Preface they derive, directly or indirectly, from Bernard's last part-time academic appointment as Stevenson Professor of Citizenship at Glasgow University from 2006–7. The main responsibility of this appoint-ment was to take charge of the programme of public lectures on 'Active Citizenship'; this he did by giving the first and last lectures, choosing and chairing the speakers in between.

Crick's approach to this appointment reflected his wholehearted endorse-ment of the rationale of the Stevenson Citizenship Trust Fund. It was set up in 1921 by a bequest from Sir Daniel Macaulay Stevenson (1851–1944) a Glasgow-born engineer, liberal politician and philanthropist who was both Lord Provost and Chancellor of the University. He was first a municipal socialist, committed to improving the horizons of Glaswegians by various means of public education (including the Sunday opening of museums and art galleries); and second, after the Great War, a proponent of international understanding and co-operation, whence he became a benefactor of the university, funding Language chairs and the lectureship in Citizenship. His brief for the Citizenship Trust Fund was as follows:

> to make provision in Glasgow for instruction in the rights, duties, and obliga-tions of citizens in relation to the city, the state, and the commonwealth of nations; and promote study, inquiry and research in subjects bearing on local

government, national polity, and international community; and thereby to emphasize the compatibility of civic or local with national patriotism, and of both with full and free international co-operation.

The first appointee to the part-time post was W. H. Hadow (as Derek Heater notes in his essay in this collection). Hadow like Crick was a Sheffield Professor who promoted 'citizenship' in the school curriculum. Sheffield and Glasgow share similar civic socialist traditions. For a period prior to Bernard's appointment there had been an implicit acceptance that the public lecture had become a lesser instrument of civic education, so the Stevenson Trust Fund had been put to diverse uses to promote citizenship education; most recently to help fund a post in the Education Faculty to develop a Global Citizenship Unit, providing school teachers with a resource – clearly in the spirit of Stevenson, but departing from the format of direct public lectures.

The Stevenson Trust Committee decided to return to Stevenson's original idea of public lectures. In Sir Bernard Crick they found the leading proponent of citizenship education in the UK to be a ready advocate for Stevenson's vision. Crick had an abiding belief that universities ought to do more to bring town and gown together. He took on the task to revive the public lectures with typical commitment (and willingness to tread on corporate toes) – 'you need inspiring speakers and better publicity'. The Stevenson Trust Committee are still working on the paradigm to the standard he set – it should be said with considerable success. (The Lectures from 2007–8 onwards are available to download on the Stevenson Trust website: www.gla.ac.uk/departments/stevensontrustforcitizenship.)

The essays that follow are somewhat less uniform in approach than was anticipated. The diversity in style in part reflects the diverse background of the contributors: they are a mixture of academic political actors and politician academics. Most of the essays significantly departed from the original lectures, and in many cases are newly commissioned. Where this is not the case, as with Crick's lectures I have not sought to edit them, or add references where they are lacking. Rather I have invited academic colleagues to modify their normal standards of scholarly notation in the interests of speaking directly to the public (following Bernard's injunction to excise unnecessary textual notes).

My approach in the following Introduction is to give occasional contextual information and briefly summarise what the essays contribute to the subject in the title of the book. Bernard would have wanted to comment more on what others have said; I have not sought to do this. Some authors acknowledge and draw on their engagement with Crick's work; sometimes

I have explained the connections. Generally, the Introduction is to provide readers with an indication of what to expect from each chapter, not provide an essay which links them.

Andrew Lockyer
November 2009

Contributors

Bernard Crick was Professor Emeritus of Politics, Birkbeck College; Honorary Fellow in Politics, University of Edinburgh; and Stevenson Professor of Citizenship, University of Glasgow (2006–7). He was former adviser on citizenship education to the Department for Education and Skills (DfES) and on citizenship and integration to the Home Office. His publications included: *In Defence of Politics* (1962, 5th edn 2000); *The Reform of Parliament* (1968); *George Orwell: a Life* (1980); *Political Thoughts and Polemics* (1990); *Socialism* (1987); *Essays on Citizenship* (2000); *Democracy: a Very Short Book* (2002); and (with D. Millar) *To Make the Parliament of Scotland a Model for Democracy* (1991).

Andrew Lockyer is Professor of Citizenship and Social Theory in the Department of Politics at Glasgow University and holder of the St Kentigern Chair. He has served as a panel member and Regional chair in the Scottish Children's Hearings System and been a government adviser on child-care law and consultant on children's rights. He has written and researched on the history of political thought, juvenile justice, citizenship and children's issues. His publications include: (with F. Stone) *Juvenile Justice in Scotland: 25 Years of the Welfare Approach* (1998) and (with M. Hill and F. Stone, eds) *Youth Justice and Child Protection* (2006).

John Annette is Professor of Citizenship and Lifelong Learning, Dean of the Faculty of Lifelong Learning and Pro-Vice-Master for Widening Participation and Community Partnerships at Birkbeck College, University of London. He is Chair of the International Centre for Education for Democratic Citizenship; is an advisor to the Department of Children, Families and Schools and has worked in partnership with local communities in London facilitating capacity building for many years. He has researched and written widely on deliberative democracy, active citizenship, community involvement and lifelong learning. His publications include: (with B. Crick and A. Lockyer, eds) *Education for Democratic Citizenship: Issues of Theory and Practice* (2003).

David Blunkett has been the Labour Member of Parliament for Sheffield Brightside since 1987. He held ministerial office in the Blair government, first as Secretary of State for Education and Employment (1997–2001) then as Home Secretary (2001–4) and later Secretary of State for Work and Pensions. He was leader of Sheffield City Council and has a BA from Sheffield University where he studied under Professor Crick. He has lectured on politics and industrial relations and written on local government and education. After leaving the Front Bench he continued to inform government policy on social issues, citizenship and the voluntary sector.

David Donnison is Senior Honorary Research Fellow and emeritus Professor in Urban Studies, University of Glasgow; he was formerly Professor of Social Administration at the LSE (1961–80) and thereafter Professor of Town and Regional Planning at Glasgow University. He was chair of the Supplementary Benefits Commission (1975–80). His publications include: *The Politics of Poverty* (1982); *Policies for a Just Society* (1998); *Towards a More Equal Society* (2001); and most recently *Speaking to Power: Advocacy for Health and Social Care* (2009).

Rona Fitzgerald is director of Fitzgerald Associates Equality and Policy Specialist Consultants. She is a graduate of University College Dublin and a Research Fellow at the European Policies Research Centre at the University of Strathclyde. She has worked for the Equality and Human Rights Commission in Scotland, and has conducted impact assessments, or provided guidance or training programmes on gender and equality for a range governments, NGOs and community organisations: these include NHS Boards, Oxfam, the Welsh Assembly, and the Irish and Basque governments. Her publications are on Ireland and the EU on gender and equality policies.

Kevin Francis is the Stevenson Fellow in Citizenship and has a joint appointment in Politics and Adult and Continuing Education at the University of Glasgow, where he is co-ordinator for programmes in Arts and Social Science, Law, Business and Accountancy. He graduated in Politics and Philosophy as a mature student. His PhD is on Democracy, Citizenship and Utopia where his teaching and research interests continue to lie. He has also taught at Strathclyde University. As Stevenson

Fellow he organises the annual programmes of high profile Public Lectures on Citizenship.

Derek Heater is a retired teacher and author. He has taught history at school, college and undergraduate level. He was a founder member of the Politics Association and has published extensively on citizenship, politics, international affairs and history. His publications include: *What is Citizenship?* (1999); *World Citizenship: Cosmopolitanism and its Opponents* (2002); *A History of Education for Citizenship* (2004); *Citizenship in Britain: a History* (2006) and (with Bernard Crick) *Essays on Political Education* (1977).

Dina Kiwan is an Academic Fellow and Senior Lecturer in Citizenship Education at Birkbeck College, University of London. She was appointed in 2002 as a member of the Home Office 'Life in the UK' Advisory Group and was Head of Secretariat to the Advisory Board for Naturalisation and Integration (ABNI). She was co-author of the Diversity and Citizenship Curriculum Review in 2007, and was a member of the Lord Goldsmith Review of Citizenship. She is author of *Education for Inclusive Citizenship* (2008).

Elizabeth Meehan is emeritus Professor in the School of Law at Queen's University Belfast where she was formerly Professor of Politics and the Director of the Institute of Governance and Social Policy. She is an elected member of the Royal Society of Arts (RSA), the UK Academy of Social Science and the Royal Irish Academy; she has received numerous academic awards and honours for her contribution to the study of Politics and European Studies, including being made life Vice-president of the Political Studies Association. Her research and publications are on women and politics; European citizenship; citizenship and participation in the UK; constitutional change in the UK; and British–Irish relations. She was also a member of the Home Office Advisory Board on Naturalisation and Integration (ABNI).

Pamela Munn is emeritus Professor of Education at the University of Edinburgh, having been Professor of Curriculum Research at Murray House Institute of Education since 1994. She chaired the committee responsible for introducing Citizenship Education in Scotland and the Advisor Group on the Implementation Programme. She was a member of many national committees and conducted extensive research on schools, most recently making proposals for improving student discipline and teacher education. She was awarded an OBE for services to education in Scotland in 2005.

George Reid is currently Honorary Professor of Law at the University of Glasgow and was the Stevenson Professor in Citizenship (2007–8). He was the second Presiding Officer of the Scottish Parliament, served eight years as an MSP and was a member of the Consultative Steering Group that set up the Parliament. From 1974 to 1979 he was the SNP Member of Parliament for Clackmannan and East Stirling, and was Director of Public Affairs for the International Federation of Red Cross and Red Crescent Societies for twelve years. Since demitting political office he has had numerous public appointments, including acting as a diplomatic commissioner and international constitutional advisor.

Matthew Taylor is the Chief Executive of the RSA. He has been extensively involved in the development of Labour Party policy and strategy. He was Assistant General Secretary of the Labour Party and Director of Policy during the 1997 General Election and Director of the Institute for Public Policy Research between 1999 and 2003. He has been a county councillor, university research fellow and director of a unit monitoring health-service policy. He has written for *Political Quarterly* and contributed to a collection on *Citizenship and Civic Culture* (2001)

Introduction

Andrew Lockyer

The first essay in the collection is actually Bernard Crick's first lecture in the 2006–7 Stevenson Lecture Series. It sets the agenda for the book.

1. CIVIC REPUBLICANISM AND CITIZENSHIP: THE CHALLENGE FOR TODAY

Crick presents a conceptual history of the civic republican tradition of thinking about citizenship and identifies within this lineage, as an alternative history of citizenship theory to the dominant liberal tradition, a corrective to what he sees as the overly individualistic, litigious and inactive nature of contemporary political life.

Crick evokes Benjamin Constant's 1820 work *The Liberty of the Ancients Compared to that of the Moderns* to highlight the contrast between the classical aim of sharing 'social power among citizens of the same fatherland' with the modern preference for the 'enjoyment of liberty in private pleasures' where 'the guarantees accorded by institutions to these pleasures' are called liberty (specifically negative liberty, to adopt Isaiah Berlin's more recent formulation). Active citizenship, Crick argues, is a learned skill that must be practiced among the groups of civil society in order for people to combine together to effectively create or resist change. This vision is contrasted with the thinner liberal conception of 'good' citizenship, which consists in obeying the law, being a good neighbour and generally relegating the good life to the private sphere.

'Is change possible or are we too far down the road to unsocial individualism and the values of a consumer society?' Crick asks. The required response he suggests is a change in the political culture 'towards far greater active participation'. This of course is the aspiration embedded in the two Crick Reports, discussed in several of the essays.

A requirement of greater citizenship participation is the dispersal of

1

power from central institutions, not just from Westminster to devolved assemblies, but from 'stifling central bureaucracy' to civil society, and within political parties from leaders to membership. Crick notes the declared willingness of political leaders to accept this, but he identifies an obstacle to devolution in what he calls the 'post-code lottery' argument – much favoured in the popular press. If there is to be genuinely local decision-making, communities will have different priorities and capacities, therefore there will be differences in the provision of even universal services. Crick thinks this is a price of local democracy worth paying.

The essays that follow address, directly and indirectly, the issues that Crick identifies either in his writing, or in his public works; they answer, or attempt to answer, what needs to be done, and what difference will more active citizenship make?

One of the formative influences on Bernard Crick throughout his adult life was his commitment to the British Labour Party. Like many party members he hoped and despaired for it; for the most part contributing to internal policy debates and publically criticising its leadership, as academic needs must. When the Right Honourable David Blunkett MP, a former Sheffield student, came to hold ministerial office in Blair's government, first as Education Secretary (1997–2001) and then as Home Secretary (2001–4), Crick was given the blessed opportunity to influence policy on active citizenship, with the endorsement of Blunkett and the Labour government. Crick was invited by Blunkett as Education Secretary to chair the committee which proposed introducing citizenship as a compulsory element in schools' curriculum – the Report of the Advisory Group on *Citizenship Education for Citizenship and the Teaching of Democracy in Schools* September 1998 (discussed in essays by Munn and Kiwan). Then again by Blunkett as Home Secretary to chair the *New and the Old* (2004) group proposing measures to encourage permanent residents to become UK citizens, with the English for speakers of other languages (ESOL) course, Test and Ceremony, and further chairing the Advisory Board on Naturalisation and Integration (ABNI) overseeing policy implementation (see essays by Meehan and Kiwan).

2. Active citizenship and Labour

The essay by David Blunkett and Matthew Taylor was commissioned to access the current thinking within the party of government at Westminster. They do not (of course) officially speak for government or Labour here, but rather address both party and country. The essay places Labour's citizenship policy in both its historical setting and the context of the reform of the public services embarked upon by the Labour government. The authors associate the collapse in levels of trust in politicians (encouraged by the press), which reached its nadir with the MP expenses scandal of 2009, together with the financial crisis, with the failings of 'consumer democracy'. This can only be reversed by 'a new way of doing politics'. What they call the 'hierarchical, antagonistic, propagandist nature of party politics' must be replaced by 'a more honest, more engaging, more transformative politics (in order to make possible) a truly empowering and collaborative welfare state.'

As they acknowledge, much of their policy thinking is an endorsement of Crick – 'Democracy cannot survive and society cannot be sustained without civil and civic engagement.' Active citizenship is not merely a policy option, it is 'an essential part of revival and the glue which holds society together'. They go beyond the Crickian mantra in thinking through what the new politics of collaboration between citizen and government might require in policy terms. Building communities with 'collective capacities and resilience' requires civic engagement strategies to mobilise and empower citizens to 'co-produce' public services; to share in their design and delivery; to have meaningful local decision-making on the use of the public purse, requiring flexibility and audit.

Their final message addresses the implication of this for party politics. A different role for opposition in the new way of doing politics is acknowledged. (It would be ungenerous to suggest they currently have an enhanced interest in the role of opposition parties; and it asks too much free-thought to bring the first-past-the-post electoral system to the table.) Blunkett and Taylor recognise that presently 'the Party' reinforces a mode of hierarchical politics; its focus is on winning elections rather than acting to contribute to civic capacity; or offering a forum for local debate; or engagement in working with community groups. Although their concluding remarks are directed to Labour, whose heritage has its roots in politics from below, their proposals and strictures are relevant to all parties.

3. The fourth principle: sharing power with the people of Scotland

The third essay reproduces the lecture given by George Reid at the point of his demitting office (November 2006) as Presiding Officer of the Scottish Parliament. He reflects upon what the Parliament has achieved in its first two terms, and what remains to be done to fulfil the aspiration of those who set it up – 'the Scottish Parliament should embody and reflect the sharing of power between the people of Scotland, the legislators and the Scottish Executive.' He claims that in the eight years of devolution Holyrood had delivered well on three of its principles – accessibility, accountability and equal opportunities – but achieving the fourth principle, sharing power between government, people and Parliament, 'has proved elusive'. Although George Reid addresses the possibilities of devolved institutions in Scotland, in contrast to Westminster, he like Blunkett and Taylor advocates 'a new way of doing politics . . . more participative, more creative, less needlessly confrontational'. Devolved government, with a more representative electoral system, is a partial answer to the democratic deficit, what remains to be done is to give more control to Parliament and people.

It is decidedly a politician's perspective to view 'trust and turnout' as the key indicators of an engaged citizenry. Reid speaks of encouraging citizens 'to participate in the policy making process' and of 'negotiated governance'. Evidence of the latter is found in the extensive use of government consultations and of the system of petitions. While there may be doubts about the former being effective participation (they may only be cosmetic), the impact of public petitions, through the petitions committee, he rightly heralds as one of Holyrood's most successful instruments of devolution. There are some concrete proposals to make government more responsive to Parliament and MSPs more answerable to their local electors. He urges revisiting the rejected proposals in Crick and Millar's draft standing orders *To Make the Parliament of Scotland a Model for Democracy*, which empower citizens (with the support of sufficient signatories) to require ministerial responses and debates on issues, and for referenda to be precipitated with sufficient support of Members.

Reid looks to the possibility of the 2007 May election producing a minority government or a coalition. He was necessarily constrained from expressing a view as to whether it would make a difference as to what party had the largest share of the vote. It has to be said that our experience of coalition and minority government in Scotland does not appear to have made party politics much less confrontational. Even if there is more consensual work in committees, the 'turnoff' factor associated with party contestation seems no less a feature of Holyrood than Westminster.

It remains an open question as to whether Scottish independence would make a difference to active citizenship. (This is conjectured upon by Kevin Francis in a later essay in this collection.) The brief of the Scottish Parliament's Presiding Officer was necessarily the furtherance of devolution. Dispersing power from the centre requires not only Holyrood acquiring powers from Westminster, but power being devolved within Scotland to local government and further to neighbourhood communities, and thence to whatever organisations in civil society provides a medium or platform for engaging citizens.

4. POWER AND PUBLIC SERVICES: FOR CUSTOMERS OR CITIZENS?

In this essay David Donnison explores the changing balance of power since the Second World War between elites and citizens in respect, particularly, of the health professions. A contemporary of Crick, Donnison offers a personal account of the decline of deference in British society before echoing a point raised in the essay with which Crick opens this volume: an excessive focus on individualistic, market-orientated values (which Crick associates with passive liberal citizenship) undermines the ethos of public services. Donnison explains how the introduction of market values, including both the profit motive and the concept of consumer choice, into the provision of public services reinforces inequality; the 'inverse care law' operates – meaning the poorest and sickest get the least good service because they are least able to agitate for their rights. This applies to services beyond health.

The provision of independent advocacy as introduced by Scottish Mental Health legislation is a particular help to protect the vulnerable against professional discretion and neglect, but individual advocacy cannot be a general solution to making public-service professions 'more effective, more accountable and more humane'. Consultation with users is of limited value, but concerted collective action by those with direct experience of services, *acting as citizens rather than as customers* offers the potential for revitalising our public services. Notably, Donnison includes public-sector professionals among these collective agitators, arguing that such actors must locate their expertise within the context of the diffuse expertise of the citizenry as a whole. He suggests that this holds out the promise of creating a new ethos where professions work alongside volunteers in the delivery of services, sometimes offering their services as good citizens.

With the failings of the market economy having an increasing impact on the availability of private provision and the funding of public services, this prospective partnership between professionals and citizenry may be increasingly necessary.

5. ACTIVE CITIZENSHIP: GENDER EQUALITY AND DEMOCRACY

In this essay Rona Fitzgerald starts from the observation that the concept of citizenship embedded in the classical republican tradition, upon which Bernard Crick's ideas of the active citizen draws, is inherently 'gender biased'. It presupposes the superiority of a public sphere that is dependent on support from the domestic sphere; the former having been (and continues to be) dominated by men and grounded on a masculine conception of virtue, while the latter is largely the preserve of women and predominantly concerned with providing care. What is needed is a concept of active citizenship fit for 'a more sophisticated polity of the twenty-first century' which is gender sensitive.

Fitzgerald explores Ruth Lister's argument that citizenship should be 're-gendered' to account for the various experiences of all citizens in the political community, not just male heads of households as has been the traditional model. She endorses the idea of 'gender pluralism' which both includes the concept of equal treatment, and also recognises the different virtues, experience and possible choices of women and men.

The author raises two points of particular importance to a re-gendered democratic theory: firstly, interests must be represented in the public sphere and as such women must be present in public life to give voice to their experience and defend their rights and identities; and secondly, account must be taken of the social significance of the caring roles, that they might be borne more equitably, and seen to be central to the obligations of active citizenship. Fitzgerald argues that Gender Budget Analysis represents a possible means of establishing the differential impacts of public expenditure on women and men and the value of care within society.

As well as drawing on feminist theory, Fitzgerald discusses the legislative requirements to promote gender equality, and draws on a substantial survey of the attitudes of Girl Guides, which reflect young females' perceptions about citizenship. They are ill informed about politics and view 'citizenship' as an alien term, but they are heavily involved in community volunteering. Fitzgerald observes that what is needed is for this commitment to serve others to be seen as an aspect of active citizenship and for the connection to be made between issues of concern to young people and political action.

The case made here comports with arguments in other essays to challenge the sharp separation of public and private spheres. Most immediately it makes the case for learning by voluntary service, and reflection upon it (see Annette's essay) to be an essential element in citizenship education.

6. What can active citizenship achieve for schools and through schools?

Pamela Munn chaired the Advisory Committee on Education for Citizenship, which applied the Crick Report to Scotland. In her essay she reflects on the progress made to date in achieving the Crick Committee aims, the barriers to their achievement and the potential benefits that might flow from citizenship education becoming embedded in schools across the UK. She does not dwell on the difference across the UK in the way citizenship appears in the curriculum: in Scotland it is an unexamined cross-curricula subject; elsewhere at secondary level it is a discrete and examinable subject.

She analyses how citizenship might appear in the different guises of the curriculum. The ethos of the school, reflected in its relationships and values (the hidden curriculum) and activities beyond the classroom (the informal curriculum), is as important as the formal curriculum, where teaching and learning about citizenship is concerned. Actively involving young people in decisions about the school and classroom life develops skills and knowledge which promotes active citizenship. Research suggests that schools' councils will promote a genuinely participatory ethos only if they give pupils a voice on matters of importance to the school.

The school and staff benefit, as well as the pupils, if the school management is genuinely open and consultative. Munn notes that 'citizenship education based on a learner-centred approach, consulting pupils about how they learn and what would improve their learning is likely to make classrooms more enjoyable, purposeful and stimulating for both pupils and teachers', which acknowledges that it is not just pupils who can feel disempowered in school. Munn suggests that Scotland might be somewhat better placed than England and Wales to implement political literacy in the curriculum (compare the studies of Kerr and the HMIe report *Improving Scottish Education*), because the former have a tradition of teaching Modern Studies to build upon, but the HMIe report concedes that 'systematic curriculum' planning to prepare pupils 'to participate in significant decisions at school is not yet common'.

The barriers to the incomplete implementation of the citizenship education agenda across the UK are common and considerable. They include the citizenship programme having to compete for time with other curriculum innovations; the difficulties of narrating progress and justifying emphasis on citizenship in the present attainment-based accounting context; the need for training to increase the confidence of teachers teaching controversial issues; increasing segregation of schools which detracts from their social inclusiveness; and the cultural challenge posed to teachers and pupils alike by learner-centred pedagogies. However, Munn argues that, by facing these challenges we can furnish young people with an education for citizenship that makes their schooling more relevant and enjoyable, inculcates habits of participation that endure into adulthood, and helps redefine young people as contributive '*citizens now*, with rights, responsibilities and views on subjects worth hearing.'

7. ACTIVE CITIZENSHIP, MULTICULTURALISM AND MUTUAL UNDERSTANDING

Dina Kiwan was a member of the 'Life in the UK' Advisory Group and its successor body the Advisory Board for Naturalisation and Integration (ABNI). Her work draws on her direct involvement with policy formation and implementation of citizenship policy in relation to multiculturalism. She examines the meaning of multiculturalism and its bearing on the two related areas of citizenship policy which were initiated by the two Crick reports: citizenship education in schools and naturalisation policy.

Kiwan's essay debates the idea of political citizenship outlined in the Crick Report from a multicultural standpoint. She maintains that the 'glue' that holds together the three strands of citizenship education – political literacy, social and moral responsibility and community involvement – is public participation based on appropriate learned knowledge and skills. Her concern is that this vision neglects the issue of motivation: what compels or encourages citizens to participate? She argues that participation requires citizens not simply to be secure in their personal identities but for these to be related to, and reflected in, the larger community.

Kiwan was party to the successful proposal that 'identity and diversity: living together in the UK' be added as a fourth strand to the 'key concepts' in the citizenship curriculum alongside 'democracy and justice', 'rights and responsibilities' and 'critical thinking'. This links with naturalisation policy which requires this to be part of the knowledge required for those seeking to become UK citizens. Kiwan views 'understanding' and 'taking a pride in' diversity as 'operationalising' the values of multiculturalism. She challenges the assumption (as it is in France) that ethnic and religious identities are only recognised in the private sphere. They should be part of what animates community cohesion and the commitment to the shared values of participatory citizenship.

8. ACTIVE CITIZENSHIP: FOR INTEGRATING THE IMMIGRANTS

Elizabeth Meehan was also a member of ABNI, bringing to it a breadth of public-service experience and academic scholarship, including in Northern Ireland and the European Union; she was also one of the Stevenson lecturers.

Meehan starts by acknowledging the precariousness of policy in the area of immigration and naturalisation. It was the intention of Blunkett and Crick to encourage those with a permanent right to stay in the UK to become 'fully citizens', not just with citizen entitlements, enabled to share in community and public life. Acquiring a 'sense of belonging' which integrates 'New and Old' is a requisite for participatory citizenship. However, it appears that there has been a significant shift from the policy of 'encouraging and enabling' to the notion that citizenship must be 'earned'. This can be associated with increasing suspicion of incomers, concern about levels of immigration, and the need for secure borders.

Meehan traces the development of language and cultural knowledge tests as a precondition for the granting of citizenship in the UK, and the provision of educational opportunities for would-be citizens to reach the threshold levels needed by the tests. Meehan notes that Crick's committee originally advocated experiential citizenship learning opportunities as a valuable step towards becoming an active citizen. They recommended offering would-be citizens with good-enough language skills the option of developing a portfolio of civic learning rather than undertaking a tick-box examination, in order to promote the ethos of active citizenship. The ceremonies were introduced to 'raise the status of becoming a British citizen' – they were not intended as an additional hurdle.

The shift in ethos to 'earned citizenship' including a probationary period where access to benefits is limited, and serving on a community body is seen as a compulsory requirement, apparently coincides with the UK Borders Agency replacing ABNI (in 2008) as the agency advising on citizenship. Meehan suggests the original reforms of the Crick committee are 'now fragile'. If she and others are right to see the direction of policy on new citizenship encouraging conformity, triggered by 'the politics of unease', it is hard to see this as promoting the form of politically active citizenship that Crick had in mind. The way forward may be rekindling the Crick–Blunkett approach to 'security' which is to extend British values of inclusion, integration and cohesion through active and critical engagement in civic and community life to would-be and existing citizens.

9. Democratic citizenship and lifelong active learning

John Annette here reflects on the plurality of opportunities presently being developed in the UK and elsewhere in the world for deliberative democratic participation of citizens to revitalise local communities. He points to the limitations of the theory of social capital which views community volunteering as the model for promoting civic renewal, without recognising the importance of the political aspect of civic engagement. This echoes Crick's concern that 'community involvement' in the schools' curriculum is too readily seen as 'doing good' by voluntary service, without contributing to student's political literacy and democratic participation.

Annette assesses New Labour's social policies on neighbourhood renewal and civic engagement (promoted by David Blunkett and supported by Hazel Blears) in terms of creating a new relationship between state and civil society, replacing government by governance. This he says looks to a new democratic politics which might include 'referendums, consultative activities, and deliberative participation'. This policy thinking gives local authorities a 'duty to involve' local communities in the planning and delivery of local services (as David Blunkett and Matthew Taylor have intimated in their essay).

Annette focuses on a particular initiative in adult learning introduced by the UK Home Office's Civil Renewal Unit, namely the Active Learning for Active Citizenship (ALAC) programme. It provides a community-based 'learning framework' which recognises difference while enabling 'a shared political identity of citizenship'. Annette finds that citizens must be supported to develop the civic skills to enable their deliberative contributions, including both 'civic speaking' and 'civic listening' to be part of active learning. Learners must be encouraged to reflect politically and critically on their experience of citizenship; the building of civic capacity must include the capacity for citizens to participate in deliberative decision-making.

John Annette's account of government thinking on participation and partnership in community regeneration is much more positive than Meehan's assessment of the direction of policy in relation to new citizens. Yet both see experiential learning as a means to advance the programme of active citizenship. More fundamentally, since many of our urban neighbourhoods are characteristically multicultural – most likely to be a mixture of established (often predominantly disadvantaged), old and new citizens and temporary residents – the need for effective policies of inclusion and empowerment in these locales suggests the need for more joined-up policies.

10. ACTIVE CITIZENSHIP FOR EUROPE AND INTERNATIONAL UNDERSTANDING

Derek Heater considers the role of active citizenship in European and international contexts. He acknowledges the predisposition to regard the city or nation state as the primary sphere of citizen's rights and responsibilities, but identifies a long-standing tradition of thinking about cosmopolitan citizenship going back to the Stoics and Romans. He notes that W. H. Hadow, the first Stevenson lecturer in 1923, conceived of citizenship with a multiplicity of identities, defining it 'as the right ordering of our several loyalties'. The commitment to transnational matters ought not to be deleterious to a citizen's other responsibilities. But active citizenship requires institutions through which to act. He asks are national institutions alone sufficient for this purpose, or is it necessary for active European or world citizens to have effective supranational institutions? He suggests the latter.

Heater outlines the existing opportunities for citizen engagement at European Union level and through international organisations and argues that these need to be widened and democratised considerably. He explains why transnational active citizenship has been weak in Britain both in terms of party policies and the deficiency of information on international matters in the popular press. However, he takes an 'idealist' perspective: the 'political illiteracy of the multitude' on European and international affairs is not irremediable.

Heater suggests that the present low levels of significance placed by the British public on global affairs can be improved in a variety of ways. A key element must be to make transnational and supranational institutions more responsive and democratic.

These include making the UK Parliament give more attention and scrutiny to matters emanating from Brussels; MEPs and MPs being more responsive to the need for reform of European institutions; advocating for a United Nations Parliamentary Assembly; and utilising the 'clout' possessed by celebrities to animate issues of global concern (particularly the climate crisis).

In conclusion, Heater suggests the best hope for changing the perspective and horizons of British citizens to make them more active as international citizens lies with two factors discussed more fully in other essays. Firstly, the education for citizenship programme in schools is where global issues (e.g. climate change, sustainability, world poverty and others) are part of the curriculum which readily engages young people. Secondly, it may make a difference that more UK citizens and residents increasingly have their country of origin or family loyalties outside the UK – or their neighbours do. This may mean the disposition of both young and new citizens to be internationally aware and active is greater than for earlier generations (outside the ruling elites). Although Derek Heater only hints at it, the use of the Internet, which has massively added to the availability of worldwide information, might also provide a means to facilitate forms of collective international action.

11. YOUNG PEOPLE AS ACTIVE POLITICAL CITIZENS

This essay looks at the making of young people into active citizens. It begins from the characterisation of 'children' as future citizens, citizens now, or citizens in-the-making. I argue that the UN Convention on the Rights of the Child presupposes children to be citizens in-the-making by granting rights to participate in political activity while denying them equal political rights.

The concept of political literacy that is entailed in the Crick Report, and supported in Crick's other writings, requires the practice of citizenship by children and young people before they have reached the age threshold at which they are in receipt of the full range of adult citizen rights. As such they may be considered to be 'citizens being-made-active' and their rights and responsibilities are part of liberal education. Their particular entitlement as children is to be treated with respect to their 'evolving capacities', which is required to fulfil their potential to be active citizens.

The argument is that 'wherever there is room for disagreement about ends, argument and compromise' there is space for political literacy; this entails respect for liberal procedural values and amounts to the exercise of political power. The argument is that this conception of political activity transcends the divide between the public and private spheres. Crucially, young people may experience politics and practice citizenship at school, and this will impact on, and be influenced by, family life. It is not necessary for institutions (schools and families) to be wholly democratic. It is sufficient, I argue, for the development of political literacy for these institutions to become non-autocratic.

There is a case for lowering the voting age to sixteen; it may encourage and promote young people to become politically active and engaged citizens. But this will lower the age at which distinctly children's rights (which recognise their immaturity and vulnerability) are replaced by adult rights and responsibilities, which will entail losses as well as gains. The idea of those below the voting age being citizens in-the-making places obligations on others to assist them to develop their civic capacities.

12. ACTIVE CITIZENSHIP AND SHARING POWER IN SCOTLAND: THE NEED TO GO BEYOND DEVOLUTION

The essay by Kevin Francis may be considered a deal more speculative than the other contributions since it proceeds from the perspective of democratic theory. But the author's opening claim is that the prospect of Scottish independence provides a realistic opportunity for radical political innovation. He insists his proposals are more than a thought experiment, as technological developments of the twenty-first century make possible new institutional arrangements which invest citizens with real power.

George Reid's analysis of the successes and shortcomings of the first two terms of the devolved Parliament in Scotland is endorsed and found to have continued to apply in the third period of Scottish government. Thus the hoped-for levels of civic engagement, delivering the fourth principle of sharing power with the people, have not been achieved. The author invites us to take Scottish independence to be a likely outcome in the not-too-distant future. In these circumstances, Crick and Millar's aspiration for Scotland to offer 'a new model for democracy' is realisable only by going some way beyond parliamentary devolution.

Francis pursues the ideas of popular sovereignty and democratic participation found in the writings of John Stuart Mill and developed by modern theorists of deliberative democracy. Mill's conception of the 'active, self-helping character' who must also be an informed and responsible voter, exercising a judgement in voting that he or she is willing and able to justify, provides the model for the citizen juror favoured by proponents of deliberative democracy. Yet where Mill concedes that participation in national decision-making must be through elected elites, and deliberative citizen juries are generally only consultative, Francis proposes a form of direct political decision-making by citizens akin to that derived from classical Athenian democracy. He suggests various ways in which bills, after parliamentary deliberation and vote, might be put to randomly selected juries of 10,000 or 20,000 for 'popular assent' or rejection. The central idea is that when citizens act as jurors they are trusted to exercise real power on behalf of their fellow citizens; arguably they act above and beyond sectional, party or local interests. In this role civic duty carries a collective responsibility which transcends partiality and particular identity.

There are doubtless utopian elements in this essay. However, it is sufficiently grounded in the history of democratic thought and experience, and it sufficiently addresses modern practicalities, not to be dismissed as simply utopian. There is what the author calls a 'hard edge' that could spark some radical thinking about instrumentalities for active political citizenship in conditions where democratic institutional innovation is likely or possible. The proposals need not be reserved for the likely, or not, advent of an independent democratic Scotland.

13. IDENTITY POLITICS: MULTICULTURALISM, BRITISHNESS AND EUROPE

This is the text of Bernard Crick's final lecture in the 2006–7 Stevenson Lecture Series. It appears here as an addendum, or final note, since it was not rewritten to address the subject of the book, as had been intended. Its inclusion is of interest not only because it outlines some of the themes of his unfinished work on the four nations of the United Kingdom; it indicates how he conceived nationality and Britishness and it gives some hints about his own multi-layered identity.

The substance of the lecture is an account of Britain as a multinational and multicultural state. The thrust of the argument might be taken to acclaim the achievement of the Union of the Kingdoms, but rather it is directed against both making the case for 'separation', and the case for maintenance of the Union, on nationalistic grounds. The identities of the separate nations of the United Kingdom are recounted and endorsed as politically important and culturally valuable (so long as they can accommodate the actuality of increasing diversity), but, it is argued, they do not require an independent nation state for their legitimate expression or survival.

Britishness, Crick argues, is not a cultural identity like being English, Welsh or Scottish; if it is 'cultural at all' it is a formal culture associated with a set of shared institutions and values. Crick's main criticism appears to be directed at the projection of 'Britishness' as if it were a superior form of national identity. He thinks Gordon Brown has (regrettably) fallen into the error of misidentifying Britishness with some distinctively English historical phenomena and mistakenly proposes that it become part of the taught citizenship curriculum. Yet Crick does not quarrel with the values and qualities that Brown associates with Britain – 'being creative, adaptable, outward looking, our belief in liberty, duty and fair play . . . manifest throughout our history' – these are 'acceptable generalities'; what he appears to object to is these characteristics being lauded as the basis of British identity without acknowledging its multinational and multicultural inclusiveness.

The analysis raises as many questions as it answers. It is clear that for Crick, Britain has the potential for greater devolution in its several parts, from state to civil society, and from government to people. The English (and perhaps Northern Irish) have a problem in locating their national identity, but political institutions should respect and accommodate different and multiple identities. If the majority of people in Scotland vote in a referendum for independence their will should be respected, but this should be a judgement about where their long-term interests lie, not about securing who they are.

Nationality, however construed, is only one aspect of identity, and actual identities might give individuals ties to several nations. Crick variously declared himself to be British, and English, and having chosen to live in Scotland since 1984, he sincerely 'hoped' some people considered him Scottish and British. 'National identities exist alongside many other meanings of identity.' What is missing from the analysis here is the link between identity and active citizenship. We can guess he would endorse Dina Kiwan's view that people should be secure in their personal identities and confident that their ethnic and religious identities are respected and relevant to their participation in public affairs.

Since Bernard Crick chose to present his own case as illustrative, we might note that alongside his national affiliations, he was also happy to be identified as a pro-European, federalist, humanist and socialist. He readily accepted the reputation of being ideologically pluralistic – never wholly in anyone's camp. For him, critical scepticism was an intellectual virtue, but this should never be an excuse for political inactivity or spurning public service. It is significant that Bernard's self perception as an academic critic and public actor permitted him to be fully engaged, as critic, party activist or government advisor, within UK institutions, with distinctively Scottish affairs, and also in the international arena. He exemplified the characteristics of a citizen who conducted his public and community service at several levels, which was consistent with having multiple identities and value commitments.

Civic Republicanism and Citizenship: the Challenge for Today

Bernard Crick

Consider this first essay in this series as a 'secular sermon'. I will preach on and around three texts. Their admonishments and message will be that while, of course, you and I all want to be good citizens, particularly for others to be good citizens, particularly for young people to be very good citizens, yet surveys, common observation and the content of the media all show that many or most of our fellow citizens are losing the desire, the will and the means to be active citizens. Some commentators now gravely discuss whether apathy is not a good thing, an indicator of contentment – and some politicians may privately agree with them. But, as it is written in my translation of the book of Proverbs, 'Do or you will be done by'. A bare 51 per cent of us were engaged enough to vote in the 2005 General Election, even to choose as if from the best of a bad job. And of eighteen- to twenty-five-year-olds, only four out of ten voted.

Sir Alistair Graham, the Commissioner for Standards in Public Life, published a survey last month, widely reported, showing that less than a quarter of us generally trust government ministers to tell the truth. Ministers are fifteenth in the pecking order of trust in the professions, hovering just below estate agents. 'Lack of trust', he said, 'leads to public cynicism and disengagement in the political system . . . damaging to the very fabric of our democracy.'

Yet too few of us are willing to stir our stumps to be *active citizens*, to work at least for a better society. We leave professional politicians to do that for us, or simply want them to leave us alone to get on with what is oddly called the quiet and private life of competitive individualism. The ten-, eleven- or twelve-hour working day of the Victorian poor is now normal for all classes, sometimes voluntarily yet more often caught up in a machine that may appear to each individual to be out of control, but is in fact encouraged by government. Successive British governments have, after all, largely opted out of the European Union's limitations on working time, at the same time as ministers expose their neglected families dutifully smiling for the cameras.

We may now be facing the inability of either politicians or publics to prevent outcomes that are actually degrading our planet. So I offer no excuses in launching this series on contemporary citizenship to begin by going back to remind us from where our political institutions and ideas have evolved. From out of the ancient Greek and Roman worlds we have fashioned – 'we' of the so-called Western or, in a non-ethnic sense, European traditions – two great and civilising cultural inventions: natural science and the ideas and practices of free citizenship. But neither can be taken for granted. Both need continual activity and now, not just institutional repair, but rejuvenation of their spirit.

So my first text, fellow citizens, if I may address you so oddly (but you probably are, else you wouldn't have come), is from the Periclean oration as related by the historian Thucydides in Athens of the fifth century BC:

> Our constitution is called a democracy because power is in the hands not of a minority but of the whole people. . . . Here each individual is interested not only in his own affairs but in the affairs of the state as well: even those who are mostly occupied with their own business are extremely well-informed on general politics – this is a peculiarity of ours: we do not say that a man who takes no interest in politics is a man who minds his own business; we say that he has no business here at all. We Athenians, in our own persons, take our decisions on policy or submit them to proper discussions: for we do not think that there is an incompatibility between words and deeds; the worst thing is to rush into action before the consequences have been properly debated.

Now modern historians tell us that in fact Pericles was a wee bit of a demagogue. And like Mr Blair he sometimes fell just a wee bit short of what he preached. But consider the ideas Pericles had to use to carry his audience; that says a lot for their level of understanding and aspirations so long ago, what I have called political literacy. His oratory was about more than maximising life chances for material advancement and spasmodic domestic bliss.

His argument that before action there must be proper public debate, but action none the less, this is at the heart of what modern scholars have come to call civic republicanism. Civic republicanism signified both a value and a theory. The value was freedom itself, specifically free public debate among others as the very essence of free citizenship. The theory was that states are stronger when their actions are understood and supported by their citizens. It is free and open debate that holds a state together not, as Plato had believed, agreement on a common core of true and transcendent values.

Some of our leaders and leader writers are now worrying themselves and us silly about the alleged dangers of multiculturalism; so they argue the need, like low-grade Platonic opportunists, for an over-riding, as it were transcendent, common core of values, which they then somewhat parochially call British. But the father of political thinking, Aristotle, said in his book *The Politics* that Plato was mistaken in his teaching about justice to try to find by philosophy an ideal, transcendent unity. On the contrary, it was the case that

> there is a point at which a *polis* [a political community] by advancing in unity, will cease to be a *polis*: there is another point, short of that at which it may still remain a *polis*, but will none the less come near to losing its essence, and will thus be a worse *polis*. It is as if you were to turn harmony into mere unison, or to reduce a theme to a single beat. The truth is that the *polis* is an aggregate of many members.

Aristotle implies that even a small city state contained an aggregation, a diversity of values and interests among its citizens. Yes, I have not forgotten that the citizen class itself was then a minority – women, slaves, debtors and foreign residents were excluded from political rights. But the unique path and practices of free citizenship had been marked and set down that could in modern times gradually be broadened out into something like democracy.

Even in medieval Europe state councillors and the learned never lost the memory of this possible something else that had once existed: the political way of doing things of the Greek city states and the institutions and laws of the Roman Republic. That republic, indeed, had a great empire, the largest ever in the world until the British Empire of the nineteenth century. Thinking of which, the philosopher Alfred North Whitehead in his book *The Aims of Education* wrote of his Victorian schooldays that he had learnt his politics from his Classics masters. They were enamoured of the Roman Republic but disapproved highly of the *Principate*, the time of the emperors (as you should if you watch the BBC's Roman epics). They blamed the fall of republican Rome on imperial expansion, therefore they were Gladstonian Liberals to a man, totally against 'on to Khartoum', 'on to Kabul', and some even against 'on to Pretoria'.

The Roman word 'res-publica' implied that things that are public must be of public concern: active citizens should and could manage the state, neither kings nor aristocratic oligarchies alone or today single parties. Citizens treat each other as equals. The public culture of politics is quite different from the private, secretive decision-making and politicking in autocracies. Republicanism did not necessarily imply democracy

– democracy was seen as a necessary element in mixed government, not the overriding principle. Property, education or extraordinary public service were the basic qualifications for citizenship, but even ancient and early modern republics were more participative in spirit than most modern so-called democracies enshrining individualistic, market liberalism.

The much-maligned Niccolò Machiavelli stated a theory of civic republicanism in his *Discoursi*. A state is stronger if it can trust a patriotic citizen class with arms. Bearing and providing arms for war and the mutual trust needed was often the qualification for citizenship. The vexed right to bear arms in the US constitution had its roots in old republican theory and practice. So freedom in a state, said Machiavelli, meant tolerating social conflict between classes; but conflict if well managed, if handled by political compromises, can be a source of strength and gives liveliness to political debate. For a republic to sustain itself and flourish, citizens must have civic spirit, what he called *virtu*, and if this *virtu* declines – or has never been present – whether by indolence, corruption, decadence or fear, there can be no republic only autocracy. *Virtu* is a nice and curious word, roughly translated as civic spirit, but then spirit of an intensity few of us now feel. It derives from the Latin 'vir' for man, or rather manliness. For courage is involved in political life, sometimes physical courage even – as Pericles of Athens famously said 'the secret of liberty is courage'. They'll take it away from you if you don't defend it. The secret of liberty is not just 'eternal vigilance', as Lincoln did not say, but eternal activity as well. Machiavelli's *virtu* has nothing to do with Christian virtues, indeed Machiavelli thought the Church was sapping republican spirit. What is proper to a man to be truly a man is courage, fortitude and audacity in public affairs; but all this is useless without political skill and knowledge. (But I note defensively that he does give one, if only one, example of extraordinary *virtu* in a militant woman.)[1]

Machiavelli's realistic restatement of an admittedly idealised picture of the Roman Republic became immensely influential. These ideas of a free and forceful citizenry helped animate the Dutch Republic in its struggles against Spain, Protestant Sweden in the Thirty Years War, England and Scotland in the civil wars, the American then the Spanish colonies in revolt, and also the French Revolution. (Somewhat bizarrely the recent statue of David Hume in Edinburgh's High Street has him be-togaed in eighteenth-century fashion). Closer to our times, an Italian Marxist in prison, Antonio Gramsci, produced a Communist variant on civic republicanism to refute Lenin's obsession with the state and one party dictatorship. Gramsci argued that the participative co-operation between industrial workers and intellectuals was now the key to the rise and fall of societies rather than Machiavelli's armed citizens or the militias of the American colonies.

Civic republicanism was strong in the early United States. Jeffersonian democracy was a cult of active citizenship which made virtues of simplicity of manners, plain-speaking, candour and high literacy – an ability to turn one's hand to anything practical as well as to read deeply and think restlessly for the common good. These virtues were to be universalised by personal example – the ideal image of the common man. Emmanuel Kant philosophised it, building on Rousseau. In the late eighteenth and early nineteenth century when, at public dinners, innumerable toasts were drunk, whether by American Democrats, British Whigs or radicals, among them was always 'To Republican Virtues, three times three'. In Britain, even here in Scotland, this could follow the loyal toast because civic republicanism, unlike 'red republicanism' or Jacobinism, was, to the disgust of Tom Paine, not against constitutional monarchy as such, in its place, up to a point.

Now to the second text of this half-learned sermon. The French writer Benjamin Constant, in an essay of 1820 (I'm getting nearer to the present day, and the point may be slowly emerging) on *The Liberty of the Ancients Compared to that of the Moderns* saw the difference between active citizenship and good citizenship clearly enough:

> The aim of the ancients was the sharing of social power among citizens of the same fatherland: this is what they called liberty. The aim of the moderns is the enjoyment of liberty in private pleasures; and they call liberty the guarantees accorded by institutions to these pleasures.

Well now, we have reached in 1820 the present day rather early. This text shows both the concept and the critique of 'the consumer society' arising long before we recently named this somewhat degrading and somewhat pleasing cultural change. R. H. Tawney in the 1920s had called it, in the title of a book still worth reading, *The Acquisitive Society*. Now, of course, Benjamin Constant in his time, which was still a predominantly rural economy, was either exaggerating or prophesying. (The American humourist Mr Dooley was to say 'a prophet is a man who foresees trouble'.) For throughout the nineteenth and early twentieth centuries all over the Western world there were ever increasing movements of the disenfranchised to gain the vote, to gain social power, to become not just legal citizens but to gain the rights of political citizens. I call this civic republicanism. But I must ask, having gained a democratic franchise, what has been done with it; or what have new elites done to the new peoples? I will suggest that after these mass movements of active citizenship, too many of the beneficiaries have lapsed back into the condition that Constant described as modern liberty: happy just to enjoy the guarantee that the state gives to personal safety and private pleasures. Scholars call this the liberal theory of the state. And yet key indicators suggest that people are not entirely happy with this social contract or unpolitical new deal. Remember those surveys telling us that government ministers, indeed most politicians, are more distrusted than even estate agents and journalists?

But, as Lenin once said, 'one step forward, two steps back'. Before coming to what can be done, I must go back to an important rethinking of the idea of active citizenship and civic republicanism that began here in Scotland in the eighteenth century: the idea of the importance for liberty of civil society. When old writers talked of civil society they simply meant the whole state, or rather those few states where civil society was an arena of political active citizens: that is John Locke's 'civil government', Emmanuel Kant's *Burgerliche Geselleschaft*, Machiavelli and Jefferson's republican government or Jean-Jacques Rousseau's *état civil* dedicated to realising the general will of ordinary people. But in the second half of the eighteenth century the concept of civil society began to take on a new meaning, largely due to the thinking here in Scotland of Adam Smith and Adam Ferguson. It pointed to the importance for liberty of semi-autonomous institutions standing between the individual and the state – those of commerce and the market, legal and clerical institutions and associations; gradually all manner of semi-autonomous groups and voluntary bodies were seen in this way, and later on political parties, pressure groups and trade unions. They were as much restraints on the state as formal constitutions and they were the training ground for active citizenship in society as a whole. I said semi-autonomous because their degree of freedom depended on reform of old laws but never on the absence of law. Adam Smith recognised that the working of free markets needed some regulation – a strong but minimal state – and a degree of common morality against fraud and for the everyday honouring of informal contracts. Hegel in his *Philosophy of Right* grandly saw civil society as the sphere of ethical life interposed between the family and the state.

Alexis de Tocqueville, in his great book *Democracy in America*, gave lasting expression to this new idea of civic republicanism as built on civil society. He saw dangers in democracy: there could be a 'tyranny of the majority' – majority opinion was and still can be intolerant (think of popular attitudes to punishment and immigrants) – and a majority could be content to sit back and let self-government be done for them; but he saw the great mitigating factor in America as being the dispersal of central power in the federal system, the liveliness of local government and the multiplicity of voluntary bodies. Following his observations thinkers and scholars slowly began a critique of the whole theory of sovereignty which had asserted that everywhere there must be some final, absolute central source of authority. Thinkers and scholars slowly evolved a theory of pluralism, that power is inherently dispersed; no state is powerful enough to override some internal groups and interests. What holds things together is simply civil society itself, the tolerance and necessary compromises of politics itself.

But somehow after Tocqueville the concept of civil society fell into disuse, even if the reality remained. Perhaps it was simply taken for granted; and nationalist ideologies needed to stress unity and sovereignty. Both popular and learned debates tended to go round and round about what should one *really* mean by sovereignty? What should one really mean by constitutional government or by democracy?

However, it was revived in the 1980s and its revival vindicated the thinking of Gramsci, that obscure unorthodox Italian Communist, when in prison in the 1930s. He had gone back to Hegel by detaching the idea of civil society from the economy, reattaching it to the state but to show that states, to retain power, cannot rely on coercion or law alone but have to gain the consent of different cultures within society. This well described what began to happen in Eastern Europe, even in Russia itself, in the last days of Communist rule. The state power could not be challenged directly but there grew up a kind of non-violent guerrilla warfare waged through cultural and educational beliefs and institutions which even would-be totalitarian Communism had failed to eradicate or to win over completely – nationality groups especially. The dissidents and then the protestors had something to build on, strong folk memories of times before the Communists. Of course, by the same token, creating democratic institutions in states that never had an articulate and varied civil society is, while not impossible, extraordinarily difficult.

I draw from this that citizenship has to be learnt and practiced among the groups of civil society, not necessarily by joining political parties with their direct relationship with the state, all the time wanting to possess it in their own interest. But politics is too important to be left to politicians. I will say that again. So now to the final text of this secular sermon.

The mission statement from the 1998 education report for England, *Education for Citizenship and the Teaching of Democracy in Schools*:

> We aim at no less than a change in the political culture of this country both nationally and locally: for people to think of themselves as active citizens,

willing, able and equipped to have an influence in public life and with the critical capacities to weigh evidence before speaking and acting; to build on and to
extend radically to young people the best in existing traditions of community
involvement and to make them individually confident in finding new forms of
involvement and action among themselves.

The advisory committee who signed up to that, including Lord Baker,
the former Conservative Secretary of State for Education, were not told
by their chairman that they had signed up to the civic republican theory
of the state and, in effect, repudiated the strict individualistic liberal
theory of the state. As chairman and principle draftsman, I didn't want
to provoke them. One of the two Blunketts signed up to it knowingly and
made it part of the compulsory national curriculum in England (that is
Blunkett the good, not Blunkett the bad). At the time it could sound New
Labour enough for No. 10 even if now it might sound like a reproach or
satire on how they have governed.

Could there possibly be a change in the political culture of this country
towards far greater active participation? Could we move away from the
simple market liberal image of the private citizen getting on with his or
her life protected by good laws and the state; or perhaps from realistically
seeing democracy, as some political scientists have done, as simply fair
competition for office by political parties mobilising a mass electorate.
Individuals can and do, of course, assert their rights more strongly than
ever before. Man-made definitions of human rights are now part of law.
Remember that they are man-made. The scepticism of David Hume about
natural rights is justified. The idea of universal human rights is good
human invention and, of course, such rights can be made and remade.
But this is a cautious digression. My main point is that the civic republic
tradition always saw rights and duties as reciprocal. That may be going too
far. People should still have rights even if they have no sense of civic duty,
sometimes even moral duty. But the theory was that rights *should* inspire
duties, just as we have a duty to respect the rights of others. Some teachers
in schools are now teaching human rights, especially the UN charter of
the Rights of the Child, as if that is citizenship. It is not. Alone it is liberal
individualism pushed to a delusionary extreme. Do we want a litigious
rights culture? Citizenship is individuals voluntarily acting together for a
common purpose. Class actions in courts can protect rights but will not
create democracy or a civic culture.

So in ordinary talk as well as scholarly one sees liberal theory as
demanding 'good citizenship', invoking 'the rule of law', good behaviour,
individual rights and at its best moral virtues of care and concern for
others, beginning with neighbours and hopefully reaching out to strangers.

But it may stop short of demanding 'active citizenship', what scholars call 'civic republicanism', people combining together effectively to change or resist change. I call that true citizenship.

Well, is change possible or are we too far down the road of unsocial individualism and the values of a consumer society? Change is possible if we go back to the sense of what I said about the rediscovery of the idea of civil society within the state, rather than the old liberal view of a direct relationship of individuals to the state mediated only by the law, rights and the market. If the civic republican theory of liberty being based on civil society is correct, the general answer is quite obvious: as much power as possible must be devolved from the centre to sub-groups, regions and localities. The difficulties are partly practical and administrative but even more so breaking from a rigid mind-set, what William Blake once called 'mind forged manacles'.

Think how many local variations in Health Service provision or school provision and practices are at once damned by the media as 'post-code lotteries'. But post-code lotteries are the price, could be the advantage, of avoiding the uniform rules of a centralised bureaucracy, a bureaucracy itself constantly pressured by ministers to change to another set of uniform rules in response to media campaigns. Devolution means inevitable variation in local decisions, so long as those decisions are reasonably transparent and open to local democratic influence or control. The alternative is what we have, especially on the vast scale of England's 50 million inhabitants, government by centralised bureaucracy. To hell with the post-code lottery argument, I say; diversity is a price worth paying for liberty, community and local democracy. To avoid it at all costs is the open licence for a stifling central bureaucracy.

Leaders of all parties now genuinely declaim the need to increase public participation and yet they don't welcome real variations in local and regional practices, unless politically they have to, as in Scottish and Welsh devolution; and these are seen in England as unwelcome exceptions not as incitements to emulation. However, may I come down to earth with a bump and point to one unexpected sign that civic republicanism could be rediscovered.

There was a brief passage in Gordon Brown's recent Labour Party conference speech that got very little attention in the media:

> I tell you: just as in the last century governments had to take power from vested interests in the interests of communities, in the new century people and communities should now take power from the state and that means for the new challenges ahead a reinvention of the way we govern: the active citizen, the empowered community, open enabling government. When I made the Bank of

England independent, and to build trust in economic decision-making, I gave executive power away and I want a radical shift of power from the centre.

How seriously should we take that, I wonder? How seriously does he take it? We may see. But it points in the right direction even if, I suspect, it is as yet more from a gut feeling – that David Cameron also shares – that something has gone wrong in the system, than any clarity as yet about what to do. A conversation on the constitution, but nothing as formal or unpredictable as a Royal Commission on the government of the United Kingdom. But if at the moment they are no clearer in the head than Edward Bear, at least they begin to think about it. Yes, I did say Edward Bear. For as Christopher Robin drags him downstairs by one leg it is

bump, bump, bump on the back of his head. It is as far as he knows the only way of coming downstairs, but sometimes he feels there really is another way, if only he could stop bumping for a moment and think of it.

NOTE

1. The reference here is to the Countess (Mistress Catherine) Girolamo whose *virtu* is evident in her ruthless deployment of her feminine attributes, though sacrificing her hostage children, to avoid conspirators, who had killed her husband, from taking the citadel at Forli. The account is to be found in Niccolò Machiavelli's *The Discourses*, edited with introduction by Bernard Crick (London: Penguin Books, 1970), Bk 3, ch. 6 'On Conspiracies', p. 419.

2

Active Citizenship and Labour

David Blunkett and Matthew Taylor

As E. P. Thompson pointed out in his seminal work *The Making of the English Working Class* (1963), around 10 per cent of the population in the mid-nineteenth century were members of mutual societies – despite levels of illiteracy, poverty and political exclusion. Membership of societies varied from craft unions (savings against likely unemployment) through to the Goose and Burial clubs, which as their name implied, were about savings for Christmas and for a 'decent burial'. Above all people came together literally in the act of survival. They supported each other through times of joy and untold misery, they started the early reading circles and self-help groups and they bolstered the 'municipal socialism' (which led the large cities to invest in clean water, the removal of sewage and the development of utilities such as gas and electricity).

Democracy cannot survive and society cannot be sustained without civil and civic engagement. The importance of civil society goes beyond underpinning political action, formalised institutions and processes of decision-taking. It reflects the philosophy of the Greek polis: that the essence of a functioning human being is participation and engagement with the world around them. This is not solely recognition of our interdependence but an acceptance of responsibility for ourselves as well as the interests of others. Our individual relationship with wider society is interlinked and, in the long term, indistinguishable. In every society there are individuals who care only for themselves, unconcerned about the future of their own family, the well-being of wider society or future generations – but these people are few and far between.

That is why active citizenship is central to the progressive vision of a good society. It embodies core values such as empowering men and women to be able to make decisions for themselves. It is vital that individuals are able to contribute, even in small measure, to their own well-being as well as their inclusion in broader society, both at neighbourhood and at civic level. Active citizenship embodies the reciprocity and responsibility which any civilised society requires for its survival.

When these core values are set aside in favour of radical utilitarian progress, and active citizenship takes second place to top-down paternalism or 'statism', the politics of the progressive left become damaged and ground ceded to the individualistic libertarian right.

The explanation for the extent of disquiet relating to revelations about MP's allowances lies in the reprehensible actions of a substantial minority of politicians and a badly designed and managed system, but it has its roots deeper in a culture of 'democratic consumerism'. As deference declined along with the importance of class affiliations, politicians faced an electorate asking difficult questions and increasingly dissatisfied with the answers. The response was too often the aggressive adoption of a set of political tactics drawn from the tools of consumer marketing and public relations. Rather than engaging citizens in the difficult issues and policy trade offs, politicians felt they had to promise the electorate they could have their cake and eat it too; understandable in the immediacy of a twenty-four hour, seven-day-a-week media, and instantaneous Internet and blogging reaction. Pandering to superficial public moods may have worked in the short term but in the long run trust continued to fall. In this atmosphere a gap grew between what MPs felt they should be paid for an increasingly difficult and thankless job and what the public themselves would tolerate. This is why the allowance system that ended in disaster developed as it did.

The very nature of a 'progressive individualist' society based solely on the rights of individuals or the expectations of market consumers fails to absorb the fundamental truths of our interdependence in a complex, highly urbanised world. The adage 'think global act local' has never been more relevant in a world where global interdependence – economic, social and political – has made joint and collaborative action a necessity not a debatable option. Of course, for most people action can only be at the local level, and that is why the recognition of the importance of formalised politics in dealing with the global challenge has to be underpinned by the ability of men and women to influence events in their own lives. When the progressive left have ignored this truth, it has resulted in top-down statism which alienates people from the very idea of democratic, active and inclusive social democracy. Labour has on occasion proved itself to be better at consumer democracy but even if it sometimes won the battles ultimately it too often lost the war: simply, to balance the demands of the individual with the needs of the society upon which every individual depends.

The critical relevance of what can be described as 'political democracy' over and above individual action of men and women as economic and social players, is very well articulated in Professor Sir Bernard Crick's book of the early 1960s *In Defence of Politics* (Crick 1962).

In today's economic climate of a 'global meltdown', active citizenship is vitally important. The challenge is to mobilise the civic and civil virtues of men and women, not only to tend to their own well-being, but to those around them. Active citizenship is a crucial aspect of a functioning society, particularly during times of instability, insecurity and stress.

Active citizenship is therefore not some sort of optional extra but an essential part of revival and the glue which holds society together. It provides a dynamic from the bottom up which complements action necessarily taken by government. Active participation is a way of mobilising, motivating and utilising the talent of the populace. At times of great threat or challenge it is the mobilisation of mutual action which has always been the hallmark of success. In periods of war, men and women come together in the defence of not just themselves and their family, but the nation's values and 'way of life'.

But what is instructive about mutuality is that it is by its very nature educative. Just as the nature of society has changed as large-scale industry has disappeared (with it the programmes of apprenticeship and mentoring), so have many of the mechanisms for active engagement. However, we must not overlook the importance of adult education in substantially reinforcing the need for progressive change. Indeed this was a major contributor to the landslide victory of Clement Attlee's Labour Party in 1945.

Within the armed services the necessity of self-preservation drove a strong sense of comradeship. The learning experience of the war paradoxically nurtured a belief that there could be a better world, and it was during this time that men and women put their faith in the notion that through government action this better world could be achieved.

There was in essence a sea change in political culture but not the corollary of continuing citizenship engagement with civilianisation and demilitarisation. Had the adult education programmes continued after the war in the way they had within the military services, the reversion to Churchill's Conservative Party in 1951 might never have occurred. While a top-down, command and control approach was a wartime necessity, in a period of post-war hope and optimism it was replaced by a desire for self-determination.

So now, in the aftermath of the global financial collapse, the necessity of government action is vitally important. However, the stimulus programmes of the US, Britain and Europe, which demonstrate the critical importance of democratic politics, need to be balanced and underpinned by a drive for active citizenship. Citizens must be part of the medium and long-term solution, not simply the supplicant victims.

As regeneration programmes and other central government funding come to an end, and as local authorities under the control of Conservative and Liberal Democrat councillors pull the plug on capacity building, the development of social capital and community-based assets, central government must step in. Not to 'do' but to support; to help offset a personalisation agenda being pushed by the political right (particularly by the Liberal Democrats). A personalisation agenda will not liberate the individual to take control, but rather distort and undermine the whole concept of strengthening a functioning, active and engaged community.

To nurture a culture of engagement requires investment in leadership skills and the creation of a substantial mass of citizens able to engage in creating a functioning neighbourhood and society. Through a well-developed culture of engagement, the social and physical capital required to tackle deep-seated intergenerational disadvantage and disengagement can emerge.

The need for continuing renewal and restoration of our most deprived neighbourhoods is self-evident. The way to achieve this is to mobilise the power, the talent and the capability of men and women in their own lives, through their lives, and in their own environment. Whether as willing volunteers or as paid employees, engagement will bring its own reward as active engagement changes not only the physical environment but also the psychology of the community.

EDUCATION

Britain in the 1990s was the least politically literate developed nation in the world. Work at York University had revealed that the citizenry in emerging nations from central and Eastern Europe had developed an understanding of political theory and institutions way beyond the norm in Britain.

This was not surprising as the traditions of working-class education (the reading circles, early technical colleges and Workers Education Association) had in many parts of the country all but disappeared. Whilst some form of education for adults existed in the larger industrial units (themselves disappearing from the early 1980s) the idea of teaching about power, influence and personal empowerment in schools and colleges, was seen as an anathema.

Organisations like the Politics Association and the Political Studies

Association battled away to keep a flame alive despite a decision in the late 1970s not to press ahead with citizenship courses in schools. In 1997 the incoming Labour government took the decision to establish a working group under the chairmanship of Professor (later Sir) Bernard Crick (Qualifications and Curriculum Authority 1998). Bernard Crick had been one of the leading lights in fighting for citizenship and democracy to be established as a mandatory element in secondary education and beyond. The wide-based working group empowered by his skills in taking people forward to understand that the issue was not about teaching party politics, helped enormously to gain consensus. But time was not on the side of those committed to opening the minds and hearts of young people to how the world really operated round them.

An unholy alliance between head teachers and educational conservatives were deeply opposed to any significant change in the curriculum. Some feared it would increase their workload. Many on the far right were very clear that teaching children about theories, institutions and processes of decision-making was a diversion – a dangerous 'left-wing plot'.

Despite fifteen million pounds being invested immediately in training and materials, years on from the laying of the order and the introduction of the first mandatory courses in 2002, many schools simply were not teaching citizenship in any meaningful sense, and some were doing so very badly.

The failure to expand the teacher training programme (although there was some effort at accelerating the in-service Continuing Professional Development), coupled with the fact that many schools did not have a specialist concentrating on developing an understanding by fellow teachers limited the impact of the course. There was a lack of awareness that particular aspects of the curriculum would have benefited the confidence of youngsters who would then perform better in other core curriculum subjects. In addition the course would improve preparation for the transition from adolescence to adulthood, and strengthen good citizenship – active not only in their community but in promoting their own well-being.

The extension of citizenship courses to those aspiring to British nationality (and the ceremonies that were developed in tandem) recognised the importance of those seeking to become naturalised citizens developing participation in, and an understanding of, the political and civic life of the nation. The notion that the indigenous population should somehow be less well informed and less engaged from active citizenship was, and remains, bizarre (Home Office 2004).

In addition, research funded by the then Department for Education and Employment at the turn of the century revealed the obvious truth that those who have an understanding of and a level of participation in civil society do better for themselves and their family, and are materially more engaged, than those who do not. In simple terms, the life, the fabric and the glue that holds society together is reinforced. The nation and the individual benefits, and an intelligent, thoughtful and engaged citizenry contribute to what the Greeks would have described as the 'polis'.

The value of education in strengthening democracy against the dangers of totalitarianism and indifference finally has been recognised. However, the battle remains to inculcate within the system a grasp of what has been achieved so far. As the primacy of unregulated markets takes a tumble it is important to recognise the links between Crick's *In Defence of Politics* and the salience of political democracy. If, as is often muted, information is power, then being informed is crucial to determining who is in power, who is powerful and how that power is to be used.

The White Paper published by the Communities and Local Government Secretary Hazel Blears, on 7 July 2008, was a step forward in recognising that there was a much broader approach required (Communities and Local Government 2008). This was not about particular initiatives but a holistic approach to changing the way in which people perceived the operation of politics, the processes of change and the critical importance of helping people through the challenge of such rapid economic, social and cultural change – without the fear, insecurity and instability so dangerous to progressive politics.

However, despite substantial steps forward such as the establishment of the Office of the Third Sector, as well as a range of initiatives from government departments in stimulating volunteering and regeneration (and New Deal for Community Programmes), there was not a central drive to ensure that people could bring about change within their own circumstances. As a consequence, much of the alienation and distrust of formal politics has remained (and in some cases worsened).

It is therefore easy for a cynical national media to undermine trust and confidence further by denigrating anything and everything which democratic politics seeks to achieve. The debate around different models of 'top-down' or 'devolved' government and the contradictions these throw up has been limited. There is a failure to understand who to hold to account for what policy. What is central government responsible for and what are the responsibilities of devolved government and decentralised agencies?

ACTIVE CITIZENS AND EMPOWERING SERVICES

As we have said many of the institutions of working-class collective support and improvement have withered away while the decline of the industrial base has removed the basis for much work-based organisation and solidarity. At the same time the welfare state, created to give working people freedom and opportunity has all too often developed an unhealthy relationship with communities; managing at its worst to foster dependence while not meeting individual needs. Policy makers are rightly suspicious of any policy that claims to meet two major objectives but there is an emerging understanding of the scope for public services to foster engagement and civic activity while this engagement is at the same time key to the renewal and sustainability of services in a period of austerity.

The next three years, and probably much longer, will see a concerted squeeze on public expenditure. Not only is the overall rate of spending growth falling fast but rising benefit and debt repayment costs mean the money available to fund services will decline as a share of expenditure. Demands arising from economic recession, population ageing and rising public expectations will add to the pressure.

This will come as a shock to a system that has become accustomed to increasing budgets. Improvements in efficiency will be important, but if we are to avoid deteriorating services and worsening outcomes more radical solutions are needed. In the search for these solutions a new alliance can be forged between the advocates of Crickian active citizenship and the champions of radical public-service reform.

For the vast majority of people the option of turning to the market will be unavailable. Even when we have got through the immediate economic downturn, the structural adjustments necessary in an economy that has relied on unsustainable levels of family and corporate debt will mean fewer can afford to turn to private education, health or social care.

Indeed, it looks as though society as a whole will have to confront as a day-to-day reality that which political and social theorists have long argued: that we cannot rely on a combination of the state and market alone to meet society's needs. We have also to build the resilience, creativity and generosity of individuals, civic organisations and communities. Thus the democratic argument for citizen empowerment and engagement is joined to social necessity.

In its twelve years in power Labour has been through various stages of public-service reform. Indeed the government often represents this as an unfolding evolution. The stages can be characterised as follows:

Phase one: Centralised reconstruction
- Role of centre – command and control
- Means of reform – investment, targets, inspection
- Overarching objective – reconstruction, driving up standards

Phase two: System reform
- Role of centre – system architect, market maker
- Means of reform – markets, contestability, choice
- Overarching objective – creation of dynamic 'self-improving' system

Phase three: Capacity building
- Role of centre – strategic enabler
- Means of reform – devolving power
- Overarching objective – empowerment and equity

Although there is inevitably some post hoc rationalisation in this story of unfolding stages (reality is more messy and implementation more patchy) there is something to the idea that failing services needed to be fixed and incentive aligned before policy makers could move to a more radical agenda of reconceptualising public services.

The new emphasis on empowerment can be seen to reflect a number of overlapping insights and aspirations. First, many of the major drivers of demand for public services arise from people's own choices. Whether it is obesity, binge drinking, poor parenting and antisocial behaviour, or reducing carbon emissions, it is clear that public services can only work by persuading people to take responsibility for their own behaviour. By engaging and supporting people, strategies of empowerment can enable them to live better lives. Second, the success of even traditional public-service interventions depend on the co-operation of individuals and communities. Parents have to get their children to school and encourage them to do homework. Doctors need patients to follow advice and take their medicine. The police need communities to work together to identify and tackle crime and antisocial behaviour. In this sense empowerment is about recognising that most public services are in essence 'co-productive'. That is to say, their outcome depends upon the combined efforts of public-service providers and recipients. This co-operation must in turn be based on citizens having greater influence (as individuals and groups) over the shape of the services. Third, public-service managers face difficult choices and trade offs, and these are set to become much more difficult in future; empowerment strategies seek to engage citizens in understanding these dilemmas, so they can shape and then support the decisions made.

There is a growing number of examples of services designed or delivered co-productively.

- The Youth Opportunity and Capital Funds provide money which young people control and decide how to spend on activities and facilities in their area. An amazing variety of processes have developed to engage young people and an even more impressive list of initiatives in areas ranging from community cohesion and sport to culture and environment (Children Schools and Families 2007).

- Direct payments enable social-care clients and carers to access payments directly and decide how to spend them. In just a few years this revolutionary idea has spread from the disability movement to being rolled out in councils across England (Department of Health 2006). As more and more people sign up, so new ways for people to collaborate on buying and providing services are starting to emerge. For this to be truly successful civil society has to develop the capacity to respond to needs in new ways (which does not simply rely on buying from large-scale providers), and which offers protection and advocacy for the most vulnerable.
- In March 2009 the government announced the £30 million Community Assets Programme. This allows local third sector organisations to apply to gain control of and refurbish underused local authority assets. This initiative, which is based on recommendations made by Lewisham Chief Executive Barry Quirk, recognises the impact that has been made by community organisations like 'friends' of local parks who have worked with councils to revive dilapidated and under-used public spaces.

However, these new ways of working are still at the margins of most public services, with, possibly, one exception. This is domestic refuse recycling where responsibility for managing domestic waste has shifted from being primarily the responsibility of the local authority to being a shared task, with assiduous householders spending a great deal more time processing their rubbish than the council.

As budgets are squeezed and expectations and needs set to rise further public services should address a new question: what is their social multiplier effect? The answer to this question and the method of increasing the effect will differ from service to service. In some cases, for example tax self assessment, simple steps such as improved interactive websites will encourage citizens to do the right thing. But for locally delivered public services there are some core service design characteristics which are likely to enhance the scope for citizen engagement and co-production:

Local flexibility is important. If public services are to feel more reciprocal citizens need to feel that their input and engagement can make a difference to local outcomes. If services are over-specified from the centre the incentives for engagement are reduced.

The message of engagement and shared responsibility needs to be consistent and measured. Most citizens have a complex, but relatively shallow relationship with the public sector. If people hear too many or contradictory messages they simply turn off. It's no good people being told their views matter by the council and then being treated with disdain by the local housing office or school. Equally, grass roots engagement in service design and delivery has to be echoed by an open and deliberative policy-making process at all levels of government.

Genuine collaboration takes time and commitment. In the short term it often seems easier to do something yourself than persuade someone else to do it with you. The targets and timescales imposed on local public services can preclude genuine engagement and co-production in favour of superficial (and often counter productive) consultation. Only by making engagement and civic capacity-building core objectives can we give services the time and space they need to renew the bonds between state provision, civic initiative and personal responsibility.

To make such engagement and decision-making meaningful there will need to be an audit of resources from the public purse specific to a geographic area with specific outcome measures. Redefining how those resources can be applied will bring alive the flexibility for truly local decision-making but will entail a supportive role for local government which entails a form of decentralisation. This rarely exists in current examples of Service Districts, which rely on the existing administration and professional top-down approach rather than a genuine reinvigoration of democratic engagement.

As this list demonstrates, there is the possibility of fusing a set of ideals about active citizenship, democratic participation and political plural-ism with the pressing need for services that are not only designed around people's needs but also able to tap into and enhance civic and individual capacity.

The government is inching towards this realisation. But at both the national and local level there are deeply embedded assumptions and modes of working that have to be challenged. These include:

Seeing the goal of engagement as legitimation rather than conversation. Thus engagement and democratic renewal are seen as ways of making the state and its managers more popular rather than as a better way of developing and delivering shared outcomes. Theodore Zeldin (1998) has argued that for a conversation to deserve the name its participants have to allow the possibility that they will have their view of the world changed by it. This is a good test for engagement strategies.

Separating the goal of engagement from the hard-headed mechanics of service delivery. It is only by genuinely reconceptualising services as co-productive that public-service managers will see engagement as a core function. So, for example, schools should see parental engagement not as an optional extra but as an essen-tial aspect of raising standards, inspiring young people and being a community resource. Similarly, ensuring schools engage with and deliver the citizenship curriculum can achieve added-value outcomes for both improved standards and preparation for functioning and engaged citizenry.

Failing to understand that engagement requires a new way of doing politics. The hierarchical, antagonistic, propagandist nature of party politics (and the obsession of the media with the game of politics rather than the substance of policy) provides a problematic backdrop for messages to service providers and the public about collaboration, empathy, duty and responsibility. Politics tends also to encourage a government-centric view of the world (if only we had the right politicians everything would be OK) rather than a citizen-centric view (it is up to people to make their future and politicians to support them in doing it). Ways need to be developed to encourage the political class to attend to the health of the public sphere as a whole; in this the opposition has as much power and responsibility as the government.

Necessity is the mother of invention. In an era when it looked like individualism and consumerism were delivering the goods the advocates of active citizenship had little to rest on other than their idealism. That era was dying even before the expenses debacle exposed the gulf of mistrust between decision-makers and citizens resulting from decades of an intensifying consumer democracy. The combined case for a more honest, more engaging, more transformative politics and for a truly empowering and collaborative welfare state is now overwhelming. But whilst understanding this opportunity we should not underestimate the challenge it involves.

CONCLUSION

We have argued that the new era into which we are moving requires new ways of thinking and acting. We have remade the case, argued throughout his working life by Bernard Crick, for the importance of active informed citizens. We have stressed the need for a thriving community and civic sphere based on principles of responsibility and mutuality. And we have connected these aspirations to the need for collaborative public services which not only meet people's expectations but build individual and collective capacity and resilience. We have also argued while this is a moment of opportunity for these progressive aspirations we should not underestimate the challenges involved in achieving this kind of cultural shift.

This is not a challenge that can be dodged by the Labour Party itself. The history of the Party and how it came to favour its particular brand of centralised social democracy has been chewed over by many scholars: what would have happened if the co-operative wing of the movement had from the start established a stake in the Party more on a par with that of the trade unions; how different would the post-war welfare state have been if Morrison had won out over Bevan in the creation of the NHS, and the Party had built on a tradition of 'municipal socialism' from which so much of the post-war settlement evolved?

Whatever history's hypotheticals, and despite a variety of reforms, the

Party continues to operate on the basis that its overwhelming primary purpose is to get its representatives elected, with its secondary (and much weaker) purpose to hold them to account, with the objective of redistributing and sharing power as part of a progressive challenge to the primacy of individualism and the market. Thus the Party reinforces a model of hierarchical politics; politics is something we elect other people to do to us. The Party does not see itself as an organisation that intervenes directly in society; it does not have a story about how its activities can contribute to civic capacity. This, despite the roots of the Party displaying the characteristics of bottom-up, contrasts with all other major political parties seeking legitimacy for existing top-down power in political institutions.

Not only does a model of party organisation geared primarily to formal elections downplay progressive values it is – over the long run – increasingly unsuccessful in attracting either activists or committed supporters. In a post deferential society we are judged by what we do, not what we say. For the Party to win credibility – especially in deprived communities – it must no longer say 'trust us we are on your side' but 'join us in making a difference'. We cannot espouse the politics of responsibility and engagement unless we transform the *raison d'être* and machinery of the organisation which is all too often detached from community life.

Our cities and towns contain thousands of people who belong to organisations with progressive values: environmental groups, development charities; and hundreds of thousands more who are active in community groups, school governing bodies, volunteer schemes and global bodies such as Amnesty International. It may not be a silent majority but it is a large and powerful constituency. The Labour Party should be the kind of organisation which offers these people a space to debate and to act so as to turn their values and commitment into the ideas and action that can make localities into the engaged, creative, self-reliant and altruistic communities which we seek. We do this not by telling these activists they should solely support us (a logic which increasingly eludes them) but by showing how we can support them in realising their shared interest and combined power.

This is a party that sees what it creates as important as who it elects, that is more ambitious in its aims and more collaborative and generous in its means. We cannot create such a party overnight, it requires a commitment from party leaders and managers that lasts more than one electoral cycle. But it is the only way our party can grow new roots into the communities of modern Britain. We know from our many conversations with him that this is the kind of party Bernard Crick wanted Labour to be. There can be few more powerful endorsements.

References

Children, Schools and Families (2007), *Youth Opportunity Fund and Youth Capital Fund: Evaluation Findings from Initial Case Study Visits*, London: Children, Schools and Families.

Communities and Local Government (2008), *Communities in Control: Real People, Real Power*, London: Communities and Local Government.

Crick, Bernard [1962] (2000), *In Defence of Politics*, 5th edn, London: Continuum.

Department of Health (2006), *Our Health, Our Care, Our Say: A New Direction for Community Services*, London: Department of Health.

Home Office (2004), *The New and the Old*, Report of the 'Life in the United Kingdom' Group, London: Home Office.

Qualifications and Curriculum Authority (1998), *Education for Citizenship and the Teaching of Democracy in Schools (Crick Report)*, London: QCA.

Thompson, E. P. (1963), *The Making of the English Working Class*, 1980 reprint, London: Victor Gollancz.

Zeldin, Theodore (1998), *Conversation: How Talk Can Change Our Lives*, New York, NY: Hidden Spring.

3

The Fourth Principle: Sharing Power with the People of Scotland

George Reid

The Scottish Parliament should embody and reflect the sharing of power between the people of Scotland, the legislators and the Scottish Executive.
(Key Principles of Sharing the Power: report of the Consultative Steering Group on the Scottish Parliament 1999)

In just under six months Scotland goes to the polls in elections to our third parliament. The same day the country votes, for the first time proportionally, for its new local councils. It is not for me to say whether 3 May 2007 will be a cusp of change or not.[1] But it would be a strange politician who was not mulling over the implications next year of minority government or of a coalition renegotiated on who-shares-what-power at Holyrood. And an even stranger one unwilling to contemplate how proportional representation (PR) will fundamentally change our political culture at grassroots level up and down the country.

The different platforms on which candidates are standing are a matter solely for the political parties, not for me as the impartial Presiding Officer. What concerns me is the relationship between the citizen and the political process – that we have not yet got right our fourth founding principle of 'the sharing of power between Parliament, people and government'.

I am acutely aware that democracy is dependent upon 'trust and turnout'. And that, in this area, the message we are receiving from the electorate is mixed. Yes, Electoral Commission research confirmed earlier surveys when it said: 'The Scottish Parliament is highly trusted and accessible. It is seen as having more integrity than the UK Parliament and as having Scotland's interests at heart . . . It is thought to be modern, accessible and likely to listen to people' (Electoral Commission 2006: 6).

But trust in Scotland's Parliament does not extend to politicians themselves. A negative view of our trade has been fuelled by sleaze at

Westminster, by perceptions of profligacy in the construction of the Holyrood campus, and by a series of spats over MSPs' expenses.

Opinion polls regularly find that around three-quarters of the electorate believe politicians make promises they do not intend to keep and put the interests of their party before those of the people who voted for them. Is it surprising, therefore, that turnout is falling? – down from 67 per cent in the 1997 Referendum, to 59 per cent in the 1999 Scottish election, and down again to 49 per cent in the 2003 election.

It seems clear, therefore, that constitutional change in Scotland has not by itself produced a new culture of political engagement.

TRUST AND TURNOUT

I shall argue that, over eight years, Holyrood has largely achieved three of our founding principles; that we are enormously accessible, very accountable, and have made real progress on equal opportunities. But that the fourth principle of the sharing of power between government, people and Parliament remains elusive.

Holyrood is a hybrid. It was conceived as a model of participative governance appropriate to the twenty-first century. But the needs of coalition – 'the primacy of delivering the programme upon which we were elected', as Margaret Curran MSP, the Minister for Parliamentary Business puts it – means that it runs largely on the rules of representative governance established at Westminster in an earlier age. An industrial age when communication was slow and when the nation divided along class lines reflected in different values on either side of the Commons.

Today, however, we live in a post-industrial age when information is instantaneous, with an electorate which is more educated, affluent and volatile. When, as research for the Power Commission has showed conclusively, electors are certainly not apathetic but want more control over the decisions which affect their daily lives and elected representatives to reflect their diversity of interests (Power Commission 2006).

The paradox of our times is that citizens are more actively engaged in issues than ever before. Party membership has fallen, however, from one in eleven people in the 1950s to one in eighty-eight (Phillips 2007: 1) and engagement is largely through voluntary and campaigning organisations outside the political process. If we really want trust and turnout, therefore, there is a case for asking whether the answer may lie in returning more power both to parliamentarians and to the people.

GREAT EXPECTATIONS 1998

Eight years ago my colleagues and I on the Consultative Steering Group (CSG) received the proof copies of our final report on practice and procedure at Holyrood, *Shaping Scotland's Parliament* (Scottish Office 1998). We were confident, we said, that we had 'set the tone for the future of Scottish politics' (Scottish Office 1998: foreword).

We had spent twelve months reviewing best practice at Westminster, in the sub-state legislatures of the Commonwealth and Europe, and in the parliaments of comparably sized independent countries. We had studied vast quantities of submissions from experts and from Scottish civic society. We were clear that we were dealing with a double 'democratic deficit' – not just the deficit of Scotland having through the '80s and '90s a government imposed on it for which it did not vote, but also the deficit of the citizen feeling disengaged and disempowered by the institutions of the state.

We had high hopes that our proposals would 'put in place a new sort of democracy, closer to the Scottish people and more in tune with Scottish needs' (Scottish Office 1998 foreword). Ours was to be 'an open and accessible Parliament; a Parliament where power is shared with the people; where people are encouraged to participate in the policy making process which affects all our lives' (Scottish Office 1998 foreword).

After the long and hard fight to secure devolution we were, I suppose, simply echoing, and encouraging, the extraordinary optimism and great expectations of the times. Witness:

the Scottish Constitutional Convention, pledging itself to 'a way of politics that is radically different from the rituals of Westminster: more participative, more creative, less needlessly confrontational'. (Scottish Constitutional Convention 1995)

Donald Dewar, introducing the Scotland Bill in the Commons on 17 December 1998: 'We want literally to create a new politics in Scotland, bringing back popular legitimacy' in order to create 'a more pluralist, outward looking democracy in tune with the modem world'. Sir Bernard Crick, as adviser to the CSG on Standing Orders, was seeking to effect 'a change in the political culture of the country' through which 'people would think of themselves as active citizens, willing, able and equipped to have an influence in public life'. (Qualifications and Curriculum Authority 1998 section 1.5)

And that shrewd observer of the 80s and 90s, the writer and journalist Neil Ascherson, advocating a new Scottish democracy which would 'cross the gap between power and people, in times when the old model of politics and representative government is losing credibility throughout the western world.' (Ascherson 2003)

LEARNING OUR TRADE

Eight years on, I want to question the extent to which the CSG proposals *did* set the tone for Scottish politics. Are citizens really 'participating in the policy making process?', as we wanted? Have we secured the 'new politics' and 'popular legitimacy' which Donald Dewar sought? Have we, in Neil Ascherson's phrase, 'crossed the gap between power and people'?

First, we should remember the Queen's perceptive comment in her address to the Parliament in Aberdeen in May 2002: 'Scotland was never going to build a new political culture overnight. After what might be considered a parliamentary adjournment of almost three hundred years, that process will inevitably take time' (Scottish Parliament 2002).

It *has* taken time, as Members – only twenty-three of whom in Session I had previous experience of serving in a legislature, reducing to sixteen in Session II – learned their trade. From the chair, however, I can testify to a major gain in self-confidence and debating skills when I compare the early days in the Assembly Hall with the Chamber at Holyrood today.

We have a solid record of legislative achievement. We have established a distinctive agenda of Scottish solutions to Scottish problems through Land Reform, the Ban on Smoking, University Tuition Fees, Free Personal Care for the Elderly, Hunting with Hounds, the Abolition of Poindings and Warrant Sales, Protection from Abuse, the introduction of PR in local elections and other measures in the 106 acts passed to date, with a further three awaiting royal assent.

With almost 900,000 visitors through the doors of Holyrood since we opened in October 2004, and with the lobbies and committee rooms filled nightly by cross-party groups and people representing every strand of Scottish life, we are clearly one of the most accessible parliaments in the world. And, beyond Scotland, we are regularly praised by European Commissioners and parliamentary Presidents as a model of participative governance and of equality for women. But constitutional change does not of itself lead to cultural change. Devolution by itself is not a quick fix for all the ills in society. And genuine engagement with the electorate remains elusive.

A CHANGE OF CULTURE

The 1990s coalition for a Scottish parliament – the Labour Party, the SNP, the Liberal Democrats, the trades unions, the civic and voluntary organisations and the churches – was fuelled largely by anti-Thatcherism and by a belief in the enduring virtues of the Keynsian welfare state.

Indeed, to this day, Scottish politics is marked principally by coalescence around classic social democratic values and differentiated largely by disputes on the constitutional issue. These values were formed in an industrial age, but by the 1990s Scotland was moving rapidly to becoming a post-industrial society.

With all the wisdom of hindsight, I now see that my CSG colleagues and I spent far too much time on institutional reform and not nearly enough on examining the massive social and economic changes, in Scotland as well as in the rest of the UK, over the last two decades of the twentieth century.

Today the majority of our citizens are better educated, more affluent, more mobile, less deferential and more politically volatile. They are living in an Internet age in which the citizen has become a consumer of public services. They are more deeply engaged in issues than ever but are disconnected from political values and institutions shaped by the classic 'top-down' culture of representative government. They want real influence over decision-making.

Bill Clinton and Tony Blair have gone some way to recognising that public space in the new millennium is wider than the political process. That the trend is away from government to governance; away from traditional models of corporatism towards models which concentrate on process rather than structure, on information rather than power; that the days when democratic decision at the polls was followed by immediate executive action probably ended with Atlee; that this is an age of negotiated governance, in which governments facilitate and the people are empowered to take actions for themselves.

In contemporary Scotland, however, there is still a tradition of civic caution. The so-called Caledonian cringe has led a whole range of commentators, particularly in our American diaspora, to criticise our poverty of ambition. We may have changed the stage on which we perform, but there is still the temptation to sing the same old songs.

We have addressed the first democratic deficit since, if we make mistakes now, they are our mistakes and it is difficult to blame London. But the second democratic deficit, of engaging the citizen sufficiently to ensure trust and turnout, remains largely unresolved.[2]

PARTICIPATION AND THE PARLIAMENT

Over the past seven and a half years the Scottish Executive and Parliament have gone to extraordinary lengths to try and accommodate participatory principles within the political framework of representative government.

In the 1980s the old Scottish Office had thirty or so consultations per year. With the coming of the Scottish Parliament, in 2000 there were 141, increasing to 188 in 2004 – somewhere around 900 consultations in total since day one of devolution in 1999. Over the same period there have been several hundred consultations by the Parliament and its Committees, in locations the length and breadth of Scotland, from inner cities to remote islands.

The methods used have broken barriers. Our Equal Opportunities Committee has taken evidence in gypsy caravans, Social Inclusion in drug-users flats, Environment in fields spread with sewage sludge, Justice 2 in prison cells. Education, in its inquiry into the languages of ethnic minorities, has put out documentation in Arabic, Bengali, Cantonese, Punjabi and Urdu. Schoolgirls have been invited to Holyrood to have their say, with force and conviction – 'You have ruined our lives' – on the impact of the Scottish Qualifications Authority fiasco upon them personally. Tiny carers have enacted their own little play on what it is like, aged ten, to have to cope with an alcoholic mother, get your siblings off to school, buy the food and pay the bills but never be able in the playground to share what life is like for fear of being seen as different.

Representatives of Scotland's business community meet annually in our Chamber, this year with thirty-four MSPs including a number of ministers. There have been similar plenary sessions with disabled people and community councillors. Events like the Carnegie Medals for Humanity Ceremony, the J8 gathering before the G8 at Gleneagles, the Malawi Partnership and the Microsoft World Government Leaders Forum next January flood Holyrood with participants from home and abroad.

Almost every night the Garden Lobby and Committee Rooms are filled with meetings organised by our sixty-two cross-party groups and other organisations – there have been 242 such participative events this year alone, and around 550 since we moved into our new campus. With 900,000 visitors off the street and through our doors in the same period, Enric Miralles' dream of his building being a place of 'constructive conversation, not sterile confrontation' has been fulfilled.

Alan Lent, Director of Research for the Power Commission Inquiry, came to the Scottish Parliament in May of this year for a Public Involvement event organised by our Futures Forum and targeted at older people. He wrote later: 'The Commission was genuinely inspired by what it saw in Scotland. Westminster has not reached even the aspiration of being participative. The very idea of holding an event like this in the House of Commons Chamber is unthinkable' (Scotland's Futures Forum 2006).

It is more difficult, though, to quantify the impact of this consultation culture; to translate outputs into outcomes, and to meet the citizens' demand that engagement means more than shared conversation. Certainly MSPs' speeches are regularly illuminated by instances of what they have learned at grassroots level. Members Business debates regularly take up themes put forward by constituents or campaigning groups. But such debates, though they regularly raise issues of concern to the citizen, do not call for any specific action. Nor are they put to the vote.

The pressures of the government's legislative and issues programme – 'a treadmill', said the Procedures Committee in 2003 – are such that opportunities for committees and Members to bring forward their own bills based on popular demand fall considerably short of what the CSG hoped for in 1999. To date, over seven and a half years, there have been only four committee and eight Members' bills, some being of a purely technical or procedural nature. There is currently gridlock on such bills lodged for consideration before the end of the present parliament. However, Tommy Sheridan's Abolition of Poindings and Warrant Sales Act and Keith Harding's Dog Fouling Act undoubtedly show how popular demand can be turned into law.

Nor should we forget that the mere introduction of a Member's bill, with committee support at Stage I, can bring leverage to prompt legislation, a change in regulations or review by the Executive. Witness Stewart Maxwell's Smoking Bill, Michael Matheson's proposals on domestic sprinklers, Colin Fox's Bill on Prescription Charging, Mike Russell's Gaelic Bill, Alex Neil's Bill on Public Appointments, Robin Harper's Bill on Organic Food, and Margo MacDonald's Bills on Prostitution.

There are signs, therefore, that engagement can bring results – particularly through petitions, to which I shall come shortly. But there remain problems in grafting participatory governance onto representative government. I want to make it clear that I am not blaming anyone for this, not least the Minister for Parliamentary Business, Margaret Curran, who has got to do the government's business but who genuinely tries to be inclusive. The problem is that we currently have a system which does not easily lend itself to our fourth principle of the sharing of power.

There is the problem of time in some committees. In total since 2003 they have spent 1,375 hours on legislation and 847 hours on inquiries and consultation. That may not seem unreasonable but several committees – Europe and External Affairs, for example – had no legislation to consider, which skews the figures. Those committees closest to the citizen's concerns, covering justice, communities, health and the environment had a much tighter schedule leaving on average, only about one-fifth of their time for consultation.

Committees also have a continuity problem. The CSG was clear that Members should serve on a committee for a full four years, gaining insight, experience and contacts in a specific policy field along the way. The CSG also took the view that being a committee convener was an alternative career path to being at least the equivalent of a junior minister. In practice Members and conveners both have been swapped around to meet the needs of party.

There is also the issue of whipping to the needs of government and opposition alike so that all sing from the same sheet. Business managers possess real power in setting the speaking order, deciding who gets a Members' debate, who receives a ministerial or leader's visit, who is nominated for an overseas visit. As one Member put it to me: 'We are tarred with tribalism. Party interest is put first. Since we are always in election mode – Westminster, Holyrood, Europe – it takes a brave soul to take an independent line.'

There is the problem that, given a tight turnaround and little time for feedback from consultations, many of those who contribute are perforce 'the usual suspects' – civic organisations built into the system, entrenched in their networks and in their beliefs. The most common complaint voiced by respondents to MORI and ICM about consultations is that many are in 'tick box' format . . . starting with a top-down proposal not the bottom-up knowledge of the citizen . . . leaving insufficient time for discussion and feedback . . . and, in consequence, are seen as 'cosmetic window-dressing'.

The public perception is that there is still a gap between the people and power. And that the sharing of power between Parliament, people and government is not yet what was promised apart, that is, from one Holyrood initiative in which we are seen to be world leaders, our Public Petitions system.

THE POWER OF PETITIONS

As a young MP I used to take petitions from Clackmannanshire to the Commons. I would bob several times at the bar, bob again at the table, bob as I passed the Speaker, and then plop the petition in the poke behind his chair. After which not much happened at all.

The CSG decided that petitions had to be formally acknowledged, considered in public and, if appropriate, be referred to a subject committee. This was to ensure that the citizen would get full feedback and, hopefully, results for his or her actions. The uptake has been extraordinary – 1,020 petitions to date, around 100 of them submitted electronically. Big petitions, like that from the Cod Crusaders, with over 160,000 signatures. Small petitions submitted by a single person. Petitions from every one of Scotland's constituencies and regions.

A petitions system which has been adopted by the German Bundestag and a number of the English regions and which is currently being studied by the French National Assembly and several Commonwealth parliaments. Compare Westminster and ask why the Mother of Parliaments receives only eighty or so petitions a year.

Now we are getting close to answering the sharing of power question. The answer is that, in this area, the Holyrood system *does* share power. The citizen raises the issue, the Parliament scrutinises it and the government can be required to change the law or regulations. It is a system with some elements of the Swiss power of popular initiative. Consider for a moment:

- The Blairingone petition of 2002, opposing the spreading of sewage sludge and animal blood and guts on village fields. The Environment Committee went to the hamlet to see for itself. In this Internet age, the American Academy of Sciences gave electronic evidence in support. The rules and regulations were radically changed.
- The Burned Children's Petition of 2004, on behalf of the 2,500 or so children scalded in Scotland each year in the bath. Thermostatic valves are now mandatory in all new and renovated properties.
- The Child Abuse Petition of 2005, seeking review of the suffering of young people in religious institutions in the 1970s. The First Minister had to respond in the Chamber, saying that what had happened was 'deplorable, unacceptable and inexcusable'. A far tighter monitoring system is now in place.

I could give other examples, but the principle is clear. In the case of petitions, the response from Parliament and the Executive is not cosmetic. There is a clear correlation between citizen action and public result.

REBALANCING POWER

There has always been a tradition of robust engagement in public life in Scotland. It is the tradition of popular sovereignty and the community of the realm first enshrined in the Declaration of Arbroath, developed by medieval philosophers like John Major, put into practice by reformers like George Buchanan, enshrined in the National Covenant, celebrated in the Disruption and reaffirmed in the Claim of Right of the Constitutional Convention.

It is also a philosophy running through Scotland's Age of Enlightenment. Thinkers like Thomas Reid were well aware that the state could not do everything, that the Parliament now sat in London not Edinburgh and that, in consequence, it should be held in check by committed citizens contributing to the commonweal through civic organisation.

The duopoly of Kirk and Crown in Parliament in an earlier age was replaced by secular or civic Calvinism. It was a position in the mainstream of both Scottish and European thought – a polis, a political community best governed by the twin assemblies of civil society and the state. Of separate but co-ordinate jurisdictions of mutually complementary bodies.

It was never a society in which the citizen would be greeted by shouts of 'hats off, strangers' as at Westminster. In the Enlightenment all could engage, regardless of rank. The concept of the community of the realm opened public space to academics, artisans, artists, doctors, economists, engineers, entrepreneurs, philosophers, scientists and writers alike. It led to a flourishing of distinctively Scottish civic organisations and, through the work of Robert Owen and the Co-operative Movement, of social organisations in the nineteenth century.

I want now to put forward some suggestions for the rebalancing of power between people, legislators and government in Scotland's third parliament. They will go some way, I believe, to restoring trust and turnout through a strengthened fourth principle.

A PARLIAMENTARY CONCORDAT

How can we give renewed voice, feedback and action to the people? How can Parliament be strengthened in its primary role of scrutiny and holding the government to account? What share of time does the Executive need over the next four years?

Should committees and individual Members be guaranteed more time and resources to bring forward their own bills and do more independent inquiries? Should their conveners be subject to election by the whole House? Should they routinely return to Acts after a couple of years, to see how they are working in practice and to address popular concerns through post-legislative scrutiny? And what measures can be put in place to ensure that when a Member joins a committee, he or she will be expected to serve there for a full parliament gaining experience, expertise and contacts in a specific field of policy?

Should the authority of Business Managers be lessened and more power be given to backbench MSPs? For the first two parliaments the Presiding Officers have largely accepted their daily nominations of who speaks in what order during debates, and their recommendations for who gets a Member's Business debate at the end of the day. While it would still be necessary to spread speaking time proportionately among the parties, would a freer hand for the Chair encourage more MSPs to contribute and to speak out on awkward issues?

Should we agree, as the Procedures Committee wants, to the introduction of interpolations at Holyrood? Such an initiative, which is available to Members of some Scandinavian legislatures or the Catalan Cortes, would enable MSPs to submit motions for a very short debate (and, unlike Member's Business, for a vote), one of which would be selected by the Presiding Officer every six weeks. In the event of the motion being carried, the Bureau would be required to timetable a full debate in the immediate future.

Should the head of government be subject to greater and more sustained scrutiny? At present First Minister's Questions are largely theatre – who's up? who's down? what are the headlines of the week? – and none the worse for that, as the crowded galleries show. But there is little opportunity to dig below the surface, to identify trends and long-term goals. In fairness to Jack McConnell, in response to questions from me as Chair of the Conveners Liaison Group in 2002, he indicated willingness to undergo wider questioning. There was no overall agreement to do so, however, by the conveners themselves.

At Westminster, the Prime Minister appears before the Liaison Committee of thirty chairmen of Select Committees 'to hear evidence of matters of public policy'. Is there not a case, in our third parliament, for similar scrutiny by our conveners?

There is also the question of the sharing of power at different levels of governance – in particular, with MPs and local councillors. In 1999 I was deputed by Sir David Steel to draw up regulations governing the relations between constituency and regional Members. The so-called Reid Principles work after a fashion, but produce regular complaints to and adjudications from the Presiding Officer, and require revisiting. Their drafting, and the necessity of securing agreement across the parties, was so difficult that the original intention of trying to obtain a similar convention with MPs, local councillors and public bodies was abandoned.

All the evidence I have suggests that this area remains messy. While some elected representatives do try to stay within their mandate, passing reserved or local matters to the appropriate representative – and vice versa – others do not. The usual defence is that if a constituent comes to them they cannot be seen to be doing nothing. But that is hardly in the spirit of devolution. It leads to duplication of effort and is profoundly confusing for the citizen. It runs counter to the European Convention on Local Self-Government of 1985 that 'the level of local autonomy is itself a direct indicator of authentic democracy'.

I believe therefore that there is a real case for trying to establish new compacts between Holyrood, Westminster and local government on the sharing of power. And thereafter for a joint publicity campaign so that the citizen knows clearly who is responsible for what. The process might well include a mandatory yearly report to constituents by elected representatives, followed by an Annual General Meeting, proposals which I shall discuss shortly.

Finally, there is a need to review our current consultation culture. If all the research done for the Power Commission and other surveys is correct, there is a widespread public belief that much of it is cosmetic, lacks feedback and displays little correlation between private input and public output. There is also, in any case, a common view that consultations are largely run in conjunction with the 'usual suspects', the large network organisations in receipt of state funding. This is a long way from what the committed citizen wants: meaningful consultation, clear feedback and a correlation between inputs and outcomes.

There is plenty in all of this for an early debate next year on the fourth principle. There are legacy papers from the Presiding Officers, the Conveners Liaison Group and the Procedures Committee, plus significant academic research, which would help inform discussion prior to the publication of the government's legislative programme in September.

A parliamentary concordat then would recognise that participatory and representative governance are not in conflict, but can enrich and strengthen each other. It would recognise that the duty of government is to try and get its programme through, but equally that the duty of Parliament is to scrutinise the Executive and to hold it to account in the name of the people. It would acknowledge that, if trust in politics is to be restored, that means more sustained and direct engagement of the citizen.

A REAL SAY FOR THE CITIZEN

There is one clear way to provide citizens with tangible power over what they see as the crucial issues of the day, even if these have been ignored by the Executive and by the Parliament. That is the right of political initiative through referendum. It enables them to bring single issues into the formal democratic sphere in a far more precise way than through a general election or membership of a political party.

The referendum is widely used in Switzerland. It has decided major questions in Ireland, Italy and New Zealand. In this month's Congressional mid-term elections in the United States, there were 200 single-issue referenda – seventy-six of them initiated by citizens groups.

I know all the arguments against. They are not part of our tradition (though there have been thirty-one referenda in the UK in the last decade). They would be hijacked by the media and by lobbyists (though that could be avoided by stipulating that public and elected representatives must first enter into dialogue on the terms). They would lead to ill-considered and populist measures (forgetting that, in other countries, citizens have refused the return of capital punishment, have voted for increased taxes and have approved the use of soft drugs for recreational use).

I think it perfectly possible for the Electoral Commission to come up with viable proposals – 5 per cent threshold of the electorate, say; a window of several months for Parliament or government to address the issue before the referendum is triggered; a requirement for 60 per cent of the electorate to participate, after which a simple majority would be sufficient for the measure to pass into law; if the proposal fails, no return to the issue for five years; and all proposals to be voted on a single Referendum Day per year (which could be held concurrently with Westminster, Holyrood or European elections).

I note that, in the Commons, government spokespeople have recently been toying with the idea of allowing citizens to initiate inquiries or hearings into local public bodies. That too is worth consideration in Scotland. Referenda return power to where it ultimately belongs, the citizen. Where used overseas in conjunction with elections, the effect on turnout is very substantial. And often the mere threat of a popular initiative is enough to spur governments and parliamentarians into action.

CITIZENS ON THE RECORD

There was a proposal brought forward by Bernard Crick and David Millar in their draft proposals to the Consultative Steering Group which, in my view, had merit but which was rejected as a step too far at the time. It addressed citizen's concerns that issues brought by them to their MSP are not officially recognised at Holyrood.

Crick and Millar proposed that where a submission on a specific issue is presented to a Minister or committee convener, is in order and is backed by 1,000 verified signatures there must be a response printed, in the Official Report of Parliament. Where the submission is supported by 10,000 verified signatures, this would automatically trigger a debate (Crick and Millar 1995). This is a relatively simple way of ensuring a correlation between citizen action and parliamentary response. It puts popular concerns at the heart of Holyrood. And, as happens with draft Member's bills, it may be enough from time to time to trigger investigation or a change in regulations. Eight years from the Consultative Steering Group, it is a proposal worthy of reconsideration.

Annual reports and AGMs

Our current allowances system permits MSPs to claim the costs of printing and delivering a report to their constituents. It is fair to say that a considerable number of these are selective, steer round contentious issues, heavily feature photographs of the Member's participation in constituency events, and are written with an eye on the next election.

I have no doubt that the vast majority of MSPs work extraordinarily hard on behalf of the people they represent. But there are still widely held public views, supported by research for the Power Commission, that they do not engage enough between elections and are more responsive to their party than to their electorate.

Currently, any reports to constituents have to be paid for out of general allowances, which also cover staff and office costs. There is a case, therefore, for separate public funding of an annual report by all MSPs to their electorate, which would be the basic document for discussion at a mandatory Annual General Meeting with constituents. At this meeting, the Member would report back on what he or she has done in the previous twelve months, take questions, and invite comments on the year ahead.

There are a number of 'best practice' proposals produced by the Power Commission (Smith 2005), which would ensure that the yearly reporting procedure would allow the greatest possible public involvement, feedback, and information. Among these is the suggestion that meetings are best designed and managed by independent facilitators to reduce the possibilities of political manipulation or hijacking by interest groups.

Thinking ahead, repositioning now

Participation in the first parliament was largely restricted to the voluntary and civic organisations which had been around since the Constitutional Convention. A number of these were firmly rooted in the social democratic consensus – providing advice one day, drawing down funding the next – to which I referred earlier. There were expressions of considerable disappointment that proposals to co-opt some of their number as non-voting members of committees did not come to pass.

There was a similar spirit running through the Scottish Civic Forum, funded by the Executive to the tune of £150,000 a year, rising to £200,000 before being halved and then ended. There were those who saw the Forum as a parallel assembly, constantly monitoring and commenting on government and parliamentary activity. It might have developed into a powerful rod to beat the back of Holyrood if, as its Chairman Campbell Christie (Campbell Christie in exchange of views with the Presiding Officer) wanted, it had focused all the disparate voices and interests on consideration of one or two themes a year. But it suffered, according to one observer, from the 'dominance of the usual suspects involved within its activities and within its structures'.

Nor did the Forum ever develop a financial base, independent of government. Contributions from civic organisations themselves remained modest, many of whom – in what is a tight competitive market – preferred to concentrate their resources on what was to become a plethora of public affairs officers and on beating their own path to ministers, MSPs and civil servants.

In the second parliament, I have tried to widen engagement along older, community of the realm, lines. To take the view that public space embraces all citizens who serve the commonweal. To include artists, academics, entrepreneurs, free thinkers, journalists and wealth creators. Not just because many of them had been profoundly critical of the Parliament in its formative years but because participation has maximum impact before a bill is ready and waiting in draft format. And, in the area of policy entrepreneurship, that is where they had valuable ideas and experience.

Scotland's Futures Forum was established in 2005. It was 'in the Parliament but not of the Parliament', since it had its own constitution and an independent board including the Head of the Civil Service in Scotland, the Principal of Edinburgh University, the Chief Executive of a leading bank, a widely successful social entrepreneur, the former General Secretary of the Scottish Trades Union Congress and three MSPs.

Futures thinking is not primarily about the future. It is about thinking out of the box, peering over the horizon at upcoming challenges and opportunities, and considering how society should reposition now. It accepts that there is a great deal of knowledge down below, if it can only be tapped. Futures thinking deals with change and unpredictable surprises; conventional thinking prefers to stick with positions and predictable trends. Futures thinking is multi-sectoral; conventional thinking is sectoral, built around ideas of 'that's not my job'. Futures thinking requires patience and perseverance; conventional thinking looks for quick wins. Futures thinking is proactive, concentrating on making the future; conventional thinking looks for opportunity, or simply drifts listlessly into that future.

The Futures Forum has brought progressive thinkers like Senator George Marshall, Bjorn Lindborg, Professor Howard Gardner of Harvard, Gary Crawly of the Science Foundation of Ireland and Lord Sutherland into Holyrood. They have dealt with such issues as conflict in society, environmental change, the nature of thought in the Internet age, innovation in small countries, and the positive impact of ageing. They, in turn, have attracted a wide range of citizens turned off by the classic political process. None of these thinkers has preached to their audiences; instead, they have all taken for granted that a great depository of practical wisdom resides among citizens committed to the public good and have wanted to listen.

The Office of the Prime Minister of France, through its *Commissariat General du Plan* – the Secretariat which, under Jean Monnet, launched the Iron and Steel Community and then the European Union itself – has been monitoring the Forum from its foundation. It is instructive to hear its current Director-General, formed in an elitist top-down tradition of governance, referring to the pool of 'bottom-up' expertise available in Scotland and quoting Voltaire during our Age of Enlightenment: 'It is to Scotland that we must look for our idea of civilisation.'

The Futures Forum will continue with this form of popular engagement. Now that significant funding is coming on stream from foundations, the commercial sector and public agencies, it will next work in marginalised communities up and down Scotland. It will start from the premise that the people know best, and tease out what parliaments and governments should do from there. A proper sharing of power in what, with vision, can be the start of a new age of Engagement and Enlightenment in the New Scotland.

THE VISION THING

It's all about vision, of course, and the four basic components of our first Enlightenment – commonweal, common sense, cosmopolitanism and optimism. It's also about understanding that we live in times of extraordinarily fast change.

In this essay I have argued that in Holyrood we have grafted the promise of participatory governance onto a system of representative government.

We have gone a long way in producing Scottish solutions to Scottish problems, and have gained in confidence along the way. We have been largely successful in securing the first, second and third principles of accessibility, accountability and equal opportunities.

But the fourth principle of the sharing of power remains elusive. In consequence, we are still not scoring high on trust. The prospect of minority government or renegotiated coalition next May provides an opportunity to think how that principle can be strengthened. I have outlined a number of ideas on how that can happen.

To do so we have to challenge a version of civic society formed in the industrial age. We have to accept that we now live largely in a post-industrial age and adventure out of our cosy consensus. We need a vision of things which moves from the first stage of constitutional reform to the next stage of developing a wider political agenda of engagement. We have to return to the older Scottish tradition of the commonweal and the whole community of the realm.

Notes

1. This essay substantially reproduces the lecture delivered by George Reid on his appointment as Stevenson Professor on 23 November 2006, given shortly before demitting office as the Scottish Parliament's Presiding Officer, six months before the May 2007 election. The lecture looked forward to a third term of the Parliament where there might be no outright majority. As it turned out the resulting election led to a minority SNP government. The full text is available on http://www.scottishparliament.uk/corporate/po/george_reid_stevenson_200.pdf.
2. In his lecture George Reid illustrates 'the pace of change' in economic and social life that has occurred in Clackmannanshire, the area he has represented as an MP or MSP from 1974. This is omitted here.

References

Ascherson, Neil (2003), *Stone Voices*, London: Granta.
Consultative Steering Group on the Scottish Parliament (1999), Report. Available at: http://www.scotland.gov.uk/library/documents-w5/rcsg-04.htm.
Crick, Bernard and David Millar (1995), *To Make the Parliament of Scotland a Model for Democracy*, Edinburgh: John Wheatley Centre.
Electoral Commission (2006), *Scotland – Poll Position: Public Attitudes towards Scottish Parliamentary and Local Government Elections*. Available at: http://www.electoralcommission.org.uk/document-summary?assetid=16169.
Phillips, Hayden (2007), *Strengthening Democracy: Fair and Sustainable Funding of Political Parties*, London: Stationery Office. Available at: http://www.partyfundingreview.gov.uk/files/strengthening_democracy.pdf.

Power Commission (2006), *Power to the People: the Power Inquiry*. Available at: http://www.powerinquiry.org/report/documents/PowertothePeople_002.pdf.

Qualifications and Curriculum Authority (1998), *Education for Citizenship and the Teaching of Democracy in Schools (Crick Report)*, London: QCA.

Scotland's Futures Forum (2006), *Public Involvement – Power to the People?* Available at: http://www.scotlandfutureforum.org/assets/library/files/application/1213712890.doc, 12 May 2006.

Scottish Constitutional Convention (1995), *Scotland's Parliament, Scotland's Right*. Available at: http://www.almac.co.uk/business_park/scc/scc-rep.htm#We_Commend.

Scottish Office (1998), *Shaping Scotland's Parliament: Report of the Consultative Steering Group of the Scottish Parliament*. Available at: http://www.scotland.gov.uk/library/documents-w5/rcsg-00.htm.

Scottish Parliament (2002), Report. Available at: http://www.scottish.parliament.uk/business/officialreports/meetingsparliament/or-02/sor0528-02.htm#Col12128.

Smith, G. (2005), *Beyond the Ballot: the Power Inquiry*. Available at: http://www.powerinquiry.org/publications/documents/BeyondtheBallot_000.pdf.

4

Power and Public Services: for Customers or Citizens?

David Donnison

The questions of governance I shall be dealing with in this essay were central to Bernard Crick's interests and I was looking forward to discussing them with him. My answers to them would have been better had I had the opportunity to do so.[1]

THE POST-WAR SETTLEMENT

In every generation there are people who remember events that occurred early in their lives which changed their world. I cannot recall where I was when news of John Kennedy's assassination broke, but I shall never forget the moment when I heard of Labour's victory in the 1945 election. I was a midshipman standing on the bridge of a cruiser steaming through the Indian Ocean in a black tropical night when the news reached us from the radio cabin. By next morning the lower decks were buzzing with it. Meanwhile, in parts of the wardroom there was considerable dismay.

Two weeks later we docked in Portsmouth to reload before returning to fight the Japanese in the Pacific. Given a forty-eight-hour pass, I soon found myself standing in the corridor of a train, crammed with service-men and stuck at Reading station. Two men with dark suits, bowler hats and briefcases came hurrying across the platform to get aboard; but seeing there was no hope of squeezing into our packed corridor, they turned away saying 'Let's try a first class carriage'. The sailor standing next to me leaned out of the open window and shouted 'First class? First class? There'll be no more bloody classes when this war's over!' – his voice echoing through the cavernous station. I could sense the support he was getting from soldiers and sailors all along the corridor.

Britain, like many other countries, was in a pre-revolutionary mood. Two hapless civil servants were seen as representatives of the class that had led these men and their families into two murderous world wars, and slumps that had condemned millions of them to poverty-stricken dependence on humiliating poor laws. When the war ended, the ruling classes of Western countries had to reach settlements with their workers that would hold their societies together – bearing in mind that, beyond the Elbe, there lay the vast Red Army; a constant reminder that other regimes were possible.

Along with full employment and the recognition of trade unions and workers' rights, these settlements included various guarantees of incomes, educational opportunities, health care, and eventually housing; provided by services which came to be called 'the welfare state'.

THE PUBLIC-SERVICE PROFESSIONS COME TO POWER

For as long as anyone could remember, British governance, as working people experienced it, had been run by the local gentry. It was they who had chaired the improvement commissions, the municipal authorities, the school boards, and the poor law, hospital and public health committees. They were also the landlords and employers of the people who depended on these services, their vicars on Sunday, their commanders in time of war, and the magistrates before whom they appeared when in trouble with the law.

Some of the gentry had been humane and radical reformers – particularly their most distinguished women, who had few other opportunities for leadership. Where would we have been without Florence Nightingale, Josephine Butler, Octavia Hill, Beatrice Webb, Eleanor Rathbone . . .? But the Peterloo massacre, in which sabre-wielding publicans, mill owners and landlords cut down a crowd meeting for peaceful protest showed what the gentry could do when frightened by threats of reform. Later, the more brutal of the Highland clearances showed what they could do when frightened by threats of bankruptcy.

The coming of the welfare state changed all that, shifting many of the local gentry's powers to central government and to the public-service professions which staffed the expanding social services. Another recollection illustrates the change. When I took up my first academic job, in the University of Manchester in 1950, Professor Metcalfe Brown, our formidable Professor of Public Health, told me how, in the 1920s, he got his first job as a medical officer of health for a rural district in Kent. He was asked only one question by the committee interviewing candidates for the post. 'Do you hunt?' It happened that he could answer 'Yes' to that question and he was immediately appointed. A few months later he felt compelled to close the local all-age school which was plainly unfit for human use. He was promptly summoned to the Hall where the chairman of his committee boomed at him as he walked up the drive, 'We only appointed you because you said you would hunt. You've never been with the hounds. And now you want to close my school!' (And it was, in a sense, 'his' school because his family had built it long ago.) By the 1950s, when I knew him, Metcalfe Brown was teaching the young doctors he trained to be medical officers that they should never call their committees together without writing the minutes of the meeting beforehand. But take care not to circulate the minutes with the papers for the meeting.

Julian Tudor Hart, in his great book on *The Political Economy of Health Care*, reminds us that before the Second World War many doctors were poor. Few were regarded as social equals by the gentry. The senior partner in the poshest medical practice in the South Wales town where he worked for most of his life always had to go into the biggest houses through the servant's entrance. Only when Lord Horder, King George the Fifth's doctor, was summoned from London to confirm the local man's diagnosis was a doctor let in for the first time through the front door. It was the NHS, Tudor Hart points out, that ensured British doctors would never be poor again.

Power was not handed over indiscriminately to the professions. It went to their dominant groups. Thus it was that we got, not the Health Service based on front-line general practices that Nye Bevan had hoped for, but a hospital-dominated service in which the most prestigious specialism's – not geriatrics or psychiatry – got the lion's share of resources. Likewise, the grammar schools and their backers in the more powerful universities hung on to their dominant role long after most other Western countries had recognised that this selective system penalised the families whose children most needed good schools. And when the Robbins Committee called for a great expansion in our universities, they brushed aside the pleas of expert witnesses who argued that these be placed, like the American City Colleges, in the centres of old industrial towns where they could be reached by families who had never been to a university before. Instead, they were set up in attractive but somewhat decayed cathedral towns with good train services enabling professors to get to London and back within a day for professional and political meetings: the kinds of places where dons like to live. There were no conspiracies. None were needed. These are the ways in which power tends to work.

The post-war settlements achieved in many Western countries – with crucial help from Marshall Aid when their first ambitious hopes faltered – brought great advances for their working people; particularly through high levels of employment, and patterns of economic development that created a steady increase in opportunities for white-collar work. For many years British society grew more equal in its distributions of housing, income and wealth.

A CHANGING SOCIAL STRUCTURE

In the early 1970s these equalising trends came to an end. Slowly at first – and then rapidly in the second half of the eighties – Britain grew increasingly unequal; partly because of changes in the economy, but largely because of changes in taxes and benefits deliberately introduced by the government. Class conflict was back, but in new forms. No longer did the main conflicts divide the two-thirds of our people who depended on manual work from the one-third who depended on non-manual work – those I glimpsed from a railway train in 1945. There were now fewer manual workers, and the main divisions ran between 'middle England' – the central strata of our society (many of them readers of our most popular newspapers, the *Daily Mail* and *News of the World*) – and diverse minorities excluded from mainstream opportunities by a variety of factors: illiteracy, racial prejudice, physical and mental frailties, lone parenthood, residence in unpopular peripheral housing estates; and often by combinations of these and other things. Their diversity explains their political weakness: the old working class had a solidarity that was a source of great strength, but there is no rainbow coalition of the excluded. Meanwhile other conflicts were to emerge at the top end of the economy as small minorities secured runaway increases in income and wealth.

Some of these social conflicts were played out across the counters, the classrooms and consulting rooms of the welfare state. The public-service professions and the services in which they worked were entangled in these divisive patterns and played their parts in the exclusion of vulnerable minorities.

Some conflicts were brutally explicit. 'What would you call a thousand dead housing officers?' ran a familiar joke on Glasgow's big housing estates. 'A start' was the reply. The people who coined that one called social security officials, on whose benefits so many of them depended, 'the SS'. And the officials, if asked by strangers what they did for a living, would demurely reply, 'I'm a civil servant'. Other conflicts were implicit but more fundamental. Research on public health long ago taught us to recognise the 'inverse care law' which seems to apply all over the world: the poorer and sicker a population is, the less the quantity and the poorer the quality of health care it will receive. Those who need most always tend to get least. It is possible to break out of that negative correlation, as Tudor

Hart showed in his own practice. But that took a great deal of work, in collaboration with his patients, the trade unions representing them, and his local authority.

Health is not the only field in which inverse care laws operate. Britain's top 10 per cent of school pupils perform about as well as any in the world; but our bottom 30 per cent generally do worse than their counterparts in other developed countries. If you look at the resources devoted to the education of each group that is not surprising. Even our tax system takes proportionately more from the poor than the rich. While the public-service professions are not entirely responsible for these patterns, they are deeply implicated in them.

The Millan Committee's report on Scotland's mental health services and the Mental Health (Care and Treatment) (Scotland) Act of 2003 which followed from it contained paragraph after paragraph designed to protect patients from unjustified incarceration, unnecessary violence, covert medication, financial exploitation, sexual abuse and other painful and humiliating experiences (Scottish Executive 2001). That was not because these things had become more common. It was because Bruce Millan's Committee was the first to include users of the mental health services among their members. They met repeatedly with them and the families caring for them, and listened carefully to what they said. Recognising the power relationships operating within mental health services, the Committee said every patient with learning disabilities or mental health problems should be entitled to the help of a free and independent advocate, and the Mental Health Act provided for that.

THE PROFESSIONS DETHRONED

These conflicts had political implications which became clear when Margaret Thatcher's governments made their assault on the public-service professions. Royal Commissions and Committees of Inquiry were drastically reduced in number; trade unions and professional associations were disempowered; so were local government and the universities. These were the power bases of the professions. Nye Bevan had to negotiate for months with the BMA (British Medical Association), the Royal Colleges and the top hospitals before he could put together the bill that eventually created the NHS. Forty years later, when Kenneth Clark carried out the biggest reforms of the NHS since Bevan's day, these bodies first heard about them with the rest of us from the *Today* programme.

When the public-service professions turned out in the early eighties under the banners of their unions and professional associations to demonstrate against 'the cuts', their patients, students, tenants, claimants and clients did not march at their side. When, in 1980, the TUC (Trade Union Council) mounted what was to be a big demonstration against the government's assault upon the welfare state, hardly anyone turned up. They did not try again. Thatcher and her colleagues noted that – and pressed on. Determined to bring the providers of social services under closer control, they developed fairly coherent doctrines for this purpose.

The purchasing and providing of services were to be split; the state doing the purchasing and, wherever possible, commercial and voluntary agencies doing the providing. Services were to be contracted out to providers who had regularly to bid for renewal of their contracts in a competitive marketplace. New plant, previously created by the state, was to be commissioned through private enterprises which rented schools and hospitals back to the state under profitable, long-term contracts. Other services remaining in the public sector were to be priced, evaluated and compared. More information was to be published about their performance. Their 'customers' (as they were encouraged to describe themselves) were in various ways to be offered more choices between the various schools, surgeons or old people's homes available to them. The process has been taken further by Tony Blair's and Gordon Brown's governments. 'Individualisation', 'monetisation' and 'choice' are central characteristics of a system designed to increase the efficiency and accountability of public services by subjecting them to market disciplines.

There is a lot to be said for some features of this regime. It is helpful to us all if politicians, central and local, can speak whole-heartedly for the users of public services, instead of speaking mainly for their providers as they often have done in the past. It is useful to know what each service costs and what it achieves. But the market regime has provoked a formidable response from distinguished critics who deplore its other effects. Vivien Stern's magisterial analysis of prison services in many countries and the malign effects of commercial enterprise in this field is perhaps the most powerful indictment of 'marketisation' within a particular service (Stern 2006). Embedded in Julian Tudor Hart's massive review of health care, informed by much research and a lifetime of clinical experience, is a passionate condemnation of the effects of market forces within the NHS; Allyson Pollock offers a well-researched and more polemical attack on the same trends (Pollock 2004). And, as I write, the current issue of *Soundings* magazine presents two articles by Peter Beresford and Sally Baker and others on social and community care that criticise the effects of 'the Government's continuing commitment to the market agenda in public services' (Baker *et al.* 2008; Beresford 2008).

These, I think, are the main reasons for the anger of these writers.

1. Priorities for the care of patients, prisoners, social work clients and other 'customers', and for the valuation of staff (now 'factors of production') depend increasingly on comparisons of the costs they impose and the revenues they attract, not on the needs of service users, the quality of care and treatment provided, or the human potential of those who care for them.
2. The staff dealing with patients and social work clients tends to become more numerous, employed by larger numbers of agencies, and they turn over more rapidly (both on a daily basis and over the longer term). So they have less opportunity to work as a team and to provide continuity of care. Co-ordination of their work becomes harder, and no-one is really in over-all charge of a patient's care. Small but essential tasks (bringing a bed pan, asking why a patient isn't eating the food brought to her and finding some more acceptable alternative) get neglected because no-one is specifically paid to do these things or to check that they are done.
3. Information and the power it confers, gain a monetary value, so people become more reluctant to share it with colleagues who have become competitors. (Tudor Hart gives a telling example of Swansea hospitals whose managers acquired deliberately incompatible computer programmes.)
4. Monetisation and marketisation produce unattractive political effects (in the general sense of the exercise of power). For example: (a) Human Rights Law that applies to the public sector does not apply to private employers, so privatised staff lose rights and protections. (b) Employment contracts may forbid public statements about the work of the agency concerned, thus prohibiting normal contributions to public debate, and whistle-blowing. (c) Directors from the private sector sit on committees which make merit awards and offer other benefits – thereby muzzling their best-informed potential critics. (d) The practice of employing expensive press officers to vet all public statements from staff, and to create rapid rebuttal units to rubbish critics is becoming more common. (e) Many of the more aggressive operators in the private sector have got jobs in ministers' private offices and as policy advisors, where they may have conflicts of interest that lead to further ill-judged expansion of the market ethos. (f) Politicians and senior officials may be reluctant to offend powerful enterprises to which they look for future employment. (g) Private sector 'philanthropy' – by pharmaceutical companies for example which fund post-graduate medical education, expensive conferences in luxurious places, and so on – is used to advance the donors' interests.
5. Economic effects can be pretty dire too. Private sector agencies which gain a large enough share of their local market – for example, for nursing and residential homes – secure monopoly power which can make them impregnable. If their contracts were not renewed or their homes closed, no other provider could be found to replace them. They may nevertheless close homes at short notice if they find it more profitable to sell the property for other uses – housing, hotels, a retail park, . . . In south-east England rising land prices have often made that an attractive option.

63

6. The aims of what should be a public service become warped. The companies that provide private prisons, Vivien Stern shows, are always more concerned to get more prisoners, rather than to achieve better rehabilitation that would reduce prison numbers. The essential point being asserted is that the private sector has a set of commercial values – a morality – inappropriate for a public service. The private prison at Doncaster (by no means the worst of its kind, I am assured) provided toilets without seats or lids, and beds without pillows because their twenty-five-year contract only required them to provide 'toilets' and 'beds and bedding'.

7. Some recent research by Paul Gregg and others at Bristol University's Centre for Market and Public Organisation suggests that the public-service ethos encourages staff to help each other out and work unpaid overtime when needed (Gregg et al. 2008). This brings massive extra resources to bear that would not be available if the same people worked in profit-making enterprises. 'Our estimate . . . suggests that an additional 120 million hours are donated in the public sector compared with similar people working in similar jobs in the private sector. This is equivalent to an extra 60,000 people'. (Which is interesting. But did they ask whether private enterprise gets harder, more disciplined work from its employees during the hours that *are* paid for? Less tea drinking? Less sick leave? We need to know the *net* effects.)

These are essentially progressive liberal criticisms of 'marketisation' within the public services. Less often heard, but equally cogent, are some hard-nosed economists' criticisms. When a product succeeds in the private sector there are investors ready and waiting to meet rising demand by producing more of it – putting less popular competing products out of business as they do so. But the state is not going to promptly expand popular clinics and schools and close down their competitors. It cannot clone the brilliant doctors and head teachers who made them successful. So more 'choice' means that queues will develop, rationing of various clumsy kinds will occur; and we know which 'customers' will be most skilled at finding their way through this jungle, and thereby exclude others less skilled at this game. Inverse care patterns will be reinforced, not eliminated.

In the private sector, more is better and 'greed is good': more output, sales, customers and profits. In the public sector, 'success' calls for fewer offenders and prisoners, fewer smokers and cancer patients, less litter to be picked off our streets and parks. The strategies required and the incentives to support them are quite different.

More generally, increasing reliance on the ethos of competitive markets tends to destroy the collective ethos – the social solidarity – fostered by a sense of shared citizenship and the mutual trust nurtured by such a culture; and mutual trust is a basic requirement of innovative and productive economies.

LOOKING BEYOND PUBLIC VERSUS PRIVATE

I do not wish to contest anything said in the progressive literature. Indeed, I agree with most of it. But the things not said bother me. None of these authors – or many others writing in the same vein – gives frank and serious attention to the failings of the public services. None recognise that the politicians who imposed market values on public services – often crude and destructive values –were contending with real problems that their electorates expected them to tackle.

Nothing is said about the massive proportion of any increase in public expenditure on our health and social services that is devoted to making life easier for the staff rather than for the service users; or the recurring failure to complete public projects within agreed deadlines and budgets. Nothing is said about our schools' and colleges' rejection and betrayal of the children of the less-skilled working class – which would be regarded as scandalous in many other Western countries. As indeed it is. Was it acceptable that much of Scotland's new Mental Health Act had to be devoted to protecting patients from the mental health services? Anyone of my age has friends and relatives who have falls, strokes and hip replacements that take them into hospitals. Is it acceptable that so many of them, after (usually excellent) attention from the doctors, end up in wards where no-one will give them a wash or bring a bed pan when they need it, no-one will ask questions if they can't eat the food (just whisking it away uneaten), no-one sweeps the floor or cleans the toilets properly . . . and this in *teaching* hospitals, for God's sake. It's not surprising that hospital-acquired infections are so common. Some of these failures can be attributed to the spread of commercial values in public services. But not all of them. There are other hospitals which do an excellent job.

I could run on. We all could. But I hope I have said enough to make it clear that anyone who does not like the corrupting effects of 'marketisation' must come up with other more convincing ways of tackling the failings of the public services, and of gaining for the public-service professions the respect and support of the communities they serve. Otherwise we shall end up with market incentives as the politicians' last resort.

To repeatedly stage discussions of our public services as an argument between those who believe that the state is always better than the private sector and those who believe that it is always worse is to insult the intelligence of both: an Orwellian chant of 'Four legs good! Two legs bad!', and vice versa. Governance is a more complex affair than this. Different services respond to different incentives and call for different kinds of management. Meanwhile this formulation of the issues rules the increasingly large voluntary sector out of the discussion altogether. Are we really sure that housing associations are always worse – or better – than Council housing services? Are we sure that Mountain Rescue, or the Lifeboat Service would work better if taken over by the state or by the private sector from the voluntary organisations that run them?

MAKING THE PUBLIC-SERVICE PROFESSIONS ACCOUNTABLE

There is not space in the closing pages of one essay to explore alternative regimes with the care they deserve. But we can briefly sketch the territory that needs to be explored. We should be looking for ways of making the providers of public services more efficient, more effective, more accountable and more humane – noting that these objectives will often conflict.

We should be asking questions about widely differing scales of action. Some of the issues to be considered are *strategic and nationwide*. (How can we get much of the work now done in hospitals out into primary care and intermediate units that will be closer and more accessible to the people who need these services?) Some will be focused on *institutions*. (How do we prevent covert social selection of pupils entering secondary schools paid for by the state? How do we give residents in care homes adequate security of tenure?) Some will be focused on *individuals*. (Who will speak up for the elderly lady in a hospital or care home who cannot get a bed pan or a wash when she needs that?)

We need to think of accountability that runs *upwards* to ministries, ministers and ultimately the electorate (Is the money honestly and efficiently used? will be one of the questions they will ask); *downwards* to service users and their families (Are the school meals nourishing? – eatable? – and eaten? Do patients feel better or worse after a course of treatment?); and *internally* to staff of the service and their governing authorities (Are rates of pay and pensions adequate? Are there fair and effective arrangements for dealing with whistle-blowers?).

We have already devised many procedures for these purposes. Each deserves a book to itself. Indeed, several already have one. To simplify and sharpen this brief discussion of them I will focus on a key question, asking of each procedure whether it is likely to strengthen our role as citizens: citizens with duties as well as rights, who share a collective concern for the needs of our fellow citizens, and for the general improvement of the public services that each of us may some day have to depend on. These questions were central to the concerns of Bernard Crick. If we rely only on the individualistic incentives appropriate for customers in a competitive market we shall be led in socially destructive directions – provoking more social conflict, wasting more human potential, excluding more marginalised people, and reinforcing inverse care patterns.

1. Public-service managers have, through politicians, some general accountability to the users of their services and the electorate at large, and politicians have incentives to seek the improvement of services for all voting citizens; which is important. But managers have much closer encounters every day with spokesmen of the public-service unions and professional associations. If their members withdraw their labour the service collapses: there is no alternative source of supply. So political accountability tends to be sporadic– too often prompted by scandals, such as the death of a child, which are apt to produce panicky and clumsy responses.

2. What countervailing power do the users of these services have? The complex and slow-moving legal procedures available (litigation and compensation, appeals to ombudsmen of various kinds, and to professional authorities such as the General Medical Council or the Law Society) are most likely to be used by the more confident and well-heeled service users – which helps a bit, but may reinforce inverse care patterns. Staff can guess who is likely to use these strategies, and who can be neglected with impunity.

3. Consultation with representative groups of service users has been a favourite prescription for many services. But the influence it exerts has not been impressive. Consultative groups often begin well, but they tend either to peter out, or to get co-opted by the professionals. More radical strategies of community *ownership* may take us further. But what works for a small housing association, owned by its residents, cannot be easily transferred to a hospital or a university.

4. Feedback surveys asking service users about their experience of the services they depend on are becoming more common. But we need to ask, Who framed the questions? Who analysed the results? And how fully and freely published were the findings? Unless users of the service were involved in all phases of this work such surveys tend to become yet another way of protecting and defending the management.

5. Social care services of various kinds are now increasingly encouraged to offer their clients individual budgets or direct payments. These are slightly different procedures, but similar in giving public services the duty to assess people's needs and resources and allocate a budget to each of them; then leaving them to select their own providers and make their own arrangements with them. This is a pure market model which makes the service users the hirers and employers of those who help them – but with the crucial difference that the state decides who needs most help. These systems can work pretty well for people with physical disabilities who are supported by loyal and well-organised families. More isolated people, and those with considerable mental health or learning difficulties need good support if they are to understand the choices available and make good use of them. Without that, the system may be used to meet the needs of the public authorities, not those

of their 'customers'. This idea originated on the far side of Canada where the families who invented it (for their children with learning disabilities) insisted on getting independent, expert advice from someone – 'brokers' they called them – who could help them get the best deals to meet their particular needs. We seem to have imported the system without recognising how important the 'brokers' are. There is a danger that it will create two-tier standards, giving the best treatment to those best able to choose and manage their own caring services while others have to make do with whatever they are given.

6. Stuart Weir and his colleagues argue that human rights laws should now be extended beyond civil and political rights to cover economic and social rights (Weir 2006). Where test cases are picked that can confer benefits on much larger numbers of people this strategy can strengthen social solidarity. It worked as a way of compelling the Prison Service to bring slopping out to an end in jails throughout Britain. It is a strategy that attempts to address the collective and competing needs of all citizens. But it operates slowly and will be more effective in tackling large-scale issues (the right to work, adequacy of social benefits, protection from homelessness . . .) than the plight of a crippled old lady lying in a hospital bed who cannot get anyone to bring her a bed pan. Who would take up such cases? Some trade unions have a good record of helping their members get their rights from public services. But it's their *members* they work for, not the unemployed; or the old lady. And their members may be precisely the people who are failing to bring the bed pan.

7. We must not forget that the professions themselves can take the initiative in helping people gain their rights from public services. Planning Aid, the charity set up by town planners, provides support and advice for people coping with the system they administer during their working day. It does an excellent job with the help of well-trained volunteers subject to the usual professional disciplines. Housing managers did something similar in creating TPAS – the Tenant Participation Advisory Service – to support people living in social rented housing who wanted to play a part in the management of their housing. Lawyers do pro bono work without charge from time to time which may help clients dealing with public authorities. Should doctors, nurses, social security officials, teachers . . . be doing something similar?

8. I have already mentioned the free and independent advocacy service for people with mental disorders introduced by the Mental Health (Care and Treatment) (Scotland) Act of 2003. Hector Mackenzie, an official of the Scottish Health Department who played a key part in getting advocacy into the Act, challenged his colleagues in other departments to contribute to a budget that would fund an advocacy service to help citizens dealing with *any* public service in Scotland. They refused. But his challenge has not gone away, and the new service is in fact expanding in various directions to serve other kinds of clients. If we go further down that road, other questions arise. Will every service need its own escorting advocacy agency? Or should one be developed to provide for all needs? Which? – The Citizens Advice Bureau?

Would such a development reinforce the customer ethos (get yourself an advocate to get your mother into the *best* old people's home, your daughter into the *best* secondary school)? Or could it help to rebuild a citizen ethos? Individual advocacy helps people to cope a bit better with the existing system. It is when people who share similar experiences of a public service get together that they start thinking of new and better ways of doing things and pressing for changes. They have the authority of hard-won experience. And they all have votes. There are groups of people with mental health or learning difficulties who have an impressive list of battle honours in helping to improve the services they depend on.

9. We have too readily assumed that 'community care', now replacing institutional care for so many people, means sending professional staff out to help them in their own homes instead of in hospitals, children's homes or old people's homes. But *real* community care begins when neighbours and relatives provide more of the support that frail and vulnerable people need. They are more likely to do this when advised and supported by good professionals. The public-service professions will still be needed – but doing a rather different job. Sixty per cent of NHS expenditure is devoted to long-term conditions: diabetes, HIV, schizophrenia, dementias . . . That means there are thousands of people out there who often know better than the doctors how to manage their condition and certainly have more time to devote to patients newly diagnosed as having it. Many of them have already formed groups set up to help fellow patients. Those groups can have an advocacy role. By working with them we may do more, and at less cost, than by expanding clinical services. It was Graham Watt, Glasgow University's Professor of General Practice, who said, 'We have to teach the professionals to ask, not "What do I do?" but "What am I part of?"'

In conclusion

Within the limits imposed on them by their duties to the state, how can public-service professions become more accountable to the people they serve – treating them, not as self-seeking customers or subservient subjects, but as responsible citizens and collaborators: co-producers of health, education and welfare? How can they avoid becoming agents of oppression, social division and exclusion? Some services will have to learn a whole new culture, from top to bottom, if they are to take down the barriers – literal and psychological – which they have built to protect themselves from the people they are supposed to serve.

Can we create a widely respected public-service ethos among the professions that helps them to become more strongly rooted in the communities they serve? If so, when their services are again drastically cut back (which could be any day now) the patients, the pupils, the tenants, the claimants and social-work clients may be out there marching alongside them.

NOTE

1. The ideas in the essay are developed further in my book about advocacy, *Speaking to Power*, published by Policy Press in 2009.

REFERENCES

Baker, Sally, *et al.* (2008), 'The rise of the service user', *Soundings*, 40, Winter 2008.

Beresford, P. (2008), 'Whose personalisation?', *Soundings*, 40, Winter 2008, editorial.

Gregg, P. (2008), *How Important is Pro-social Behaviour in the Delivery of Public Services?*, Centre for Market and Public Organisation Working Paper 08/197, Bristol: Bristol University.

Pollock, A. (2004), *N.H.S. plc: the Privatisation of our Health Care*, London: Verso.

Scottish Executive (2001), *The Millan Report: New Directions. Report on the Review of the Mental Health (Scotland) Act, 1984*. Available on: www.angus. gov.uk/ccmeetings/reports/socialwork/soc2001/444-01.pdf.

Stern, V. (2006), *Creating Criminals. Prisons and People in a Market Society*, London: Zed Books.

Tudor Hart, J. (2006), *The Political Economy of Health Care. A Clinical Perspective*, Bristol: Policy Press.

Weir, S. (2006), *Unequal Britain. Human Rights as a Route to Social Justice*, London: Politico's Publishing.

5

Active Citizenship: Gender Equality and Democracy

Rona Fitzgerald

INTRODUCTION AND CONTEXT

This essay will address the question of what active citizenship would do for gender equality and thereby, for democracy. The model of active citizenship in the classical republican tradition that has been endorsed by proponents like Hannah Arendt, and that has influenced work by Bernard Crick, is considered gendered. The feminist critique of classical civic republicanism suggests that the historical articulation of active citizenship favours masculine virtues and that it presupposes a sharp division between the public and private spheres. In addition, academic feminists make the case that this version of civic republicanism is gender-biased because it undervalues women, ignores the fact that women and men have historically stood in a different relationship to citizenship, considers the domestic sphere as a support for the public sphere, and fails to recognise the role of care in citizenship (Lister 2003).

If our starting point is that civic republicanism, as Bernard Crick suggests, 'is people combining together effectively to change or resist change', then part of the question to be addressed here is how to increase participation of women and girls in this collective action – in public life. The statement itself raises questions about what active citizenship is, and, about what characteristics we would consider essential for active citizenship in a more sophisticated polity of the twenty-first century.

The focus of this essay on gender equality is deliberate. This is because the questions to be addressed are not just about women and their exclusion from participation and representation. I will suggest that a more useful line of inquiry takes account of the fact that socially constructed roles shape expectations and assumptions about what women *and* men do in society. We need to acknowledge that these gendered norms may play a part in how women view political participation in general and active citizenship in particular. In addition, the focus on gender fits with legislative and policy priorities expressed in recent UK legislation like the Gender Equality Duty (2007). Furthermore, this recognition of the role of gendered behaviour and values in how women and men act in society enhances consideration of the case for gender parity in politics (Phillips 1998) and, importantly, it compliments the case for the possibilities of re-gendering of citizenship by working towards a women-friendly citizenship. Lister's work builds on the *pluralist citizenship* approach and argues for broadening the concept to include recognition that care is part of citizenship (Lister 2003).

In asking the question about what active citizenship can contribute to gender equality and to a renewed democracy, the focus here is on identifying key issues from debates in feminist literature, on discussing some examples of initiatives for supporting or encouraging women into public life and to highlight some questions that emerged from a recent report on activism by the Girl Guides. The initiatives discussed will include legislative provisions like those found in the Sex Discrimination Election Candidates Act 2002 and practical measures like those adopted by the Scottish Parliament to build equal opportunities into the fabric of the devolved Parliament. These initiatives raise questions about how gender equality might enhance democracy and how democratic participation and representation might reinvigorate political and social life. They chime with the notion of re-gendering citizenship as articulated by Lister and suggest a direction for future progress.

Questions about active citizenship and about the barriers to participation are outlined in the report of a recent survey produced by the Girl Guides in partnership with the Fawcett Society. The report of the survey is called *Active Citizenship: Girls Shout Out. Political outsiders: we care, but will we vote?* The survey provides a point of contact for this article with the experience and views of an important cohort of young women. It also provides a touchstone in respect of making conceptual debates relevant to them.

In the survey, one thousand young women in the Girl Guides between the ages of fourteen and twenty-five were interviewed. The survey found that girls in guiding are committed volunteers who care deeply about a diverse range of issues including domestic violence, equal pay and knife crimes. However, it also emerged that they are largely sceptical about politics and that they question whether getting involved can really help to make a difference. Many of the young women interviewed indicated that there is a good chance that they will not vote; they also suggest that while they are active in society, they would not consider being involved in politics. 'When I think about active citizenship, I don't think about politics, I volunteer but politics just never occurred to me' (Girl Guides 2009: 9).

In making the case for a gender-sensitive model of citizenship that can be women friendly, it is critical that it includes a specific challenge to assumptions and expectations about what women and men do in society. In particular, it requires challenging current gender norms through a renegotiation of the value given to the contribution of women and men to society.

THE CONTEXT

There has been substantial change in the last thirty years or more in the relationship between the public and private spheres in the United Kingdom. The growth of feminism combined with substantial legislative, demographic and political change has required a renegotiation of historic roles. Women participate in the labour market in equal numbers to their male counterparts, albeit that their working patterns are significantly different. Girls are out performing boys at school in most subjects – resulting in concern and some remedial action by educational authorities. Women make up half of the university student population; 57 per cent of first-degree graduates in 2007/08 were women, the same as in the previous year (Higher Education Statistics Agency 2009).

Nonetheless, in a report on *Sex and Power: Who Runs Britain* (Equal Opportunities Commission, EOC 2007), the answer is still, overwhelmingly, that men predominate in positions of power in Britain and that women are less well represented in public life. For example, after thirty years of the Sex Discrimination Act, women represent fewer than 20 per cent of Members of Parliament at UK level, they occupy about 24 per cent of posts in public and voluntary bodies and just 10 per cent of directors at FTSE 100 companies are women (EOC 2007). Public policy responses to gender inequality have included provision for flexible working and family friendly labour market policies – thus facilitating different patterns of participation for women with childcare and other care commitments.

However, the fact that these policies are largely aimed at women may mean that they perpetuate gendered roles among couples. For example, the concern to maintain income means that few men work flexible patterns. It also means that when women take time out for childcare and other care provision, they are considered to be less skilled in the labour market in respect of human capital formation. The result is that they are paid less over their working life. Combined with the fact that women tend to live longer, this may mean that they are more likely to have an impoverished old age.

In their critique of gender-blind policy responses, Bellamy and Rake make the following point:

> However, these policies have not been guided by an over-arching aim of gender equality with the result that they have failed to narrow the economic gender gap for all women or to tackle the underlying gender inequalities which cause it. Labour's strong emphasis on paid employment as the key route to citizenship may actually reinforce the gender and motherhood gaps experienced by many women as the opportunity cost to unpaid care work increases. In addition, work-life balance policies and new maternity legislation have brought immediate benefit to many women, but in the long term may reinforce the notion that women are primarily responsible for caring work. (Bellamy and Rake 2005: 3)

While active citizenship is not exclusively about political representation and participation, political participation and representation may be critical to a vigorous modern democracy and for the renewal of our democratic institutions. Bernard Crick has made the case for this renewal. He raises the issue of lack of engagement and complacency including the fact that it may be perceived as being normal in a stable democratic state. While stability may be part of the reason for disengagement from political activity and voting, it may also be a sign that cynicism and disenchantment have become endemic in public life.

In this essay, I will focus on arguments relevant to consideration of the impact of active citizenship on society, on politics and for gender equality. Additionally, I will raise questions about how we might formulate a re-gendered notion of citizenship drawing on feminist literature. It may be that this notion of active citizenship will be broader than representation and participation in politics. We may need to encompass social, community and political life in the broadest sense and provide recognition for caring as part of active citizenship (Dietz 1998; Lister 2003).

GENDER MAINSTREAMING

The context for our deliberations is made more urgent by the fact that there is both a legal and policy imperative for promoting the participation of more women in political and social life. The Gender Equality Duty (GED) was introduced in Britain in 2007. This represents the most significant change to sex equality legislation since the equal pay and anti-discrimination acts of the 1970s. The Gender Equality Duty is a form of legally enforceable 'gender mainstreaming' in that it will require public authorities to build gender equality considerations into all of their functions including workforce issues like pay, occupational segregation and promotion. It further requires that gender equality considerations be integrated into service delivery issues across a range of services from health, education, local government and transport.

This shift to mainstreaming marks a considerable change from the anti-discrimination or legal-based framework characteristic of the 1970s and the positive action approach to designing programmes for women of the 1980s. Furthermore this change in direction has been heavily influenced by policy developments and legislation emanating from the European Union (Campbell *et al.* 2009). I will argue that bringing gender equality into the mainstream of political, economic and social life will provide the opportunity for better policy outcomes for women and men and for society as a whole.

WHY GENDER MATTERS

In asking the question why gender matters a number of answers could be advanced; the first is a practical one about participation and unequal experiences. For example, it matters because women are paid on average about 17 per cent less than men for full time work; it matters because there is evidence that health outcomes for women and men are influenced by behaviour that is gendered; it matters because boys are under achieving at school; it matters because girls are opting not to study science and maths thus restricting their subject choices at third level.

Significantly, it matters because as indicated above, currently one-in-five Members of the UK Parliament are women, although women make up over half of the adult population. Out of the twenty-seven EU member states, the UK ranks fifteenth in terms of women's representation in national parliaments. In global terms, the UK Parliament is fifty-first of the countries included in the 30 November 2007 Inter-Parliamentary Union's monitoring report. These figures for women's representation have prompted the extension of the Sex Discrimination Election Candidates Act 2002 mentioned above.

Another critical reason why gender might matter is the bearing it has on the functioning of democracy and the justice system. This includes the loss to women in terms of their rights and their interests (Phillips 1998: 239).

Taking a rights-based approach to thinking about participation and representation for women can identify a range of areas where they have a distinct interest and where sex and gender intersect. For example, reproductive rights and the criminal justice system. In terms of reproductive rights, the 1995 United Nations *Beijing Declaration and Platform for Action* provides a definition, listing control over sexuality and reproduction amongst women's human rights. However, this recognition is the subject of ongoing struggle, both at national and international levels. As recently as May 2008, MPs voted to retain twenty-four weeks as the upper time limit for abortions. This was the first time that MPs were asked to vote on cutting the limit since 1990. There were calls for a reduction to twelve, sixteen, twenty or twenty-two weeks. Whether women are for or against extending the time period within which abortion is legal, this is an area of particular interest to them with potentially differential impacts on their lives.

At international level concern has been raised about issues like Aids/HIV policy in respect of the differential impact on women notably in countries like South Africa. The UN Millennium goals have a focus on gender equality and empowerment for women. In 2008, women held 18 per cent of parliamentary seats worldwide.

In the UK, the criminal justice system has received attention in recent years in respect of how women are treated. From Helena Kennedy's book *Eve was Framed* (Kennedy 1992), to the Fawcett Society's annual reports on Women and Justice, the case has been made for improvement in the criminal justice system for women, as offenders, victims and staff. This is an area where advocacy has resulted in action by public authorities and government and there is now an annual system of reporting by the Home Office providing statistics, outlining policies, and procedures that have been changed.

However, one area where there has been less progress is convictions for rape. In a recent article in the *Guardian* newspaper (6 February 2008) on the low conviction rates for rape and discrimination against pregnant women in the workplace, Katherine Rake, the director of the Fawcett Society, makes the point that this is the price that women are paying for under-representation in power. She goes on to remind readers that consideration of, and actions about, domestic violence are recent initiatives that coincide with the advent of more women in Parliament since 1997. Rake acknowledges that men can address sexism and she is careful not to claim a causal relationship between representation and policy agendas. Nor does she suggest that women have a common political agenda, but she does make the point that more women representatives provide an opportunity to influence policy priorities. If there are more women in Parliament, issues that impact on them differentially have a better chance of being aired and being acted upon.

Katherine Rake's themes are echoed in the feminist literature about politics and citizenship. Questions are posed about the issue of identifying women's interest; about how and why representation for women matters. Importantly for the theme of this essay, there is consideration of how we frame the argument for re-engendering democracy within the concept of civic republicanism and active citizenship. In identifying women's interest, there is an acknowledgement that women are not a homogenous group (Phillips 1999; Lister 2003). A further aspect to consider beyond concern for women's interests is the loss, through their under-representation, of their contribution to democracy as a whole. There is also considerable literature about gender and citizenship that discusses feminism and citizenship making the link with more participatory and democratic practices (Dietz 1998).

SEX VERSUS GENDER

Definitions are important for clarity. Sex refers to the biologically determined differences between men and women that are universal. This is the model that was at the centre of health policy for a considerable period. Gender refers to the social differences between women and men that are learned, changeable over time and have wide variations both within and between cultures. More recently the medical model has been challenged to incorporate a more gender-sensitive approach to designing and implementing health policy. Gendered roles shape women and men's lives and increasingly we have evidence across a range of public policy areas about the impact this has on, for example, health outcomes (Doyal 2001).

GENDER AND CIVIC REPUBLICANISM

Iseult Honohan's book on *Civic Republicanism* provides a useful starting place as she discusses both the concept and historical evolution of civic republicanism and a brief overview of some of the contemporary debates. She identifies the central strands in civic republicanism: freedom, the civic virtues, participation, the common good, and public versus private interests. Her contention is that the re-emergence of civic republicanism was as a counter to liberalism because of the political challenges presented by the pluralism and interdependence of modern societies. Honohan provides some discussion of the feminist critique of virtue – the fact that for women it was associated with respectability and with concerns about sexual propriety. She makes the case that republican civic virtue is not essentially gendered but that it is a concern for common goods that may take various forms. She cites Wollstonecraft's claim that defining virtue in terms of self-reliance rather than grandiose public action could include women as equals (Honohan 2002: 167).

THE CASE FOR RE-GENDERING CITIZENSHIP

In her article on citizenship and gender, Lister focuses on key debates about what she terms the *re-gendering* of citizenship. She makes the case that the veil of neutrality has obscured the gendering of citizenship to the disadvantage of women (Lister 2001). The notion of *gender neutrality* is used and promoted by policy makers and, in particular, by economists. Economists argue that financial allocations in budgets are gender neutral. This ignores the fact that the outcomes of the expenditure are often different for women and men. Mackay and other economic feminist writers have made the point that expenditure is more likely to be gender blind and therefore that it risks both a differential impact and the possibility of discriminating against women (Mackay 2009).

Lister's case for re-gendering is multifaceted. She reviews the various perspectives and discourses from feminists on citizenship. On the question of rights and participation, she cites Dietz (1998), who formulates *a feminist civic republican* model of citizenship – arguing for a more participatory and expressly democratic model. However, this embracing of civic republicanism is tempered by the work of Phillips (2000) who suggests that civic republicanism traditionally defines the political in narrow terms and ignores domestic constraints on many women's political participation.

In her review of the various feminist perspectives on the question of citizenship, Lister offers an analysis of concepts such as the gender-neutral citizen, the gender-differentiated citizen, through to the notion of the gender-pluralist citizen. While acknowledging the case for both the neutral- and differentiated-citizen approach in the literature (Bryson 1992; Voet 1998) she makes the strong case for the notion of a gender-pluralist citizen (Lister 2001: 8). This latter point is important and relevant, as mentioned earlier; equality legislation in the UK now provides both an impetus and a legal imperative to adopt a multi-strand approach acknowledging the interrelationship between different characteristics on the choices about how people live their lives.

While supporting the gender-pluralist approach, Lister is clear that it offers only one half of the equation in articulating a theory of citizenship that is gender sensitive:

> Gender-pluralist approaches are best equipped to accommodate the range of social divisions, such as sexuality, class, 'race', religion and age, which intersect with gender to shape the citizenship of women and men. They help to diffuse the gender binary at the centre of the equality vs. difference dichotomy. However, they do not offer guidance on one of the key questions for the re-gendering of citizenship which it raises: the respective value to be accorded to

unpaid care work and paid work in the construction of citizenship responsibilities and rights. And a purely pluralist approach means that citizenship no longer offers a universal yardstick against which marginalized groups can stake their claim. (Pascall quoted by Lister 2001: 9)

Therefore, the final building block in working towards a women-friendly citizenship is 'the incorporation of care as an expression of citizenship, in line with a gender differentiated model' (Lister 2001: 9). This requirement or demand is echoed in a range of arenas from feminist economists to policy makers. For Mackay, the fact that gender analysis and statistics are not part of the preparation and construction of the national budget implies that budgets are 'gender blind'. As discussed above, this blindness is often presented as 'gender neutrality' in that the nature and level of budgetary allocations do not normally depend upon whether they apply to men or women. However, the impact of patterns of public expenditure is gendered, therefore steps should be taken to ensure that the focus on neutrality should not allow policy to be 'gender blind' (Mackay 2009).

In response to this recognition, there are a number of initiatives around gender budget analysis both at European level and at international level. The term gender budget analysis refers to a process of analysing the government budget to establish the budget's differential impact on women and men. The process is sometimes called gender budgeting or gender-sensitive budgeting. The objective is to trace the relationship between policy objectives and priorities and the resource allocation process.

Gender budget analysis is not about providing a separate budget for women and men but about ensuring that spending meets the needs of women and men. The starting point is that the implications and impact are likely to differ because of the different social and economic positioning of males and females (Elson 2000). As part of this adjudication on the impact of the budgetary allocations, feminist economists have made the case for the recognition of the value of unpaid work at family and societal level that women undertake. For example, Waring has made the case that Gross Domestic Produce (GDP) does not adequately measure unpaid work predominantly performed by women, such as housework, childcare and eldercare (Waring 1988).

The inclusion of social care in a gender-sensitive model of active citizenship also addresses some of the concerns expressed in the Girl Guides' study about issues that they care about and that have an impact on their lives, like domestic violence, bullying, unequal pay and tackling knife crime.

Lister, too, has done some work on citizenship and young people. Some of the points and themes identified in this work are reflected in the Girl Guides' study. For example, the need to communicate about active citizenship though more modern media like Internet sites or using iPods; the fact that many of the young people consider the term citizenship to be dated with the result that it does not inspire them to get involved in political activities to effect change; the fact that education or information about citizenship is delivered by older people who don't seem to make it relevant to the lives of young people. Importantly for the Girl Guides interviewed, lack of relevant information is considered a large part of the problem:

> Over a quarter of girls ascribe their lack of political engagement to insufficient information about how and why they should take part. But skepticism also plays its part, with the remaining top five reasons for disengagement all indicating disenchantment with politics and cynicism about whether it can make any difference to the issues they care about. (Girl Guides 2009: 12)

THE IMPETUS FOR CHANGE

As indicated above, the Gender Equality Duty (2007) places the onus on public authorities to tackle discrimination and to promote equality. When a more pro-active approach has been taken, as with elections to the devolved institutions in Scotland and Wales, the proportion of women elected is greater – nearer 50 per cent as compared with 20 per cent in Westminster.

The Equality Bill 2009 extends the Sex Discrimination Election Candidates Act 2002 until 2030. The act allows political parties to select candidates based on gender with the purpose of increasing the number of women in Parliament. The efficacy of mechanisms like this is limited by commitment in political parties to elect more women, by a perception that gender equals women and that women's inequality has been successfully tackled because women are now more evident in public life and across the labour market. However, drawing on the literature identified here, there is still a lot of progress to be made. Recognition that gender is about men and women is critical. Otherwise women present as an *extra system* demand and will be considered as a problem for policy makers instead of being essential to the renewal of democracy.

SCOTTISH PARLIAMENT

In a recent article for Hansard that marked ten years of equal opportunities in the Scottish Parliament, Mackay has outlined some of the non-legislative measures that have brought equal opportunities into the work of the Parliament (Mackay 2009: 4).

The institutional 'blueprints' of the parliament contained important statements and mechanisms for promoting equal opportunities. Key features included: 'family friendly' working hours for the parliament and the recognition of Scottish school holidays; a purpose-built visitors' crèche; a Parliamentary Equal Opportunities Committee with a remit for equal opportunities issues both inside and outside the parliament; an Equality Unit within the Scottish Executive, tasked with promoting multiple strands of equality; the commitment of both parliament and the executive to 'mainstreaming' equality – including gender equality – across all their areas of work including legislation and policy-making; the requirement that memoranda accompanying executive Bills include an equal opportunities impact statement. The other key principles have provided enabling conditions for the promotion of EO [sic] through more open, accessible decision-making processes and more participatory politics. (Mackay 2009: 4)

In other work, Mackay makes the point that while there is some disappointment with the achievements of the first ten years of the Scottish Parliament and the strong presence of women, there is agreement that issues like domestic abuse and equality proofing the budget are a result of both the commitment to equal opportunities and the championing of these issues by women (Mackay 2003, 2006).

WHAT WOULD MAKE A DIFFERENCE: ISSUES FROM THE GIRL GUIDES' STUDY

For the Girl Guides interviewed, the barriers identified above are lack of information about politics and about issues; the methods and manner in which they are communicated with (what media are used); a feeling of lack of relevance; and perhaps that the very term *citizenship* was outdated and does not have resonance for them. The findings of this survey are interesting for a number of reasons: the fact that the girls interviewed are active in their community with a high level of volunteer activity – 96 per cent of those interviewed engage in some kind of volunteering activity. This is noteworthy as the government's view is that increasing participation in volunteering is the way to get more active citizenship. The results of this survey seem to challenge that premise and/or suggest that another step is important to make the leap from volunteering to active participation in public life.

When asked about the issues that might motivate them to get involved in politics or volunteering, the girls were most inspired by the prospect of being able to make a real difference to the lives of girls, women and young people. They were most committed to playing a part in stopping domestic violence against women and children. Other inspiring issues were speaking out about gangs and knife crime; preventing bullying; equality for women in the workplace; and combating the pressure on young women to have sex before they are ready.

CONCLUSIONS

The essay has identified both theoretical and conceptual issues in respect of active citizenship and gender. Some areas for progress have been identified and the scale of the challenge as illustrated by the Girl Guides' study has been discussed. In arguing for a gender-sensitive model of active citizenship, some key issues have emerged including the critical question of what elements or characteristics should be part of a model of citizenship that is inclusive, gendered in the best way and that enhances democracy. In this essay, I have shown that there is considerable learning from the literature, from the Girl Guides' study and from Fiona Mackay's Scottish findings mentioned above.

Re-gendering the model of active citizenship requires a more pluralist citizenship that challenges the classic republican model. It means expanding or recasting notions like virtue to encompass, as Wollstencraft suggests, self-reliance rather than grandiose public action. It means considering caring as part of citizenship and working towards a more equal share of this between men and women. In other conceptual debates some writers have suggested that parenthood be considered a craft (Sennett 2008). Others have argued that well-being or happiness should be part of public policy considerations for government (Layard 2005). This points to a revaluing of parenting and other caring responsibilities that would broaden out the responsibility for these matters to society and to policy makers.

For the Girl Guides interviewed, improved communications both in terms of content and using more modern media are part of the route to progress and greater engagement. Obviously the way in which the MPs expenses crisis of 2009 is resolved will make a difference to perceptions about politics, politicians and democratic participation as citizens.

The case has been made for gender-sensitive analysis in public policy, in institutional change and in budgetary allocations. Linking issues for women with more participative and democratic practices is strongly suggested to be the direction for reform. To modernise Aristotle and insist on practically wise women, I am convinced by the capacity of a gender mainstreaming approach to support the kinds of change that we need. However, I can also see that this approach is not well understood and is considered as being wholly about women.

Consequently, if the valuing or revaluing of care does not result in a more equal responsibility among men and women for delivering that care, we will be focusing on a major issue for women but not bringing gender to the mainstream of public policy-making. From the literature discussed here and the findings of the Girl Guides' survey, this will have serious implications for reforming or renewing our democratic institutions and for making political participation relevant to young people.

REFERENCES

Bellamy, K. and K. Rake (2005), *Money, Money, Money, is it Still a Rich Man's World?* An audit of women's economic welfare in Britain today. Fawcett Society. Available at: http://www.fawcettsociety.org.uk/documents/auditfull-report.pdf.

Bryson, V. (1992), *Feminist Political Theory*, Basingstoke: Macmillan.

Campbell, J., R. Fitzgerald and L. Mcsorley (2009), 'Structural funds and gender equality: the impact of gender mainstreaming in Western Scotland', *Local Economy*, online. See http://www.informaworld.com/smpp/title~content=t713705644.

Dietz, M. (1998), 'Context is all: feminism and theories of citizenship', in A. Phillips (ed.), *Feminism and Politics*, Oxford: Oxford University Press.

Doyal, L. (2001), 'Sex, gender, and health: the need for a new approach', *British Medical Journal*, 323: 1061–3. Available at: http://bmj.com/cgi/content/full/323/7320/1061.

Elson, D. (2000), *Gender Budget Initiatives as an Aid to Gender Mainstreaming*, paper delivered to the Ministerial Conference on Gender Mainstreaming, Competitiveness and Growth, OECD, Paris, 23–4 November 2000.

Equal Opportunities Commission (2007), *Sex and Power who runs Britain?* Available at: http://www.opportunitynow.org.uk/document.rm?id=472.

Girl Guides (2009), *Active Citizenship: Girls Shout Out. Political outsiders: we care, but will we vote?*, Fawcett Society. Available at: http://www.girlguiding.org.uk/about_us/girls_shout_out/active_citizenship.aspx.

Higher Education Statistics Agency (2009), *Higher Education Student Enrolments and Qualifications Obtained at Higher Education Institutions in the United Kingdom for the Academic Year 2007–8*. Available at: http://www.hesa.ac.uk/index.php/content/view/1356/161/.

Honohan, I. (2002), *Civic Republicanism, the Problems of Philosophy*, London: Routledge.

Kennedy, H. (1992), *Eve was Framed: Women and British Justice*, London: Chatto and Windus.

Layard, R. (2005), *Happiness: Lessons from a New Science*, London: Penguin.

Lister, R. (2001), *Citizenship and Gender*. Available at: http://www.socsci.aau.dk/cost/gender/Workingpapers/lister.pdf. [Reproduced in K. Nash and A. Scott (eds) (2001), *The Blackwell Companion to Political Sociology*, Oxford: Wiley-Blackwell, pp. 323–32.]

Lister, R. (2003), *Citizenship: Feminist Perspectives*, 2nd edn, Basingstoke: Palgrave/Macmillan.

Mackay, F. (2003), 'Women and the 2003 elections: keeping up the momentum', *Scottish Affairs*, 44: 74–90.

Mackay, F. (2006), 'Descriptive and substantive representation in new parliamentary spaces: the case of Scotland', in H. Sawer, M. Tremblay and L. Trimble (eds), *Representing Women in Parliament: a Comparative Study*, London: Routledge, pp. 171–87.

Mackay, F. (2009), *Travelling the Distance? Equal Opportunities and the Scottish Parliament*. Prepared for inclusion in Hansard publication.

Phillips, A. (1998), 'Democracy and representation: or why should it matter who representatives are?', in A. Phillips (ed.), *Feminism and Politics*, Oxford: Oxford University Press.

Phillips, A. (1999), *Which Equalities Matter?*, London: Polity Press.

Phillips, A. (2000), 'Feminism and republicanism: is this a plausible alliance?', *Journal of Political Philosophy*, 8(2): 279–93.

Rake, K. (2008), 'Equal measures', *Guardian* Interview, 6 February 2008. Available at: http://www.guardian.co.uk/society/2008/feb/06/equality.gender.

Sennett, R. (2008), *The Craftsman*, London: Penguin.

Voet, R. (1998), *Feminism and Citizenship*, London: Sage.

Waring, M. (1988), *If Women Counted: a New Feminist Economics*, London: Macmillan.

6

What can Active Citizenship Achieve for Schools and through Schools?

Pamela Munn

INTRODUCTION

For the first time ever throughout the United Kingdom young people will be leaving school having done 'citizenship', in one form or another. In England, citizenship education became a statutory foundation subject in secondary schools in 2002 and non-statutory guidelines were also given at primary-school level in the same year. The creation of citizenship as a statutory part of the timetable followed government acceptance of the recommendations of the Advisory Group on Citizenship, chaired by Bernard Crick and set up in 1998 by David Blunkett, then Secretary of State for Education. In Scotland, the Advisory Committee on Education for Citizenship, chaired by the author, saw its recommendations accepted by the Scottish Executive too and implementation began around the same time. The focus in Scotland was strengthened further by the major programme of curriculum reform 3–18 entitled *Curriculum for Excellence*. The creation of responsible citizens is one of the key purposes of the curriculum set out in this programme and programmes of study in primary and secondary schools will be required to demonstrate how they are contributing to this purpose.

The goals of citizenship education in schools of the UK are similar, and owe much to the theorising about the nature and meaning of citizenship developed by Sir Bernard Crick and outlined earlier in this collection. These goals are to develop political literacy, community involvement and social and moral responsibility in young people. The ways in which these goals are enacted in schools vary across the UK and indeed within each of the four countries of the UK.

In some schools, citizenship lessons appear on the timetable in the same way as English, mathematics or history. In other schools, citizenship is less likely to appear as a definite timetabled slot, but young people will be undertaking a huge variety of activities designed to increase their knowledge and skills of what being an active citizen means. These activities include, for example, mock elections, membership of school or classroom councils, setting up a Fair Trade tuck-shop, making a film about an issue of local community concern, petitioning national or local governments, making the school an eco-friendly one, and so on.

Many commentators would argue that the development of active citizens has long been a key, if implicit, purpose of schooling and that the way this has been achieved is by increasing access to a liberal academic curriculum based securely on subject disciplines. Lindsay Paterson, for example, in his keynote address to the British Educational Research Association in 2008, argued that

> we know from research in several countries that liberal education makes people more
>
> - liberal as opposed to authoritarian;
> - respectful of diversity;
> - opposed to invidious discrimination;
> - trusting of their fellows;
> - likely to take part in worthwhile social activities.
>
> In short, generally more aware of, and in support of, the essential tenets of liberal democracy.

In the same address, Paterson acknowledged that widening access of the whole school population to this liberal curriculum has been very slow and that lively and imaginative teaching is required to engage young people in 'the best that has been thought and said'. Nevertheless, he reminds us of the centrality of a broad and balanced academic curriculum as a means to promoting cultural inclusion and of developing the virtues by the cultivation of the mind, Matthew Arnold's vision of the purpose of schooling. Recognising the centrality of the whole school curriculum to the development of active citizenship, are there additional particular features of schools which explicitly and directly cultivate active citizenship? This essay draws on recent research to describe these features. It then highlights some of the social and cultural barriers with which schools have to contend in providing opportunities for active citizenship to be exercised. The essay concludes by considering what an inclusively focused citizenship education could achieve for individuals, for constituent communities and for the functioning of democratic institutions in the UK.

CHARACTERISTICS OF SCHOOLS COMMITTED TO ACTIVE CITIZENSHIP

It is commonplace in studies of the school curriculum to distinguish three main but interlocking strands. These are the hidden curriculum, the formal curriculum and the informal curriculum. The *hidden curriculum* is a term used to describe what is taken for granted about the way a school operates and what it includes, for example, the nature of relationships between pupils and teachers, the values displayed by the subjects which get most time on the timetable, the nature of school assemblies, the kinds of pupil achievements that are valued via prize-giving ceremonies and so on. The hidden curriculum is very important in sending implicit messages to pupils (and staff) about who or what is valued in school and conversely about who or what is less valued. The *formal curriculum* refers to the subjects on the timetable and links to the hidden curriculum via practices such as setting and streaming of pupils by ability and the kinds of teachers who are allocated to different sets or streams. The *informal curriculum* refers to school clubs and societies, and includes activities such as the production of a school play or musical, chess clubs, debating societies, sports and so on. These activities aim to stimulate pupils' interests and enthusiasms outside the formal subjects on the timetable and also develop, sometimes implicitly, skills of communication, turn taking, and general pro-social behaviour.

A PARTICIPATORY ETHOS

This brief description of interlinking aspects of curriculum is important for understanding the characteristics of schools committed to active citizenship because the *ways* in which provision for learning and teaching about citizenship are made are almost as important as the provision itself. Most writers on education for citizenship in schools agree that young people learn more effectively about active citizenship by actively participating in decisions about school and classroom life. They suggest that in being involved in real decision-making, which will require consideration of the consequences of doing one thing rather than another, collecting information and persuading people of the rightness of the decision, young people build up a repertoire of skills and knowledge which will equip them for life beyond school. Such participatory activities go beyond the acknowledgement of the formal rights of young people, to encompass an understanding of notions of mutuality of purpose and of community. Such activities also enable young people to begin to understand political and civil power.

Many schools who have been quick to introduce pupil councils as part of their management structure have embraced this feature of education for citizenship. However, the ways in which these councils and other forms of participatory decision-making work, send important messages about whether they are tokenistic, severely circumscribing the kinds of matters on which pupil voices are heard, or a genuine attempt to open up the decision-making structure of the school empowering pupils and indeed staff.

We know a little from research about how elections to the council take place, how agenda items are decided upon and how decisions are made and conveyed to the school as a whole. The tendency in many schools, perhaps unsurprisingly, has been for teachers to exert control and there is some evidence of tokenism as Wyness (2006) reveals in his research on young people's participation. The following extract is from pupils in a Marylebone school:

> Robin: I think most of the things they bring up like food in the school, it just gets ignored basically or rejected so it really doesn't make any difference.
> Interviewer: Who rejects?
> Robin: The teachers, senior staff who are in the meeting they don't seem to listen to us much . . . Some suggestions wouldn't work or are impractical, but some of them are quite reasonable suggestions but they just get banged on the head.

There are some interesting counter-examples of some financial power being delegated to councils although we cannot be sure how much spending decisions are for School Council members alone. In Scotland for instance, one account revealed that the school council had a budget of £2,000 per annum, designed to signal that it was a serious committee with the power to do things (Ross *et al.* 2007).

Much of the focus of the early work of school councils has been on the school environment, with improvements in the playground or in the toilets being most common. There has been some pupil decision-making about the curriculum especially in the area of personal and social education – an area not subject to national examinations. While it is easy to criticise this focus as diverting attention away from really important matters of teaching and learning, this is to misunderstand the importance of the school environment to pupils. For example, whether toilets are attractive and safe places and whether pupils have somewhere to store their books and other belongings are hardly trivial aspects of the working environment. Moreover, a study of the school's energy footprint and the design and access to the school playground can be part of a project on climate change.

Reports of other forms of pupil participation abound and include classroom- as well as school-level matters, for example on behaviour, peer counselling, and buddy schemes whereby an older child befriends a younger one and 'looks out' for them. Most often these kinds of schemes relate to ways of tackling bullying and helping to develop a sense of belonging in the transition from one school to another.

In general, research on participation mechanisms for pupils conveys the impression of pupils being incorporated into the organisational structure of the schools to improve ways of doing things rather than to challenge the existing systems. The mechanisms seem to be being used to enable the schools to do what they always do, but more efficiently and effectively. The paired reading, buddy and peer counselling schemes, for example, all intrinsically worthwhile, might be seen as helping to develop capability for thoughtful and responsible participation in social life, helping others and particularly those in difficulty of one kind or another. It is not clear whether they also involved discussion and debate about why such schemes were needed in schools at all (Ross *et al.* 2007; Deuchar and Maitles 2008). If such discussion did take place it would be interesting to know how much explanations lay in the individual agency of pupils and how much lay in considerations of the structures and functions of schooling.

What would a genuinely participatory school ethos look like and what would it do for schools? The short answer is that school management practices would be open and consultative, genuinely and routinely seeking the views of staff and young people about how the school operates and identifying aspects in need of improvement. The Teaching and Learning Research Programme commissioned a major study on pupil voice and Rudduck's (2003) summary of the benefits of taking the pupil voice seriously is reproduced in Figure 6.1.

CURRICULUM PLANNING

Knowledge and skills are essential to effective participation in decision-making. Knowledge about how school, local, national and international decision-making systems operate is clearly important to understanding how to make one's voice heard. This is a major part of what it means to be politically literate. Thus a characteristic of a school committed to active citizenship would be imaginative plans about how to develop young people's political literacy. Curriculum agencies in the four constituent parts of the UK as well as the education departments of the four Parliaments/Assemblies, the European Union and a host of voluntary organisations provide a wide range of resources here ranging from the local to the global.

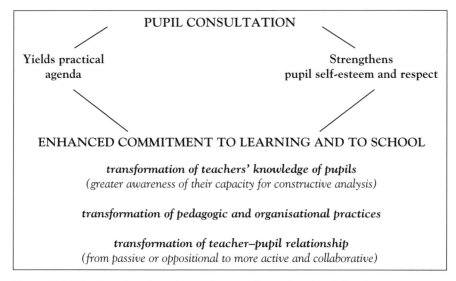

Figure 6.1 The benefits of pupil consultation. Reproduced with kind permission of Professor Andrew Pollard, Director of the Teaching, Learning and Research Programme.

There is a wealth of material available and so our ideal school would have clear plans with built-in progression in terms of complexity of local, national and international governance arrangements. Teachers would be confident enough in their teaching to take advantage of local, national and international events to illustrate decision-making systems at work. Not all schools have specialist staff in these areas and it is worrying that a recent report by Kerr *et al.* (2007) of the implementation of citizenship education in England highlighted that 'political literacy is an area of particular weakness due to teachers lack of confidence in the subject matter and the fact that it is perceived to be dry and difficult to teach.' The same report drew attention to the fact that in England, 'four years on from the introduction of statutory citizenship over half of teachers teaching citizenship have still not received any citizenship-related training.'

Even in Scotland, where there is a strong tradition of the teaching of Modern Studies (Maitles 2008) from the first year of secondary education, which includes many elements of political literacy, curriculum continuity and progression remain an issue. Not all young people continue with the subject into third and fourth years and the provision of specialist units for those who do not is still in its infancy. In the absence of major longitudinal research on the implementation of education for citizenship in Scotland, Her Majesty's Inspectors of Education (HMIe) are an important source of information. In its landmark report *Improving Scottish Education*, providing an overview of the system as a whole, HMIe (2006) summed up its view of the state of progress in education for citizenship in Section 3.1.

> Schools also have increased their emphasis on citizenship. Many are giving some more attention to involving young people in decision-making. Some have used curriculum inserts to explore issues such as citizenship and the law or anti-racism. However, practice is uneven within and across schools. The development of pupils' understanding of values and citizenship, including the ability to hold informed views and make judgements, depends on the acquisition of knowledge and critical thinking skills. Systematic curriculum planning to ensure that pupils are well prepared for political, social, economic and cultural involvement in society and to participate in significant decisions at school is not yet common.

This summary reminds us that as well as knowing *about* systems of government and decision-making, young people need to think through their views on *the substance* of contemporary issues. In other words as well as understanding the ways in which they can influence decision-making, they need to be well informed about which directions they wish decisions to take and to be aware of, and respect, alternative viewpoints. The Qualifications and Curriculum Authority in England sums up this point in its official guidance to schools on the importance of citizenship education.

> Citizenship addresses issues relating to social justice, human rights, community cohesion and global interdependence, and encourages students to challenge injustice, inequalities and discrimination. It helps young people to develop their critical skills, consider a wide range of political, social, ethical and moral problems, and explore opinions and ideas other than their own. They evaluate information, make informed judgements and reflect on the consequences of their actions now and in the future. They learn to argue a case on behalf of others as well as themselves and speak out on issues of concern. (QCA.org.uk)

In these matters, which might be summed up as the teaching of controversial issues, schools throughout the UK have a rich resource in their specialist teachers of, for example, history, geography, the sciences, and religious and moral education who are accustomed to teaching about competing views on a matter and about how to present reasoned arguments. All too often these staff are in subject-specialist 'silos' with little incentive to engage in cross-curricular planning on a topic such as climate change or poverty because of the demands of an accountability system which focuses on the key performance measure of pupil attainment, particularly in national qualifications. Yet a recent systematic review of thirteen studies on the impact of citizenship education on student learning and achievement (Deakin-Crick *et al.* 2005) suggests that the benefits of meaningful curricula and a learner-centred pedagogy can be considerable in terms of improvement in pupils' attainments. Similarly, Rudduck and McIntyre (2007) highlight the benefits to be gained by consulting pupils about their learning. Drawing on a number of school-based projects, they report increased pupil motivation, improved attendance and improved attainment. They emphasise that their work is small scale and not open to statistical generalisation and so caution that their claims are based on the potential of consulting pupils about their learning based on the patterns which emerged from their case studies.

Thus citizenship education based on a learner-centred approach, consulting pupils about how they learn and what would improve their learning, is likely to make classrooms more enjoyable, purposeful and stimulating for both pupils and teachers. It might also re-engage teachers and pupils with the true joy of learning. David Hargreaves (Rudduck and McIntyre 2007: 199–200) observed, 'It is possible . . . to increase student test performance while weakening their commitment to learning.' Thus the potential of education for citizenship based on a learner-centred pedagogy and a curriculum which actively engages with pupils' concerns and experiences is to transform learning from an instrumental chore relevant only to securing qualifications to something which is fun, sometimes difficult but intrinsically enjoyable and worthwhile, with clear connections to the real world outside school.

SOCIAL AND CULTURAL BARRIERS TO ACHIEVING SCHOOLS COMMITTED TO EDUCATION FOR CITIZENSHIP

The potential benefits of engaging fully in the practices of education for citizenship are large. They include more democratic forms of school organisation, more active engagement of pupils with their own learning leading to better motivation, attendance and achievement and, by implication, a better motivated and engaged teaching force. Above all there is the potential to rediscover learning as being about more than passing exams. Why then has education for citizenship not fully taken off across UK schools? There are many reasons.

Firstly, any curriculum change takes time. Education for citizenship was introduced as a statutory subject only in 2002 and it takes time for teachers to become aware of new expectations, use programmes of work and adapt them for their own classes and engage in curriculum planning. Moreover, citizenship is one of many innovations with which teachers have to cope and since there is no national qualification for which to prepare pupils, it should be no surprise that changes in assessment and qualifications in subject disciplines which frame accountability systems took priority.

Secondly, and related to accountability frameworks, teachers are accustomed to numeric performance targets such as the number of pupils obtaining five or more GCSEs at levels A* to C. We have not, as a system, derived good narrative performance measures of accountability where teachers or schools can describe what they have achieved in terms of, for example, curriculum planning, or pupil consultation. Much of the work relating to education for citizenship relates to hard-to-measure activities such as pupil-teacher relationships or active engagement with local community issues. A sad fact of our current system of accountability is that if something is not easily measurable it tends to assume a lower level of priority in the busy lives of teachers.

Thirdly, there is the pragmatic lack of training for teachers and associated lack of confidence already reported.

Fourthly, our admissions systems to schools, particularly but not solely in England, can sometimes lead to increasing social segregation in terms of pupil intakes. In a presentation to a conference on this topic, Whitty (2007), taking data from the national audit office at face value, suggests that academies were exploiting their freedom to recruit more affluent and biddable pupils. He argued the need for longitudinal research tracking the attainment of pupils in academies entitled to free school meals. There is much debate about whether all schools are the same in terms of funding, status and governance or whether new types of schools could be used to advantage in advancing the equality agenda. A detailed consideration of these matters is well beyond the scope of this essay. In terms of inclusive citizenship education, however, the very fact that in some parts of the country schools choose pupils rather than the other way round, sends messages about the inclusiveness of our school system. Furthermore, even where there is a social mix in schools, this is not the same as social mixing. This is what makes the hidden curriculum of schools so important in attempts to develop inclusive citizenship.

While these barriers are real enough, they are not impossible to fix if there was the political will to do so. If they were the only barriers to the full implementation of citizenship education across the UK then we could argue that it was only a matter of time and political will before citizenship education was fully embedded in the school curriculum. However, there are deeper cultural barriers at work going to the heart of the organisation of schooling and classroom relationships which are more difficult to overcome. As Sir Bernard Crick has indicated, 'Teachers need to have a sense of mission . . . to grasp the fullness of [citizenship education's] moral and social aims' (Deuchar and Maitles 2008). Even if teachers were to do so, it takes considerable courage for teachers to relinquish some of their control and to engage in learner-centred pedagogy. The move from the traditional didactic form of teaching – the sage on the stage – to more personalised learning – the guide by the side – needs more than simple technical training. It requires a reconceptualisation of the role of the teacher. Such a reconceptualisation would need to involve parents and pupils in understanding the benefits to be gained by a more learner-centred pedagogy. Of course, such a pedagogy would need to be accompanied by high levels of expectation and respect for all pupils if we are not to reinvent social segregation by denying some pupils access to a broad liberal education on the basis of their social origins, race or gender.

An equally difficult issue is the duty of schools to promote social cohesion based on respect for different traditions, cultures and races within the broad liberal values of the British state. Kerr *et al.* (2007) report that teachers feel 'most confident' teaching about rights and responsibilities and different cultures and ethnic groups. Yet Kiwan (2008: 119) cites evidence from the Commission on Racial Equality that up to one third of schools do not have a race equality policy. While having such a policy is no guarantee against racism, it signals an intent to adopt inclusive processes and practices, as Kiwan makes clear. Deuchar and Maitles (2008) also suggest that race and debates about institutional racism are important, but so far neglected, areas in education for citizenship in Scotland. In a study undertaken in twenty-four schools in four local authorities in Scotland, Intellectual Assets Centre (2005) reported that

> most teachers related the promotion of race equality to working with minority ethnic pupils. Race equality was often spoken of in terms of how well the school was supporting bilingual pupils through its interaction with the English as an Additional Language (EAL) service, or as having a strong stance on racist incidents and the promotion of multiculturalism through faiths and festivals. Few teachers focussed on how they used the curriculum to take forward anti-racist issues or what the benefits of race equality work would be for majority ethnic pupils or for themselves as teachers.

Following the terrorist attacks in London on 7 July 2005, questions have been raised about the limits of multiculturalism and the best ways of achieving community cohesion within a multicultural society. In 2007, Sir Keith Ajegbo chaired an independent review on *Diversity and Citizenship Curriculum* (Department for Education and Skills 2007) which, amongst other things, recommended that the secondary curriculum for citizenship education should include a new element entitled 'Identity and diversity: living together in the UK'. However, these are deep and difficult issues.

The risk is that issues concerning diversity and inclusion are discussed blandly and neglect the very real dilemmas facing pupils and teachers in their daily lives. Riddell and Kakos (2008), in a literature review on religious education, draw attention to similar difficult issues in the teaching of religious education. They quote Barnes (2006) who maintains that much religious education in UK schools reflects the Protestant liberal position, favouring a phenomenological approach to religions, describing their contours and according them parity of esteem, but certainly not pitting their truth claims against each other. Barnes suggests, however, that whilst this approach might have merits in terms of quelling religious intolerance and ignorance, there are clear drawbacks and it might be seen as patronising and as diminishing vital elements of particular religions, which are actually based on making truth claims which are incompatible with those of other religions.

The Department for Children, Schools and Families has responded to requests from teachers for practical advice and guidance on teaching controversial and sensitive issues by launching a *Learning Together to be Safe* toolkit on 8 October 2008. This is designed as a resource for schools and shows schools the positive contribution they can make in tackling violent extremism. The toolkit highlights the desirability of working in partnership with local communities and of teachers being responsive to local issues. The toolkit is essentially a guide for teachers in evaluating their practice, together with some examples of resources provided by outside agencies. It makes it clear that it is not a specific programme of work and despite the good intentions underlying the toolkit, one feels that more dedicated and specific in-service training is required if hard-pressed teachers are to increase their confidence in teaching about racial and religious identity.

There are thus a number of social and cultural barriers to be overcome if education for citizenship is to bring about the ambitions held for it. We know the centrality of teachers in any curriculum innovation and that it is folly to imagine that one can design a 'teacher-proof' curriculum. The demands we are making of teachers are substantial, including more democratic classroom and school practices, confidence in engaging with sensitive and controversial issues, more personalised learning and re-thinking the nature of their professionalism including new teaching approaches and a greater emphasis on inter-disciplinary working. We are asking this of teachers at a time when the accountability regime under which they operate focuses on narrow measures of pupil performance. That so many have risen to the challenge is heart-warming. In the concluding section of this essay, we turn to what an inclusively focused citizenship education could achieve for individuals, for constituent communities and for the functioning of democratic institutions in the UK.

THE POTENTIAL IMPACT OF EDUCATION FOR CITIZENSHIP

Very little systematic empirical evidence exists about the impact of education for citizenship. This is hardly surprising given the relatively short time – six years – that education for citizenship has been formally part of the school curriculum. The review by Deakin-Crick *et al.* (2005), mentioned earlier, on the impact on student learning and achievement, points to the small number of studies available and to the fact that many of them preceded the implementation of education for citizenship. The nine-year evaluation of citizenship education carried out by the National Foundation for Educational Research (NFER) is assessing effectiveness in terms of models of delivery and the embeddedness of citizenship in the mainstream curriculum rather than on the impact on individuals, schools and communities. This final section, therefore, considers the *potential* impact, what education for citizenship might help to bring about. Moreover, citizenship education is being implemented in different ways in different parts of the country and so a scientific before-and-after implementation research approach would not be possible.

For individual pupils we are gradually accumulating evidence that one aspect of education for citizenship, active participation in school and classroom decision-making, can make pupils feel more highly valued by their teachers and peers, can increase a sense of belonging and can have a positive impact on motivation and achievement. We also know that a curriculum which engages in imaginative ways with matters of real, direct concern to pupils can stimulate deeper learning and can develop skills of rational debate and coherent presentation of argument. The hope is that these impacts will remain long after a young person has left school and will encourage young people to take an active interest in local, national and global affairs, enhancing a sense of mutuality and collective agency in the face of pressure of competitive individualism. On a more pragmatic level, the key features of citizenship education should make schools more enjoyable, engaging and pleasant places in which to work.

As far as local communities are concerned, a more engaged and active youth in local good causes would surely do much to counteract the image of the out-of-control lads and ladettes so often portrayed by the popular media. We have some evidence of this from studies by Wyness (2003, 2006) drawing on case studies of young people's participation in the civic and political sphere. He points out, however, the tensions between an adult desire to control the nature and extent of young people's participation in civic forums, youth parliaments and the like and the danger that too much regulation of young people's participatory rights would stifle diverse forms of activity. We would also expect to see more active involvement in local politics stemming from the experience of active participation in local issues and a greater understanding of these. The hope is that habits of participation and the establishment of networks through schools and through new technology will lead to greater collective engagement with local political processes.

At a national level the potential of education for citizenship is to reshape a conception of children and young people as citizens in waiting to citizens now, with rights, responsibilities and views on serious subjects worth hearing. Even more ambitiously, of course, it is hoped to help reinvigorate parliamentary democracy by encouraging young people in the democratic process and holding politicians more rigorously to account. These are ambitious aims indeed and, of course, not within the power of schooling alone to bring about. There are many influences on political participation, not least the behaviour of politicians themselves. Much depends on what teachers and pupils see as the key purposes of citizenship education. This essay began by outlining the three main strands of political literacy, community involvement and social and moral responsibility in young people. It is possible that schools will be tempted to focus on the social and moral responsibility elements, partly as a response to a rise in youth crime and the moral panic that accompanies reporting of incidents of indiscipline and violence in schools. This could be an understandable reaction to their core business of teaching and learning and socialisation of young people into acceptable ways of behaving. We have already seen how pupil participation can be harnessed to improving the existing ways of doing things in schools rather than challenging these. We can also see how the informal curriculum can be used to provide opportunities for community involvement. And yet, if we are to achieve the aim of a change in the political culture of the UK and develop young people who are willing, able and equipped to have an influence in public life, we must support schools more effectively in their endeavours. Going beyond one's comfort zone is never easy and schools need much greater recognition and encouragement as they strive to incorporate the more radical aspects of education for citizenship. We need more resources, better training of teachers and a system of accountability that encourages rather than discourages their efforts. We need the sharing of practice among schools but we also need a more active intellectual engagement with teachers about the nature of the enterprise they are engaged in and the challenges and dilemmas they face in putting education for inclusive citizenship into practice.

REFERENCES

Barnes, P. (2006), 'The misrepresentation of religion in modern British (religious) education', *British Journal of Educational Studies*, 54: 4, 395–411.

Deakin-Crick, R., M. Taylor, M. Tew, E. Samuel, K. Durant and S. Ritchie (2005), 'A systematic review of the impact of citizenship education on student learning and achievement', in *Research Evidence in Education Library*, London: EPPI-Centre, Social Science Research Unit, Institute of Education, University of London.

Department for Children Schools and Families (2008), *Preventing Violent Extremism – a Toolkit for Schools*, London: DCSF.

Department for Education and Skills (2007), *Diversity and Citizenship: Curriculum Review (Ajegbo Review)*, London: DfES.

Deuchar, R. and H. Maitles (2008), 'Education for citizenship', in T. G. K. Bryce and W. M. Humes (eds), *Education in Scotland: Beyond Devolution*, 3rd edn, Edinburgh: Edinburgh University Press, pp. 285–94.

Her Majesty's Inspectors of Education (2006), *Improving Scottish Education*, Edinburgh: HM Inspectorate of Education.

Intellectual Assets Centre (2005), *Minority Ethnic Pupils' Experiences of School in Scotland*, Insight 16, Edinburgh: Scottish Executive Education Department. Available at: http://www.scotland.gov.uk/Publications/2005/03/insight16/1.

Kerr, D., J. Lopes, J. Nelson, K. White, E. Cleaver and T. Benton (2007), *Vision Versus Pragmatism: Citizenship in the Secondary School in England*, (DCSF Research Brief RB845 Citizenship Education Longitudinal Study, Fifth Annual Report), Nottingham: DCSF.

Kiwan, D. (2008), *Education for Inclusive Citizenship*, London: Routledge.

Maitles, H. (2008), 'Modern studies education', in T. G. K. Bryce and W. M. Humes (eds) *Education in Scotland: Beyond Devolution*, 3rd Edn, Edinburgh: Edinburgh University Press, pp. 534–9.

Paterson, L. (2008), Keynote address, British Educational Research Association Annual Conference, Heriot-Watt University, Edinburgh, 3 September 2008. Available at: www.bera.ac.uk.

Riddell, S. and M. Kakos (2008), *Religious Education in a Multi-cultural Society: School and Home in Comparative Context – a Literature Review*, Edinburgh: Centre for Research in Education Inclusion and Diversity, University of Edinburgh.

Ross, H., P. Munn and J. Brown (2007), 'What counts as student voice in active citizenship case studies? Education for citizenship in Scotland', *Education Citizenship and Social Justice*, 2(3): 237–56.

Rudduck, J. (2003), *Consulting Pupils about Teaching and Learning*, (TLRP Research Briefing Number 5), London: TLRP.

Rudduck, J. and D. McIntyre (2007), *Improving Learning through Consulting Pupils*, London: Routledge.

Whitty, G. (2007), 'Social selection, social sorting and education', paper presented at the Mayor of London's Conference, City Hall, 12 October 2007.

Wyness, M. (2003), 'Children's space and interests: constructing an agenda for student voice', *Children's Geographies*, 1(2): 223–39.

Wyness, M. (2006), 'Children, young people and civic participation: regulation and local diversity', *Educational Review*, 58(2): 209–18.

7

Active Citizenship: Multiculturalism and Mutual Understanding

Dina Kiwan

INTRODUCTION

Over the last ten years, there has been widespread interest in citizenship, and this is particularly evident in ethnically and religiously diverse societies, as is evident in both academic and policy discourses in the UK. Clearly, 'citizenship' is a contested concept, with many competing (and overlapping) conceptualisations, including citizenship framed in moral terms, as a legal status, in terms of active participation, and in terms of identifying with the political community (whether this be local, national or global). Indeed, Bernard Crick and Andrew Lockyer take as a starting point in the Preface of this book the question of 'good' citizenship and 'active' citizenship, setting out the remit for each contributor to consider how to achieve an 'active' citizenship culture, and to consider what might be the consequences of such an endeavour.

Bernard's opening essay, 'Civic republicanism and citizenship: the challenge for today' discusses the 1998 Crick Report, 'Education for citizenship and the teaching of democracy in schools'. The rationale in the Crick Report for this citizenship initiative is presented primarily as a means to address concerns of voter apathy, especially amongst the young. Indeed, in my own research on policymakers' views on what the key influences driving the citizenship agenda were, political apathy of young people and society in moral crisis were the two most commonly cited reasons given (Kiwan 2008a). Interestingly, diversity and immigration issues were relatively less frequently cited, although it could be argued that with the focus on debates relating to Britishness, integration and community cohesion, citizenship and the perceived challenges of ethnic and religious diversity are now seen as much more central to the citizenship agenda than five years ago.

The heightened policy focus we have witnessed on the interrelationship between citizenship, integration and diversity, has been framed in terms of how to balance 'unity' and 'diversity'. This essay examines the meaning of 'multiculturalism' in the United Kingdom contemporary political context, as well as exploring its contested theoretical meanings in relation to active participatory citizenship. The relationship between 'citizenship' and 'multiculturalism' is examined in two key policy areas – citizenship education policy in schools (Qualifications and Curriculum Authority 1998; Ajegbo *et al.* 2007) and naturalisation policy (Home Office 2003, 2007). I conclude by highlighting key areas for future policy focus.

THE POLITICAL CONTEXT

The UK is both a 'multination' state – made up of England, Northern Ireland, Scotland and Wales, and a 'polyethnic' state – consisting of a large number of ethnic and religious groups, in large part a result of mass immigration since the Second World War, although it should be noted that there have been waves of immigration to the UK throughout history.[1] British national identity has historically been an implicit concept, rather than being explicitly defined (Grillo 1998). British national identity was a construct that was superimposed over Welsh, Scottish and English identities, although it has not superseded these regional identities. It is of note that the English have not developed a separate English identity to the same extent as in Scotland, Wales or Northern Ireland. This has been changing over the last few years with symbols such as the flag of St George being reclaimed from far-Right groups, and the notion of 'Englishness' being openly discussed (Blunkett 2005). Whilst it has been argued that, historically, defining 'Britishness' was not inherently racialised, racialised discourses have been implicitly coupled to discourses on national identity from the mid-twentieth century onwards in the context of post-war mass immigration predominantly from the former colonies of the British Empire (Grillo 1998).

In recent years, the UK has witnessed a number of legal and political events shaping the socio-political landscape, including the political and legal recognition of institutional racism (Macpherson 1999), the introduction of new requirements for the acquisition of British citizenship and permanent settlement (Home Office 2005), increased globalisation, migration and social pluralism (Home Office 2001) and the occurrence of key international events such as 11 September 2001, and the London bombings in July 2005. Islam, which has recently been high on the public agenda both nationally and internationally, has further challenged the sometimes implicit relationship between religion and the state. Islam is typically cast as being in opposition to Britain's liberal ideals, exemplified by the Rushdie Affair (Modood 1992). In a study of Muslim elites in Europe, it was shown that the majority of Muslims in the UK (71.4 per cent) advocate a 'neo-orthodox' approach to integrating Islam (Klaussen 2007), which is conceived of in terms of resisting attempts to 'Westernise' Islam and that Islam's institutions should not be integrated into existing European frameworks. This is not to say that neo-orthodoxy perceives itself to conflict with liberalism, but that this position supports the right to exist and live as a religious minority. It is interesting to note that this stands in marked contrast to Muslim elites in France, the majority of whom (60 per cent) are characterised as 'secular integrationists', who advocate equity with respect to existing church-state relations, with Islam integrated into existing institutional frameworks. In an attempt to explain this difference, Klaussen (2007) observes a relationship between ethnic origin and preferred policy approaches to integration, where most Muslims from Pakistan and Bangladesh take a more conservative neo-orthodox view, with British Muslims tending to originate from these countries.

The loyalty of British Muslims has also continued to be a topic of debate, with a concern that British Muslims' loyalty is first and foremost to Islam, rather than to the state. Yet in a Gallop Poll, 73 per cent of Muslims in London were supportive of elections, compared to 60 per cent of non-Muslims, and Muslims were also found to be more supportive of the police (78 per cent) compared to non-Muslims (69 per cent; Klaussen 2007). Furthermore, Islam is also presented in public discourse as dangerous and violent, often implicitly conflated with perceived threats to liberties arising from international terrorism. Yet at the same time, the problem of 'Islamophobia' is acknowledged, with the British government stressing the need to clearly distinguish between the 'war on terror' and Islam.

UNDERSTANDING MULTICULTURALISM IN RELATION TO CITIZENSHIP

Citizenship, historically, has been, by definition, an exclusionary concept (Heater 1990), with the rights and responsibilities of citizenship conferred to only a subset of people within a society. However, with the relatively recent expansion of citizenship to include all members of society – including gender, social class, disability, ethnicity and religion – there is an increasing interest in inclusive theorisations of multicultural citizenship (Kymlicka 1995; Parekh 2000).

Yet there has been a growing criticism of the policy and practice of multiculturalism particularly in the media and public policy discourses

(Kiwan 2008a). Whilst multiculturalism is clearly a contested term, it has come to be misconstrued as synonymous with minorities, with the image of different communities living separately from one another, which is seen to undermine 'shared values', integration and social cohesion. Indeed, anti-racist critiques of multiculturalism dating back to the 1980s argued that multiculturalism as a policy approach is ineffective and tokenistic, with one of the most well-known catchphrases critiquing multiculturalism coined by Troyna: 'the three S's – saris, samosas and steelbands' (Troyna 1984). But the development of multiculturalism in the 1960s and 1970s should be put in the context that at this time it was an extension of liberal tolerance rather than aiming at participation.

Proponents of multicultural citizenship argue that accommodating diversity is necessary for the development of an inclusive citizenship (Kymlicka 1995). I have also argued that the accommodation of diversity is necessary for a participative citizenship (Kiwan 2008a). Liberalist theorists argue that it is not the aim of public institutions to represent or account for difference, and that the assumed neutrality of our public institutions is the price citizens must pay in order to be treated as equals, regardless of ethnicity, race, religion or sex. However, multiculturalists argue that individuals need 'a secure cultural context' that should be considered a 'primary good' (like religious freedom, freedom of conscience, free speech, right to vote, etc.), and therefore public institutions should be required to recognise difference, rather than ignore it.

Recognition that diversity need not undermine unity or integration was reflected in the 2002 White Paper, *Secure Borders, Safe Haven: Integration with Diversity in Modern Britain* (Home Office 2002). Diversity is recognised as being an integral part of living in modern Britain, and also that diversity and integration need not be mutually exclusive. Yet, this White Paper implicitly assumes a public/private sphere distinction, with no consideration of the process by which ethnic and religious minorities can contribute to a process of developing a 'shared' public culture (Kiwan 2008a).

In the remainder of this essay, I examine conceptualisations of citizenship in relation to multiculturalism in recent policy developments in two domains – citizenship education policy and naturalisation policy.

CITIZENSHIP EDUCATION IN SCHOOLS

In 1998, a policy review of citizenship education, set up by David Blunkett – then Secretary of State for Education – was undertaken by the Advisory Group on Education for Citizenship and the Teaching of Democracy in Schools, chaired by Professor Sir Bernard Crick (QCA 1998). Key recommendations included that citizenship education be a statutory 'entitlement', and also that citizenship become a separate subject in the curriculum rather than a cross-curricular theme (QCA 1998). Citizenship was conceptualised in terms of the three 'strands' of political literacy, social and moral responsibility, and community involvement, drawing from T. H. Marshall's conceptualisation of citizenship as being made up of three elements: civil, political and social citizenship (Marshall and Bottomore 1992). Citizenship was introduced as a statutory subject in secondary schools in England in 2002.

Although the Crick Report references T. H. Marshall in its conceptualisation of citizenship (QCA 1998), the issue of social inclusion is not substantively addressed, even though T. H. Marshall's primary concern was with social inclusion (Marshall and Bottomore 1992). This downplaying of diversity might seem paradoxical in theoretical terms, given Crick's (2000: 18) conceptualisation of the nature of politics: 'politics arises from accepting the fact of the simultaneous existence of different groups, hence different interests and different traditions, within a territorial unit under a common rule'. Crick also sees this as a 'process of discussion' between different groups. One explanation for the relative downplaying in particular of ethnic and religious diversity in the original Crick Report may be that this was an act of politics itself – a compromise based on perceived political sensitivities at the time (Kiwan 2008a). Crick is not a critic of multiculturalism; in his opening essay, he makes a rebuttal to critics of multiculturalism quoting Aristotle: 'it is as if you were to turn harmony into mere unison or to reduce a theme to a single beat'. However, Crick's civic republican conception of citizenship is more accommodating of political diversity than of ethnic and religious diversity in the public sphere.

As well as being considered politically problematic, diversity and multiculturalism are conceptualised in terms of a potential barrier to citizenship in the Crick Report (QCA 1998), rather than as an integral aspect of citizenship. It is explicitly linked to dissent and social conflict – with the 'knowing and understanding' of 'the nature of diversity, dissent and social conflict' outlined as an expected learning outcome for students by the end of compulsory schooling (QCA 1998: 44). The Crick Report proposes that the way to deal with the 'problem' of diversity is to 'find or restore a sense of common citizenship, including a national identity that is secure enough to find a place for the plurality of nations, cultures, ethnic identities and religions long found in the United Kingdom' (QCA 1998: 17). However, Crick was not proposing an assimilatory national identity, but rather a civic republican conception of citizenship in terms of commit-ment to political principles and institutions. For Crick, citizenship is not about national identity; rather, it is about active participation.

The concept of 'active citizenship' is constructed as a 'habitual interac-tion between all three' (QCA 1998: 11) strands – the political literacy, social and moral responsibility and community involvement strands. Participation is presented as the pervading 'glue' of citizenship that links these strands together. Crick has often argued for the importance of learn-ing and practicing citizenship. However, this assumes that active citizen-ship is dependent primarily on having acquired appropriate knowledge and skills for participation. The problem with this assumption is that it does not address what might actually motivate people to participate at all. I have argued that identity should be recognised as a significant com-ponent in understanding what motivates participation (Kiwan 2008a). Unless participatory approaches to citizenship do not also address and accommodate people's diversity of identities, they are unlikely to achieve an inclusive empowerment of all types of young people. This is because in order to be motivated to participate, one must be able to identify or relate one's own personal identity/ies with those reflected in the larger community.

Over the last three years, UK public policy has increasingly sought to conceptualise citizenship in relation to identity, diversity, com-munity cohesion, 'Britishness' and 'shared values'. In 2006, the DfES[2] commissioned a curriculum review of diversity and citizenship, which I co-authored with Sir Keith Ajegbo. We recommended a fourth strand, entitled 'Identity and diversity: living together in the UK', consisting of the following five sub-themes:

1. Understanding that the UK is a 'multinational' state, made up of England, Northern Ireland, Scotland and Wales
2. Immigration
3. Commonwealth and the legacy of Empire
4. European Union
5. Extending the franchise (e.g. legacy of slavery, universal suffrage, equal opportunities legislation). (Ajegbo *et al.* 2007)

Whilst the original Crick Report deliberately avoided the relationship between citizenship and national identity, we proposed that identity, including a historically contextualised understanding of national identity, is crucially important to developing both the knowledge and skills for a participative and inclusive citizenship. Although there is some reference to diversity in the Crick Report in relation to 'key concepts, values and knowledge and understanding', diversity is not considered in relation to active participation under 'skills and understanding' (QCA 1998). The Qualifications and Curriculum Authority has subsequently incorporated the proposed fourth strand, 'Identities and diversity: living together in the UK' as a 'key concept', alongside 'democracy and justice', 'rights and responsibilities', and 'critical thinking' into the new Citizenship Programmes of Study at KS3 and KS4 (QCA 2007). Since autumn 2007, secondary schools in England have been required to teach this revised citizenship programme. It is hoped that an explicit focus on ethnic and religious identities in the context of a participatory conception of citizenship will achieve a wider, more inclusive participation amongst those from a wide range of different ethnic and religious backgrounds.

In the following section on naturalisation policy, I illustrate how conceptions of citizenship in this policy domain have drawn on the work in citizenship education policy.

Naturalisation policy

It is important to contextualise developments in naturalisation policy in relation to policy developments in the domain of citizenship education as well as with reference to the national and international socio-political events leading up to and during this period (Kiwan 2007, 2008b). As discussed in the preceding section, citizenship and nationality were kept quite separate in the original Crick Report and subsequent citizenship education curriculum documentation. In contrast, these concepts were explicitly brought together in the domain of naturalisation. In 2002, a Home Office Life in the UK Advisory Group was set up by the then Home Secretary, David Blunkett, to develop proposals for language and citizenship education for immigrants applying for naturalisation to become British citizens. This was also chaired by Sir Bernard Crick and I was a member of this group. The report of the group, *The New and the Old*, was published in September 2003 (Home Office 2003).

The rationale for the work of the Life in the UK Advisory Group refers to the government's stated intention in the 2002 White Paper *Secure Borders, Safe Haven* of raising the status of becoming a British citizen, and is framed with reference to broader government policy aims including 'a wider citizenship agenda', 'encouraging community cohesion' and 'valuing diversity'. The Nationality, Immigration and Asylum Act 2002, requires those applying for British citizenship to be able to show 'a sufficient knowledge of English, Welsh or Scottish Gaelic' and to have 'sufficient knowledge about life in the United Kingdom' (Home Office 2003). The details of these requirements are discussed in full in Elizabeth Meehan's essay, 'Active citizenship: for integrating the immigrants'. In summary, we recommended that applicants for British citizenship must either: (1) successfully pass a 'citizenship test' – for those with higher levels of English language,[3] or(2) successfully complete an accredited ESOL (English for Speakers of Other Languages) with citizenship course – for those with lower levels of English language.[4] Since November 2005, applicants for British citizenship have been subject to these requirements. In addition, they must also attend a citizenship ceremony.

As a member of the Life in the UK group, I drafted the report's definition of 'multicultural' in the context of being British:

> We see a multicultural society as one made up of a diverse range of cultures and identities, and one that emphasises the need for a continuous process of mutual engagement and learning about each other with respect, understanding and tolerance – whether in social, cultural, educational, professional, political or legal spheres. Such societies, under a framework of common civic values and common legal and political institutions not only understand and tolerate diversities of identity but should also respect and take pride in them. (Home Office 2003: 10)

This definition focuses on operationalising multiculturalism, by emphasising mutual engagement and learning in all spheres – social, cultural, educational, professional, political and legal. It also challenges the assumption that ethnic and religious identities operate only in the private sphere. The word 'process' was chosen to indicate an ongoing active participation and contribution inherent to an understanding of operation in all the above-mentioned domains – political, legal and professional, as well as the less problematically perceived social and cultural domains. Whilst there is a commitment to shared values – achieved and developed through contribution from all those actively participating through the 'continuous process of mutual engagement' – there is an implicit recognition that shared values can indeed change (Kiwan 2008a).

The strong educative component is evident and indeed not unexpected given the involvement of both Blunkett and Crick in both the citizenship education and naturalisation policy initiatives. What is also significant is that the expertise of at least eight of the fourteen members of the Advisory Group was in the domain of education. Both the content of the 'citizenship test' and the language and citizenship courses were strongly influenced by the citizenship education programme of study offered in English secondary schools. The nature of the 'assessment' proposed by the Advisory Group also reflects contemporary thinking in the domain of education with regard to optimal approaches to teaching, learning and assessment. The notion of 'progress' as opposed to a common standard illustrates the strong educative purpose that the new naturalisation requirements were expected to fulfil. Support for lifelong learning underpinned the recommendations of the Life in the UK Advisory Group, with the naturalisation requirements being conceived of as a learning 'entitlement' rather than a hurdle; it was hoped that this learning experience would be an encouragement to continue to learn and develop skills (Home Office 2003). This educative approach viewed the naturalisation requirements as the first step to communicating and participating with one's fellow citizens, learning and integrating into a new culture. This notion of progress is evident in the title of the Life in the UK Handbook, *Life in the United Kingdom: a Journey to Citizenship* (Home Office 2004, 2007). Here 'journey' signals that citizenship is conceived of as a continual process, with the formal acquisition of the legal status of citizenship as only the starting point (Kiwan 2007).

In public discourse, the citizenship test is often referred to as a 'Britishness' test. However, at the launch of the Life in the UK test, hosted by the Advisory Board for Naturalisation and Integration (ABNI) in November 2005, the then immigration Minister, Tony McNulty stated: 'This is not a test of someone's ability to be British or a test of their Britishness. It is a test of their *preparedness to become* citizens' (Taylor 2007). This suggests that the test should be seen as a step in the journey of integration towards citizenship.

For those with lower levels of English, the course route – in contrast to the test – is intended to be learner-centred and focused on speaking and listening. The course route to citizenship, therefore, has the potential to fulfil the proposed integrative purpose of the 'journey' to citizenship, with its focus on social interaction with, and participation of learners. It also recognises the importance of being able to communicate verbally in the language of the receiving society in order to avoid exclusion, and to facilitate and promote participation in social, economic and civic domains. Indeed, in the Life in the UK Advisory Group Report *The New and the Old* we had intended that the test route would also entail some participative opportunities for applicants – either in the form of a short course, or through distance learning to develop a portfolio of evidence of civic learning and participation (Home Office 2003: 22–3). However, this part of our recommendation was not taken up by government.

MOVING POLICY FORWARD

Over the last five to seven years, we have witnessed a shift in how citizenship has been conceptualised in education policy, with the original Crick Report presenting citizenship predominantly in terms of skills for participation. With the introduction of the fourth strand, bringing identity issues to the fore, citizenship has been contextualised explicitly in relation to how we live in the UK as a multicultural society. In pedagogical terms, it is important that students go beyond merely 'learning about' diversity to actively operationalising this understanding with respect to participation.

In the domain of naturalisation policy, if the government seriously wants to promote integration, there should be funding available for new immigrants who intend to settle, in order to attend English language and citizenship courses (Kiwan 2007). Currently, in England (although not in Scotland), there exists what is referred to as the three-year rule, which is a rule that immigrants are not entitled to free English language classes until they have been resident in the country for three years. Whilst there are clearly financial considerations, this constraint must be weighed against the costs of not actively supporting integration at the time when this makes most sense. In addition, further structural and financial support should be prioritised and made available to further education institutions and those other providers of English language and citizenship courses.

It is important that the role of social interaction in promoting mutual understanding and integration should not be underestimated. This was our rationale in the recommendation we made in the Life in the UK Advisory Group Report when we proposed that those taking the test route should nevertheless also attend a short course, or develop a portfolio of evidence of civic learning or participation (Home Office 2003: 22–3). However, this part of the recommendation was not taken by government. I would propose that this be reconsidered, and combined with support for mentoring of new immigrants and new citizens, across social, civic and economic domains. It is also important that mentoring take place across different ethnic and religious groups (Kiwan 2007).

Whilst supporting multicultural understanding between different ethnic and religious groups is clearly recognised by policymakers as important in promoting community cohesion, it is at least equally important that efforts are made towards strengthening trust between citizens of different ethnic and religious communities and the legal and political institutions of the state (Kiwan 2008a). This is also particularly appropriate in the contemporary UK context, given that the majority of UK Muslims favour a neo-orthodox approach to integration. Therefore, rather than blocking funding for a predominantly single ethnic or religious group, as recommended by the Commission for Integration and Cohesion (2007), it is important to continue to support multicultural funding policies, where support for community activities develops social capital and also strengthens this trust relationship.

Notes

1. For detailed accounts of UK history and migration, see Colley 1992; Grillo 1998.
2. Now renamed as DCSF (Department of Children, Schools and Families).
3. At or above English for Speakers of Other Languages (ESOL) entry level 3.
4. Whose English is below ESOL entry level 3.

References

Ajegbo, K., D. Kiwan and S. Sharma (2007), *Curriculum Review: Diversity and Citizenship*, London: DfES.

Blunkett, D. (2005), 'A new England: an English identity within Britain', Speech to the Institute for Public Policy Research (IPPR), 14 March 2005.

Colley, L. (1992), *Britons: Forging the Nation 1707–1837*, London: Pimlico.

Commission on Integration and Cohesion (2007), *Our Shared Future*. London: DCLG.

Crick, B. (2000), *In Defence of Politics*, 5th edn, London and New York: Continuum.

Grillo, R. D. (1998), *Pluralism and the Politics of Difference*, Oxford: Clarendon Press.

Heater, D. (1990), *Citizenship: the Civic Ideal in World History, Politics and Education*, London: Longman.

Home Office (2001), *Community Cohesion: a Report of the Independent Review Team (Cantle Report)*, London: Home Office.

Home Office (2002), *Secure Borders, Safe Haven: Integration with Diversity in Modern Britain*, London: Home Office.

Home Office (2003), *The New and the Old*, the Report of the 'Life in the United Kingdom' Advisory Group, London: Home Office.

Home Office (2005), *Life in the United Kingdom: a Journey to Citizenship*, 2nd imprint, London: TSO (on behalf of the Life in the United Kingdom Advisory Group).

Home Office (2007) *Life in the United Kingdom: a Journey to Citizenship*, 2nd edn, London: TSO.

Kiwan, D. (2007), 'Becoming a British Citizen: a learning journey', (Briefing paper for Lord Goldsmith's Review of Citizenship), London: Ministry of Justice. Available at: http://www.justice.gov.uk/reviews/publications.htm.

Kiwan, D. (2008a), *Education for Inclusive Citizenship*, London and New York: Routledge.

Kiwan, D. (2008b), 'A journey to citizenship in the UK', *International Journal on Multicultural Societies*, 10(1): 60–75.

Klaussen, J. (2007), *The Islamic Challenge: Politics and Religion in Western Europe*, 2nd edn, Oxford: Oxford University Press.

Kymlicka, W. (1995), *Multicultural Citizenship*, Oxford: Oxford University Press.

Macpherson, W. (1999), *The Stephen Lawrence Inquiry: Report of an Inquiry by Sir William Macpherson of Cluny*, London: HMSO.

Marshall, T. H. and T. Bottomore (1992), *Citizenship and Social Class*, London: Pluto Press.

Modood, T. (1992), 'British Asian Muslims and the Rushdie Affair', in J. Donald and A. Rattansi (eds), *'Race', Culture and Difference*, London: Sage and the Open University.

Parekh, B. (2000), *Rethinking Multiculturalism*, Basingstoke and London: Macmillan Press.

Qualifications and Curriculum Authority (1998) *Education for Citizenship and the Teaching of Democracy in Schools (Crick Report)*, London: QCA.

Qualifications and Curriculum Authority (2007) *Programmes of Study: Citizenship (KS3 and KS4) at the Secondary Curriculum Review*. Available at: www.qca.org. uk/secondarycurriculumreview/.

Taylor, C. (2007), *ESOL and Citizenship: a Teacher's Guide*, Leicester: NIACE.

Troyna, B. (1984), 'Multicultural education: emancipation or containment?', in L. Barton and S. Walker (eds), *Social Crisis and Educational Research*, Beckenham: Croom Helm.

8

Active Citizenship: for Integrating the Immigrants

Elizabeth Meehan

INTRODUCTION

Active citizenship is an aspect of recent reforms of nationality and immigration policies in the United Kingdom. There are both ideological and conceptual difficulties in addressing the question of what active citizenship, as outlined by Bernard Crick in the opening essay in this book, could achieve for the integration of immigrants. The answer depends largely on the framework from which one starts. As Kymlicka (2009) points out, some critics argue that the new citizenship agenda 'panders to xenophobic sentiments', reinforcing 'ideological assumptions about the essential homogeneity of existing citizens and of the alien otherness of newcomers'. Conversely, 'defenders argue that it is based on a good-faith commitment to enabling integration, reflected in . . . pro-active campaigns to encourage naturalisation, and a commitment to providing resources to enable immigrants to meet the new tests'. The second motivation was the foundation for the first UK reforms and remains so, albeit in a difficult political climate, amongst advisers on so-called 'earned citizenship'.

Surveys (Carrera 2006; Etzioni 2007) of developments elsewhere suggest that such programmes are increasingly used to control inward migration rather than to foster the social inclusion of immigrants. Etzioni claims that it was anti-immigration, not pro-integration, forces that led to the introduction of citizenship and settlement tests in the United States some hundred years ago. And critics of the latest UK reform are sceptical or uncertain about the government's intention in introducing 'earned citizenship'.

It is difficult to know whether the new UK agenda is seen by would-be citizens themselves as enabling or coercive. There is little systematic information about whether the new rules have assisted integration or inculcated a fuller sense of citizenship than for those naturalising under the previous rules. But, in contrast to Etzioni's modern claim about the US, there was a contemporaneous call for citizenship education for would-be citizens and settlers that was not based on anti-immigrant sentiment. This was written in 1917 by Grace Abbott, Director of Chicago's Immigrants' Protection League, based on her intimate knowledge of the lives of immigrants and underpinned by a philosophy of integration similar to that of the first UK reformers, David Blunkett and Bernard Crick.

This essay begins with the conceptual issues. It then outlines the development of new UK rules for would-be citizens and immigrants seeking permanent residence. It continues by explaining the original measures and the new proposals in the light of ideas about active citizenship. The measures developed by Bernard Crick and his colleagues, together with the new proposals, could represent a significant contribution to both political efficacy on the part of immigrants and the mutual integration of them and existing communities. However, it is suggested in conclusion that the ideological context of migration policy means that the motivation imbuing the original reforms is now fragile.

CONCEPTUAL ISSUES: CITIZENSHIP, NATIONALITY AND IMMIGRATION

Bringing together 'citizenship', 'active' and 'immigration' throws up some confusions and normative issues that need to be addressed before the essay's main topic. Citizenship is a contested concept but there is agreement about its possession of two meanings (Honohan 2005). On the one hand, it denotes a person's formal relationship to a state – that is, nationality, for which it is regularly used interchangeably (see also Kiwan 2008: 67–9, 71–2). Although by modern custom and practice, the rights, benefits and privileges of citizenship tend to depend on possession of nationality, they are not the same and it can be misleading to use them as synonyms. This can be seen in the following conundrum. On the one hand, people who are co-nationals of the same state may be denied the same citizenship rights as one another. On the other hand, residents in a state who are not nationals of it may be granted some of the same rights of citizenship that are enjoyed by those who are nationals.

The first part of the conundrum is illustrated by the case of women in all early liberal democracies. The second is illustrated by the existence of, for example, the European Union and other systems where, for reasons of history or special relationships, voting rights are granted to non-nationals (Shaw 2007: 76–82). Often this is restricted to local elections but, in the UK for example, Irish and Commonwealth nationals have full voting rights. Incidentally, Lord Goldsmith (2008) thought these should be phased out, nationality and citizenship being made coterminous so as to emphasise the significance of being or becoming a British national/ citizen. Contrary to his view, there is a growing, albeit disputed, interest in the idea that lawful residence, rather than the possession of a particular nationality, should be the basis for full membership of a political community.

Though it is doubtful that theoretical debates about membership were uppermost in ministers' minds, they brought an element of it into conditions for non-nationals. In announcing the extension of the rules for naturalisation to permanent settlement, Home Office Minister Liam Byrne referred to aspects of membership such as helping people to integrate into local communities and generating 'a greater understanding of the rights and responsibilities that come with living in Britain' (Home Office 2006). The Home Office went further in its first explanatory leaflet, stating that the new rules would 'encourage people [seeking permanent settlement] to become full and active citizens and play a full part in their wider community' (Home Office n/d).

CITIZENSHIP, MEMBERSHIP AND ACTIVE CITIZENSHIP

Citizenship as full membership of a political community is, in some accounts, the holding, on an equal basis with others, of a set of rights and responsibilities. Here, active citizenship refers to carrying out the basic activities of being a citizen, such as voting and, when necessary, using legal rights and social protection, but more often simply being free to pursue lawful private purposes. This is how it is for Benjamin Constant's 'moderns' as quoted in Bernard Crick's essay. In other accounts, it is a more ambitious idea – similar to its meaning for Constant's 'ancients'. A 'new modernity' that harks back to 'the ancients', but which is inclusive, is to be found in Crick's essay where he refers to the outcome of citizenship education; that is, the 'transformation of political culture' so that 'people are active citizens willing, able and equipped to have an influence in public life and with capacities to weigh evidence', and so on. As Kiwan (2008: 47, and in her essay in this collection) points out, this means that active citizenship is more than volunteering to do 'good works' but is also about using such experience to reflect on public and political affairs.

In modern conceptions of citizenship, enabling people to be full members of the community also entails social rights or assistance. Under the new idea of 'probationary citizenship', people who seek permanent settlement or naturalisation, although taxpayers, will not have the equal protection of the social policy regime. This was criticised by the Northern Ireland Human Rights Commission (2009) and in the House of Lords by, for example, the former trade union leader, Lord Morris (HL Hansard, 11 February 2009: col. 1176). But, since this book is about active citizenship, the material basis for equal citizenship is not addressed here – despite its undoubted importance.

Enabling people to be active citizens is one thing. Promoting active citizenship is not necessarily the same. In the case of immigrants to the UK, enabling people to be full members of the community was the motivating force behind the first policy innovations. However, the intention was for more than what Constant described for 'the moderns'. The well-known disadvantages of being an immigrant were to be alleviated, identification with the UK polity was to be fostered, and, through these, social inclusion and cohesion were to be achieved. As Kiwan (2008: 69) puts it, while 'a sense of belonging or identity may promote participation, the experience of participating can enhance a sense of belonging'.

To promote active citizenship, the original thinking included the idea of combining voluntary action and experiential learning as an effective alternative to the new test or as a supplement to a classroom-based method of teaching English and inculcating knowledge of life in the UK. This would be, it was thought, more meaningful for immigrants themselves and involve adaptation and learning on the part of the 'host' society. However, the way in which this idea now manifests itself as 'earned' citizenship is not supplementary but additional, on a voluntary basis, to the test or classroom experience.

CONDITIONS FOR THE ACQUISITION OF BRITISH NATIONALITY AND PERMANENT LEAVE TO REMAIN

Following a White Paper, *Secure Borders, Safe Haven* (Home Office 2002), the new conditions were set out in the Nationality Immigration and Asylum Act of the same year. This act introduced a requirement that foreigners seeking British nationality, after five years residence, should be tested to show that they had both 'a sufficient knowledge of English, Welsh or Scottish Gaelic'; and 'a sufficient knowledge about life in the United Kingdom'. The route to becoming a British national was to culminate in a citizenship ceremony, involving, among other things, a pledge to observe the rules and customs of democratic citizenship. The government's stated intention was not to create hurdles but 'to raise the status of becoming a British citizen and to offer more help to that end' (Home Office 2004: 3) – and, indeed, to encourage permanent residents to apply for naturalisation. The then Home Secretary, David Blunkett, appointed an advisory group, called here 'The New and the Old' after the title of its report, under the leadership of Sir Bernard Crick, to advise on the implementation of the naturalisation requirements.

The need to demonstrate knowledge of English (or Welsh or Scottish Gaelic) and of life in the UK was extended in 2007 to those seeking the right to remain indefinitely. This could be seen as inconsistent with the aim of encouraging naturalisation but stemmed from recognition that, in some cases, significant disadvantages are incurred in a person's state of origin if he or she takes on a new nationality. In January 2009, the government introduced into the House of Lords a new Borders, Citizenship and Immigration Bill. A wide-ranging bill, it deals with border policing, sex discrimination in the inheritance of nationality, children, judicial arrangements relating to appeals, and so on. Its relevance to this chapter is its introduction of the ideas of 'probationary' and, especially, 'earned' citizenship.

After five years' residence, refugees and highly skilled and skilled workers may apply for naturalisation. On demonstrating knowledge of English and of life in the UK, they will undergo a period of 'probationary' citizenship during which time access to the full range of benefits is restricted. The transition from 'probationary' to full citizenship can be 'speeded up' (or 'slowed down' in the event of crimes attracting non-custodial sentences and put at an end in the event of custodial sentences – Home Office, UK Border Agency 2008) if citizenship is 'earned' through a demonstration of active citizenship in a voluntary capacity. Details of how this will work are still at the design stage. (The qualifying periods differ in length for those seeking the right of permanent settlement and for family members of each category. In all cases, full access to benefits and social housing is restricted until naturalisation or the right to remain has been granted.)

During the bill's passage through both Houses of Parliament, concerns were expressed that 'earned citizenship' would be a burden rather than the form of empowerment that was intended in the original philosophy of promoting active citizenship. Even peers and MPs who are well disposed to the idea of active citizenship remained worried about how earned citizenship would operate in practice for immigrants and the voluntary organisations and local authorities that will be involved in arranging such activities. These concerns were expressed most extensively in the House of Lords, especially by Baroness Hanham. She chairs the England Volunteering Development Council which is part of Volunteering England. Volunteering England is represented on the UK Borders Agency's (UKBA) Design Group which is advising on the implementation of earned citizenship. The preliminary findings by UKBA and the Design Group (Home Office UKBA 2009) on the operation of earned citizenship were provided for the House of Lords and further explanations were given in a letter to Liberal Democrat spokesperson Lord Avebury by Lord Brett, Minister in the Government Whips Office and Spokesperson for the Home Office. But uncertainties remained when the bill moved to the House of Commons (2009).

ENABLING PEOPLE TO BE ACTIVE CITIZENS

The report to David Blunkett by The New and the Old Group (Home Office 2004) had fleshed out arrangements for the acquisition and assessment of knowledge of English and life in the UK. The group also recommended the establishment of the Advisory Board on Naturalisation and Integration (ABNI) to advise on the implementation of the new arrangements and other matters relating to integration. It was established in November 2004 and remained in existence for four years. Its remit was

> to provide independent advice to the Government on its citizenship and integration programmes, and to advise and report on the processes of assessment of the understanding of language and civic structures, as required by the Nationality, Immigration and Asylum Act 2002.

Its first chair was Sir Bernard Crick and he was succeeded by Mary Coussey who had also served on the original group. Several other ABNI members had been on The New and the Old Group and many were specialists in adult education and the teaching of English for speakers of other languages (ESOL). The selection of experts in these fields was deliberate (Crick, 'Farewell to ABNI', in ABNI 2008). All members shared the founding philosophy that the need to show knowledge of English and life in the UK was not to be a barrier to keep people out but a support to ensure a better life within. And, indeed, the intention was to encourage people to become naturalised and full members of the polity and society.

TWO ROUTES FOR DEMONSTRATING KNOWLEDGE OF ENGLISH AND OF LIFE IN THE UK

Two routes to citizenship came into effect on 1 November 2005. Applicants able to demonstrate an existing command of English at ESOL level 3 can go straight to a test of English in which the questions are based on the material in a handbook, *Life in the United Kingdom: a Journey to Citizenship* (ABNI 2004, 2007). Applicants with a weaker command of

English must follow an ESOL course that uses materials which are about life in the United Kingdom, slightly adapted for the different parts of the UK. (*Citizenship Materials for ESOL Learners*, commissioned by the Department for Education and Skills and the Home Office; managed by National Institute of Adult and Continuing Education (NIACE) and LLU+ at South Bank University, London. Available at: www.esolcitizenship.org.uk.) Passing, in this case, means satisfying ESOL examiners that people have shown adequate progress from one level to the next. In either case, the formal granting of the status of citizen is no longer a piece of paper in the post but conferred at a special ceremony, introduced before the new language rules.

How the learning and assessment systems work

The test for those already possessing the right linguistic competence is overseen by Learn Direct and carried out in 109 test centres, mostly in England but with five in Scotland, four in Wales and two in Northern Ireland. There is a support website that includes information about the test, where it can be taken, an exercise to gain familiarity with the computer, an interactive on-line tutorial to assist in preparing for the test, and a means of self-assessment. (A sample test is available at www.britishness-test.co.uk/.) The revised edition of *Life in the United Kingdom: a Journey to Citizenship* (ABNI 2007) contains nine chapters:

1. The making of the United Kingdom
2. A changing society
3. UK today: a profile
4. How the United Kingdom is governed
5. Everyday needs
6. Employment
7. Knowing the law
8. Sources of help and information
9. Building better communities

The test involves twenty-four questions, different for each person, drawn from the material in chapters 2–6.

For people following the ESOL route, the materials are, like the handbook, about life in the UK. The development of the course materials and the training of ESOL trainers (some 1,000 throughout the UK) were carried out by the National Institute of Adult Continuing Education (NIACE), with the London Language and Literacy Unit. (NIACE's title includes 'England and Wales' in brackets but it was commissioned by the

Home Office to work with Scotland and Northern Ireland, too, on training teachers and adapting the course materials to life in those parts of the UK.) ESOL learners explore twelve themes:

- What is citizenship?
- Parliament and the electoral system
- The UK – geography and history
- The UK as a diverse society
- The UK in Europe, the Commonwealth and the UN
- Human rights
- Working in the UK
- Health
- Housing
- Education
- Community engagement
- Knowing the law

The materials are designed so that teachers can adapt them to reflect features of their locality or to bring in other websites. BBC Northern Ireland, for example, has websites on the history of the conflict and the development of the Good Friday Agreement. Others include those of the major newspapers, the Refugee Council, the Home Office and that of the Department for Education and Skills on *Making Sense of Citizenship*. ESOL courses also involve practical elements such as visits to museums and local sites of historical or political interest and social relevance, as well as visits to classes by, for example, legal specialists, political representatives, service providers and community activists. In pilot tests of the materials, some learners said they would have enjoyed visits by Tony Blair and David Beckham!

Feedback on the course materials received by ABNI indicates that the materials are being used creatively by ESOL teachers and are enjoyed by learners. Seemingly, they have provoked lively debate on topics which, in the past, have not often featured in ESOL materials; that is, citizenship, human rights and Parliament. Both teachers and learners reported satisfaction with how interesting they were and how they had expanded horizons and confidence.

There are a number of ongoing issues relating to the learning of English and about life in the UK. Many of these represent practical impediments for individuals in becoming active citizens, including the costs of the test and courses, waiting lists for courses, and the difficulty of attending courses for those working long hours or caring for dependent relatives. These, and other practical impediments, are outlined in ABNI's Final Report, along with related recommendations for any successor body (ABNI 2008). But, here, the focus is on the relationship, if any, between enabling people to be active citizens and promoting active citizenship, an aim expressed in The New and the Old Group, deliberated upon within ABNI and the subject of a recommendation for its successor group.

Promoting active citizenship

There are three main issues complicating the likelihood that 'enabled citizens' will become 'active citizens'. Two have been considered by ABNI: the limitations of the test route as it currently operates; and the possibility of an experiential learning component in ESOL classes and as an alternative to the test. A third issue, relating to the relationship between identity and participation, has been identified by Kiwan and is dealt with in her essay in this book. Her argument for institutional multiculturalism is relevant to this essay's later reference to how some citizenship ceremonies are developing.

Limitations of the test route

As noted, *Life in the United Kingdom: a Journey to Citizenship* is now in its second edition. Aspects of the first edition raised questions of historical, political or social interpretation among ABNI members, as well as about the level of literacy required to understand it. It was never going to be easy to write an account of the history of the making of the UK that would not be contested. Add to that the need for the handbook to enable newcomers to know about the whole of the UK, not just the part where they had chosen to reside. At the same time, the extent of differences in different parts of the UK was not to overload the reader in need, on the one hand, of a general picture and, on the other, of particular knowledge about his or her chosen region. It was not easy to capture in a single document the complexities of the different laws and regulatory or administrative systems in the UK as a whole, England, Northern Ireland, Scotland and Wales. Further problems lay in the need for it to be written at a language level that can be managed by ESOL level 3 speakers and, simultaneously, will not irritate those who are fluent or may be speakers of English as a first language. For example, in many countries with multiple ethnic-minority languages, English is the lingua franca, as in India and Nigeria. Other settlers or aspirant citizens who take the test are from English-speaking countries; for example, Canada, Australia and the US.

A comparative textual analysis of the two editions by an independent commentator, Patricia White (2008), suggests that the text of the first is more akin than the second to the idea of an active citizen. The first, she argues, implies or assumes that 'the typical citizen is someone who is community-minded and keen to participate'; the second 'gives the impression that the typical citizen is an obedient rule-follower' (pp. 225–6). She also argues that both the test and the handbook in its new style suggest that British society is one that wants citizens 'who can efficiently tick boxes' (p. 227), rather than those who know (and identify with) 'what determines the quality of life in a democratic community' (pp. 228, 230). Though White (p. 227) does concede that the second edition is better for test preparation, the critical context of her concession does not do due justice to the seriousness of ABNI concerns that the revised handbook should be written in a way that was helpful to those preparing for the test. Indeed, pass rates have improved since the publication of the second edition (see also Kiwan 2007: 6).

On the more philosophical point about activism and reflection on the democratic community, it should be noted – as, indeed White (2008: 229) does – that the test, as implemented, does not reflect what The New and the Old Group had intended. Their recommendation, which would have avoided her 'tick box' charge, had been that applicants with good enough existing language skills would either attend a short course on citizenship in a recognised institution or, through distance learning, 'develop an appropriate portfolio or other evidence of civic learning, volunteering or civic participation'. Only then would they take a short written test (Home Office 2004: 20–3).

ACTIVE CITIZENSHIP THROUGH EXPERIENTIAL LEARNING IN ESOL AND AS AN ALTERNATIVE TO THE TEST

The New and the Old Group also recommended the involvement of voluntary associations in the provision of teaching materials (Home Office 2004: 26). And, as noted, ESOL teachers have injected elements of active citizenship through visits by civic and political actors to colleges and visits to relevant sites outside colleges. Kiwan (2007: 12) notes that social or political efficacy can be fostered through the social interaction opportunities provided by ESOL courses – with likely lasting effects in life, at work and in the community.

At one time, it seemed that the Trades Union Congress (TUC) might provide a vehicle for integration and active citizenship. In an agreement with the Confederation of British Industry and the government, it undertook, among other things, to encourage migrants to join trade union organisations. During ABNI's deliberations, it was thought that an active citizenship curriculum could include reflection in a learning portfolio on involvement in a trade union. Other experiences that could similarly be reflected upon included engagement in, for example, youth groups, residents' and parent-teacher associations, and volunteering in voluntary or statutory agencies. Such activities all feature as potential routes to 'earned citizenship', though issues remain to be resolved over what kinds of activism in trades unions (and political parties) could be said to be voluntary in the sense that personal benefit is not involved (HL Hansard, 2 March 2009: cols 553–4, 565–70).

With or without voluntary activity combined with experiential learning, ABNI, throughout its life, promoted the idea of a more active citizenship approach in the teaching of English. It supported suggestions in this area by Lord Goldsmith (2008 ch. 7) in his report on citizenship (see also his contribution to House of Lords debates, especially 11 February 2009: cols 1145–6,). These include: delivering ESOL through appropriate partnerships with courses embedded into life contexts, including participation; learning pathways towards economic participation and active citizenship; and mentoring. Notably, he talks of 'gathering credits' which contrasts with the government's words, 'probationary' and 'earned'. The latter attracted adverse comment on their 'punitive' air when the Prime Minister announced the plans in February 2008 (Institute for Public Policy Research 2008). Similar remarks were made during the new bill's passage through the House of Lords (e.g. HL Hansard, 2 March 2009: cols 517–19).

ACTIVE CITIZENSHIP AND EARNED CITIZENSHIP

ABNI (2008: 28) made recommendations on the proposal for earned citizenship. But the philosophy underlying the new provision is not yet fully clear. Lord Brett (House of Lords 2009) did, indeed, say in his letter, noted above, that 'active citizenship is designed specifically to aid integration'. And the UKBA (Home Office UKBA 2009) paper provided for peers opens by saying (emphasis in the original):

> We want to do more to encourage all migrants who wish to stay in the UK permanently to **integrate fully** into society.
>
> This includes:
> * bringing migrants into **contact with the wider community**
> * showing British citizens that those seeking to join them are **earning their citizenship by being active participants in British life**
> * encouraging those who become citizens by opening them up to new experiences which could become **lifelong roles**.

Clearly, these intentions represent more than allowing people to do 'good works' in return for nationality or residence. But there is little to be gleaned of what might be consistent with Crick's idea that citizenship education could transform political culture, involving both existing citizens and newcomers. The Lord Bishop of Lincoln said in the Second Reading debate that he suspected the proposals of seeking to promote 'a culture of conformity' rather than the 'mutual enrichment' of cosmopolitanism (HL Hansard, 11 February 2009: cols 1143–4). Such concerns were less obvious in the House of Commons debates.

While there is little about mutual adaptation in the UKBA document, it would be fair to say that the last bullet point just quoted does embody an educative element for 'new citizens' by demonstrating an ambition for immigrants to develop themselves as reflective citizens. But it is not yet clear how an educative or developmental element will be built in. In ABNI's deliberations such activities were not 'stand alone' but embedded in a learning curriculum. The UKBA document merely outlines potentially acceptable activities in two categories: formal volunteering or civic activism. The first includes volunteering in, for example, local hospitals, schools, museums, lunch clubs for the elderly, and so on. The second includes serving on a community body, such as a board of school governors. But there is nothing about learning; all that is required is for 'a person in a supervisory capacity with personal knowledge of the applicant's active citizenship' to confirm that the volunteering has taken place.

CITIZENSHIP CEREMONIES

In its final report, ABNI (2008: 28) identified itself with the view expressed by The New and the Old Group that; 'successful and thriving culturally and ethnically diverse societies depend on interaction between the various groups'. This understanding also underlies how some of the citizenship ceremonies are organised – which could, in a few cases, be taken as models of Kiwan's institutional multiculturism. Ceremonies were introduced in 2004 – before the new arrangements for knowledge of English and life in the UK. They are occasions when new nationals swear or affirm, whichever they prefer, allegiance to the Queen and pledge that they will observe the rules and customs of democratic citizenship. David Blunkett intended them to be celebratory, a welcome from the local authority into the community and a chance for the authority to 'encourage participation in the democratic process' (Rimmer 2007: 3). To emphasise the local welcome, many of the first ceremonies in Great Britain took place in town halls, usually with the mayor presiding. Because of the contested nature of locality, identities and their overlap in Northern Ireland, all ceremonies there take place at Hillsborough Castle and are presided over by one of the Lords Lieutenant. (According to one account of them – Mary Fitzgerald, 'Welcoming Ulster's new citizens', *Belfast Telegraph*, 22 March 2005 – the participants did feel that the occasion was, indeed, a special one. I attended one ceremony in Northern Ireland and can confirm the newspaper report. I found similar atmospheres at ceremonies in London.) The first ceremony was conducted by Mark Rimmer (Head of the Registration Service in the London Borough of Brent and, among many other things, national local government spokesperson on Citizenship and Nationality) on 26 February 2004 in the presence of David Blunkett and Prince Charles. Three years on, in the context of a 'perceived cooling of enthusiasm for ceremonies in central government', he (Rimmer 2007: 4–5) called for citizenship ceremonies to be 're-energised' and linked with citizenship education and community cohesion. At Rimmer's suggestion, ceremonies have also been held in 'iconic' buildings such as the British Library and The Banqueting Hall. His own London Borough of Brent pioneered involving local schools in the ceremonies and using venues other than local government buildings – schools and colleges. With the co-operation of teachers, he also pioneered linking the new citizens' experiences with the schools citizenship curriculum. Similar initiatives have taken place in a small number of other English authorities.

Conclusion: active citizenship in the context of 'a politics of unease'?

ABNI's efforts to promote opportunities for interaction and mutual adaptation are consistent with standards advocated by the Council of Europe in its 1999 Declaration on Education for Democratic Citizenship. But the '*Journey to Citizenship*' has been criticised at home from the standpoint of equal treatment. In February 2009, members of the House of Lords (Hansard, 11 February 2009: cols 1128–213) repeated what others had been saying – that no native-born UK national had to take a test or be inducted into society through a citizenship ceremony. On the other hand, the government claims that existing requirements and the additional 'probationary' and 'earned' elements have public support as part of a 'firm but fair system'. It quotes one respondent's view in the consultation process that it was 'fair' that anyone wishing to become a British citizen 'should demonstrate themselves as having integrated into and contributed to British society' (Home Office 2008: 4, 9).

Indeed, there is a range of theoretical literature which argues that encouraging equality does not necessarily imply the same treatment but may require specific measures. Usually, this literature is directed at making the life-chances of the vulnerable comparable with those of the more secure through, for example, affirmative action. The reduction of inequalities through some judicious combination of the same and specific treatment may have a public policy purpose, such as social cohesion, but there is also a moral dimension. Jonathan Seglow (2005) reminds us that 'the right to be a permanent visitor' has moral implications for the host country that go beyond what follows from 'the right to visit' that country as a passer-through or on holiday.

However, key factors in whether specific measures are seen as a matter of justice or otherwise are their purpose and ideological context. Lord Goldsmith (2008: 119), anticipating comments about the new bill, noted that 'most people born in the UK would struggle to pass the test and this creates a deep impression of unfairness among people who have to take the test.' In an international survey of citizenship rules and practices, Goldston (2006) highlights a number of countries where, via direct or indirect discrimination, citizenship tests are used as deliberate obstacles to certain groups of people. It is possible that, in the UK, a sense that different treatment for existing and would-be citizens is unfair could be alleviated by the fact that, as all children take citizenship classes at school, 'in time, there will be no substantive difference between their citizenship learning and the naturalisation requirements for those applying for British citizenship' (Kiwan 2007: 8).

However, that depends on the climate. A recent analysis by Huysmans and Buonfino (2008) of parliamentary debates in the House of Commons from 2001 sought to uncover whether immigration and asylum featured in a nexus with terrorism. Their findings are that migration and asylum were occasionally used as a 'vehicle' in debates about counter-terrorism, becoming embedded in a politics of a perceived need for exceptional policies in the face of exceptional danger to the state. This they call 'a politics of exceptionalism'. More often, they argue, this was not the case. But they also identify a 'politics of insecurity' in relation to lower threats – to 'the legal and social order in various sites within the state'. Here, they argue, references to migration and asylum play a significant part. They call this 'a politics of unease'.

I think they would agree that the language used by the government in the new Borders, Citizenship and Immigration Bill is consistent with 'a politics of unease', while that of critics, especially those in the House of Lords, is not. The proposals on integration are in a bill that introduces a unified border policing force and deals extensively with illegal behaviour.

Lord West, Home Office Parliamentary Under-Secretary of State, introduced the bill in the context of the need for 'robust systems in place to control those coming here' (HL Hansard, 11 February: col. 1130). This outlook and its converse were commented upon by the Lord Bishop of Lincoln whose sentiments were taken up by other Members during the various stages of the bill – rather more strongly in the Lords than the Commons. In the Second Reading debate, he said the following:

> After all, what is a border? Is it a barrier or is it a meeting place? I imagine that most of us want to believe that a border can be a meeting place. Therefore, I imagine that most of us would rather not be debating a Bill which is predicated on a pathology of suspicion and a predetermination towards exclusion rather than welcome. I guess that most of us would rather be debating a Bill driven by the spirit of hospitality rather than hostility towards those who wish to settle in this country . . . (HL Hansard, 11 February 2009: col. 1142)

The principal reason for which the UKBA is known is its role in controlling borders as barriers, while issues of citizenship and integration involve a range of bodies that are more about fostering meeting places – departments dealing with domestic affairs, local authorities, community and voluntary associations. One of Lord Goldsmith's recommendations (2008: 108–9) – supported by ABNI (2008: 18), having previously made a similar recommendation – was that there should be an Office of Citizenship. It would bring together the acquisition of citizenship and the promotion of participation amongst both old and new citizens. For as long as 'probationary' and 'earned' citizenship are dealt with in the space where there is 'a politics of unease' instead of a more 'hospitable' – to quote the Bishop of Lincoln – framework, it will be hard for the Design Group to convince immigrants that the provision is there to encourage rather than impede. Nor will it be easy for advocates of participatory and multicultural citizenship to sustain a belief in the prospects for Bernard Crick's ambition for integrated and active new citizens at least and, at best, a 'transformed political culture' involving all citizens. The paraphrased words of the bard of the country that Bernard adopted seem an appropriate ending:

> An' forward tho' I canna see, I [hope but] fear
>
> (Robert Burns, 'To a Mouse')

REFERENCES

Abbott, Grace (1917), *The Immigrant and the Community*, New York, NY: The Century Co. (reprinted by Kessinger Publishing's Rare Reprints).

Advisory Board on Naturalisation and Integration (ABNI) (2004), *Life in the United Kingdom: a Journey to Citizenship*, London: The Stationery Office/Home Office (published on behalf of the Life in the UK Advisory Group).

Advisory Board on Naturalisation and Integration (2007), *Life in the United Kingdom: a Journey to Citizenship*, London: The Stationery Office/Home Office (published on behalf of the Life in the UK Advisory Group).

Advisory Board on Naturalisation and Integration (2008), *Final Report of the Advisory Board on Naturalisation and Integration (ABNI): November 2004– November 2008*, London: ABNI (Home Office).

Carrera, Sergio (2006), 'A comparison of integration programmes in the EU: trends and weaknesses', *Challenge Papers*, No. 1, March 2006. Available on the website of the Centre for European Policy Studies: http://www.ceps.be.

Etzioni, Amatai (2007), 'Citizenship tests: a comparative communitarian perspective', *The Political Quarterly*, 78(3): 353–63.

Goldsmith, Lord (2008), 'Citizenship: our common bond'. Available at: http://www.justice.gov.uk/reviews/citizenship.htm.

Goldston, James A. (2006), 'Holes in the rights framework: racial discrimination, citizenship and the rights of noncitizens', *Ethics and International Affairs*, 20(3): 321–47.

Home Office (n/d), *UK Settlement: Introduction of Language and Citizenship Testing*, London: Home Office.

Home Office (2002), *Secure Borders, Safe Haven. Integration with Diversity in Modern Britain*, London: Home Office.

Home Office (2004), *The New and the Old*, (Report of the 'Life In the United Kingdom' Group), London: Home Office.

Home Office (2006), Press release, 4 December 2006. Available at: http://press.homeoffice.gov.uk/press-releases/migrants-english-tests.

Home Office UKBA (2008), *The Path to Citizenship: Next Steps in Reforming the Immigration System: Government Response to Consultation*, London: Home Office.

Home Office UKBA (2009), Document made available to the House to illustrate the government's emerging thinking on active citizenship, 20 March 2009.

Honohan, Iseult (2005), 'Active citizenship in contemporary democracy' (paper for the Democracy Commission), in Clodagh Harris (ed.) *Engaging Citizens: the Case for Democratic Renewal in Ireland*, Dublin: Taskforce for Action on Social Change and New Island Publishing, pp. 169–80.

House of Commons (2009), Borders, Citizenship and Immigration Bill [HL]: Second Reading, HC Hansard, 2 July 2009: cols 170–256. Committee Stage, HC Hansard, 9 June 2009: cols 3–35, 39–68; 11 June 2009: cols 71–92, 95–128; 16 June 2009: cols 131–66, 169–204; 18 June 2009: cols 207–28, 231–56. Report Stage and Third reading, HC Hansard, 14 July 2009: cols 177–257.

House of Lords (2009) Borders, Citizenship and Immigration Bill [HL] 15: Second Reading, HL Hansard, 11 February 2009: cols 1128–214. Committee Stage, HL Hansard, 2 March 2009: cols 511–93. Report Stage, HL Hansard, 25 March

2009: cols 712–15; 1 April 2009: cols 1081–1152. Third Reading, HL Hansard, 22 April 2009: cols 1535–43. Letter from Minister in the Government Whips Office to Lord Avebury, 6 April 2009.

Huysmans, Jef and Alessandra Buonfino (2008), 'Politics of exception and unease: immigration, asylum and terrorism in parliamentary debates in the UK', *Political Studies*, 56(4): 766–88.

Institute for Public Policy Research (2008), Prime Minister speaks on managed migration and earned citizenship. Available at: http://www.ippr.org.uk/events/archive.asp?id=3015&fID=239.

Kiwan, Dina (2007), 'Becoming a British citizen: a learning journey', Briefing Paper for Lord Goldsmith's Citizenship Review. Available at: http://www.justice.gov.uk/reviews/publications.htm.

Kiwan, Dina (2008), *Education for Inclusive Citizenship*, London: Routledge.

Kymlicka, Will (2009), 'Multicultural citizenship within multination states', International Centre for Education and Democratic Citizenship, London, 13 March 2009.

Northern Ireland Human Rights Commission (2009), Submission on the Borders, Citizenship and Immigration Bill for the House of Lords Second Reading, 11 February 2009. Belfast: Northern Ireland Human Rights Commission.

Northern Ireland Human Rights Commission (2009), Briefing Paper on the Borders, Citizenship and Immigration Bill for the House of Lords Committee Stage, 25 February 2009. Belfast: Northern Ireland Human Rights Commission.

Rimmer, Mark (2007), 'The future of citizenship ceremonies', Briefing Paper for Lord Goldsmith's Citizenship Review, October 2007. Available at: http://www.justice.gov.uk/reviews/publications.htm.

Seglow, Jonathan (2005), 'The ethics of immigration', *Political Studies Review*, 3(3): 317–34.

Shaw, Jo (2007), *The Transformation of Citizenship in the European Union: Electoral Rights and the Restructuring of Political Space*, Cambridge: Cambridge University Press.

White, Patricia (2008), 'Immigrants into citizens', *The Political Quarterly*, 79(2): 221–31.

9

Democratic Citizenship and Lifelong Active Learning

John Annette

This essay explores to what extent should attempts to introduce more deliberative democratic engagement, in the form of citizen juries, citizens' assemblies, participatory budgeting, and so on, be part of a citizenship education for lifelong learning informed by a 'political' or civic republican conception of citizenship which had been espoused by the late Professor Sir Bernard Crick. This can be compared to a liberal individualist conception, which emphasises individual rights, or a communitarian conception, which emphasises moral and social responsibility. It also considers how people are finding new ways to engage in civic participation which can provide the basis for certificated or accredited lifelong learning for democratic citizenship. It examines, in particular, the 'Active Learning for Active Citizenship' programme which was funded by what was previously the Civic Renewal Unit of the Home Office and also considers the possibility of learning democratic citizenship based on the theory and practice of deliberative democratic engagement.

CITIZENSHIP EDUCATION AND THE CONCEPT OF CITIZENSHIP, EVERYDAY POLITICS AND CIVIC ENGAGEMENT

It could be argued that the conception of citizenship underlying UK lifelong learning for citizenship is a civic republican one which emphasises democratic political participation. This reflects the influence of Bernard Crick and the ex-Minister David Blunkett. One of the key challenges facing the introduction of citizenship education in the UK is the question about whether and in what respects citizenship is 'British'. Elizabeth Frazer has written about the 'British exceptionalism' towards discussing citizenship (Frazer 1999) and David Miller has written that citizenship – except in the formal passport-holding sense – is not a widely understood idea in Britain. People do not have a clear idea of what it means to be a citizen . . . Citizenship is not a concept that has played a central role in our political tradition. (Miller 2000: 26)

The question concerning to what extent British people are familiar or comfortable with the concept of citizenship raises questions about the extent to which the political language of citizenship and civic republicanism can increasingly be seen as a tradition of 'British' political thought which can provide the basis for a transformation of the more dominant liberal individualist political traditions.

In the UK the current 'New Labour' government has espoused a programme of civil renewal and now community empowerment that links the public, voluntary and community sectors to work for the common good. This is informed by a set of beliefs and values involving faith traditions, ethical socialism, communitarianism and, more recently, civic republicanism. According to David Blunkett, when he was the Home Secretary,

The 'civic republican' tradition of democratic thought has always been an important influence for me . . . This tradition offers us a substantive account of the importance of community, in which duty and civic virtues play a strong and formative role. As such, it is a tradition of thinking which rejects unfettered individualism and criticises the elevation of individual entitlements above the common values needed to sustain worthwhile and purposeful lives. We do not enter life unencumbered by any community commitments, and we cannot live in isolation from others. (Blunkett 2003: 19)

It is this civic republican conception of politics (see Bernard Crick in this collection) which I would argue animated key aspects of New Labour's policies from citizenship education to its strategy towards revitalising local communities.

This reconsideration of the concept of citizenship and citizenship education should also be informed by the recent work on the 'politics of everyday life' which can broaden our understanding of what 'the political' could mean in the lives of all citizens (Crick 2005; Ginsbourg 2005; Stoker 2006). We need more research into how people understand the 'political' as it relates to their everyday concerns in their communities as compared to the more formal political sphere of voting, political parties and holding public office. This broader conception of the political reflects the decline of formal political participation and lack of trust in formal politics at a time when there is evidence of continuing forms of civic engagement which may escape the radar of Robert Putnam's research into social capital (cf. Sirianni and Friedland 2004; Power Commission 2006).

This also reflects the important distinction that should be made between volunteering which leads to active citizenship and a more political form of civic engagement in the community which can lead to democratic citizenship.

POLITICS AND COMMUNITY INVOLVEMENT

In his short book on democratic theory Bernard Crick has written,

> I remain concerned, though, that the interpretation of 'community involve-ment' that underpins the Citizenship curriculum will involve a conception of the community that sees it simply as a place or neighbourhood where students are merely 'active': *doing good* rather than *political good (i.e. informed, effective citizens)*. That is, the new curriculum will result in forms of volunteering that will fail to challenge the students to think and act 'politically' . . . (Crick 2002: 115)

In contemporary political thinking the concept of community has become both philosophically and politically significant. Community has also become increasingly the focus of government policy in the UK and the USA. From the 'Third-Way' communitarianism of New Labour, to the emergence of communitarian-based 'Compassionate Conservatism', the idea of community is now seen as a key to rethinking the relationship between civil society and the state. Government social policy concern-ing neighbourhood renewal and urban renaissance stresses the role of citizens in inner-city areas in designing and rebuilding their communities (Newman 2005).

Linked to this challenge is the perceived sense of the loss of commu-nity in contemporary British society. This lost sense of community also underlies the idea of social capital, which has recently been popularised by Robert Putnam in his study of the decline of civic engagement and social capital in the USA (Putnam 2000). The concept of social capital has pro-vided a theoretical basis for understanding the importance of community, which according to the neo-Tocquevillian analysis of Robert Putnam and his colleagues has important consequences for citizenship and political participation. While Putnam and others have analysed the decline of tra-ditional volunteering in the USA it is interesting to note that in the UK there has been a much smaller decline (Hall 2002).

CIVIC RENEWAL AND ACTIVE CITIZENSHIP

David Blunkett in his Edith Kalm Memorial Lecture (Blunkett 2003) and various publications and speeches called for a new *civic renewal* or *civic engagement* which emphasises new forms and levels of community involvement in local and regional governance. This work was carried on by Hazel Blears as Minister for the Department for Communities and Local Government as part of its community empowerment strategy. This new democratic politics, which would include referendums, consultative activities and deliberative participation, has found support from organisations as diverse as the Local Government Association and the prominent thinktank Institute for Public Policy Research (IPPR 2004) and more recently was the focus of the think tank 'Involve'. One outcome of this shift in thinking, which might be termed a switch from *government* to *governance*, is the obligation upon local authorities to involve local citizens in decision-making concerning local governance and public-service delivery. These partnerships seek to involve local communities in the development of community strategies and the more recent 'duty to involve' in public-service delivery. Previously, the Home Office established a Civil Renewal Unit, which has begun piloting an 'Active Learning for Active Citizenship' programme through which it was intended that adult learners will develop the capacity to engage in deliberative democracy at a local level. This unit is now the Community Empowerment Unit in the Department for Communities and Local Government and the 'Take Part' cross-departmental strategy is being supported by the new 'Community Empowerment Strategy' which is being facilitated by the Community Development Foundation (Brannan *et al.* 2007). While recent research by Charles Pattie, Patrick Seyd and Paul Whitely (Pattie *et al.* 2004) provide a framework for examining attitudes in the UK towards citizenship and there is growing research on the nature and forms of political participation, much more research is needed to more fully understand the complex political attitudes of people in order to establish more meaningful and effective forms of political participation. Research in this area also needs to go beyond the limited conception of politics that can be found in the literature of political socialisation.

In the USA this 'civic renewal movement' has led commentators to challenge the assumption of Robert Putnam and others that there has been a fundamental decline in social capital and civic participation. Carmen Sirianni and Lewis Friedland have mapped out the different dimensions of this movement and while recognising the decline of more traditional forms of civic engagement and political participation, like membership of formal organisations, voting and membership of political parties, they argue that there are new and changing forms of civic renewal and call for greater and more creative forms of civic engagement (Sirianni and Friedland 2004). Internationally, there is evidence of new global networks emerging which promote these new forms of civic engagement and deliberative democracy (Fung and Wright 2003).

This recent work on civic renewal also points out the limitations of social capital theory by recognising the need to go beyond both bridging and bonding social capital and enable political action through linking social capital. Without vertical political networking, for example, poor communities do not necessarily gain access to new forms of political influence (Field 2003).

ACTIVE LEARNING FOR ACTIVE CITIZENSHIP

In 2004 the Civil Renewal Unit of the Home Office, which was established under the influence of the then Home Secretary David Blunkett, enabled the development of the 'Active Learning for Active Citizenship' or ALAC programme for adult learning in the community for citizenship. In a scoping report by Val Woodward, entitled 'Active Learning for Active Citizenship', a participatory and community-based pedagogy was proposed (Woodward 2004). This learning framework is analogous to one which is proposed by Pam Coare and Rennie Johnston which they argue should be inclusive, pluralistic, reflexive and promote active citizenship (Coare and Johnston 2003). They emphasise the need to listen to community voices in determining what forms of learning meet the needs of different communities. In the action research-based evaluation by Rooke and Mayo they recognise that the ALAC programme did not result in a formal national curriculum but instead provides a learning framework which is participatory, community-based, one which recognises difference while enabling a shared political identity of citizenship and which enables an understanding of global interdependence (Mayo and Rooke 2008). The interest in lifelong learning for active citizenship may be more with building social capital (cf. Putnam 2000) and community cohesion and not always for capacity building for democratic political participation (Annette 2003).

An important feature of participatory politics which has recently been emphasised is that of the need to enable the capacity to participate in deliberative democratic engagement. From citizens' juries to community visioning the deliberative engagement of citizens has become an increasing feature of the new localism and also public-service delivery (Fung and Wright 2003; Brannan *et al.* 2007). More recently, there has been growing international interest in participatory budgeting from the more famous example of Porto Allegre in Brazil to developments in the UK like the experiment in Lewisham in London. The work of the Power Commission and think tanks like the IPPR, the New Economics Foundation, Involve, and so on now promote a more participatory and deliberative form of citizen engagement (IPPR 2004; Power Commission 2006). What has been lacking has been an analysis of what form of capacity building is necessary for citizens to participate in these activities and in what ways does participation in deliberative democratic engagement provide a form of education for democratic citizenship. This involves a consideration of how deliberative democratic theory, like the emphasis on inclusion and voice in the work of Iris Marion Young, can influence educational practice. It also means that the analysis of the institutional practice of deliberative democratic engagement must develop an understanding of experiential learning and the means to analyse its learning outcomes. We need to know more about how citizens can develop the civic skills necessary for deliberative democratic engagement. A particular civic skill which is necessary is that of 'civic listening' and not just 'civic speaking'. This would include both levels of emotional literacy and intercultural understanding. We also need to learn more from the experience of 'participative governance' activities taking place abroad: from participatory budgeting in Latin America, citizens' assemblies in Canada, and rural participatory action research in India (Cornwall 2008).

In conclusion, I would like to note how the New Labour government's programme for the modernisation of local government and its community empowerment strategies provide the opportunity for local people to get involved in local government and regeneration partnership boards. This is part of a shift from local government to local governance and such activities provide rich opportunities for non-formal lifelong learning for active citizenship (Newman 2005). This non-formal experiential learning would benefit from being informed by the theory and practice of community-based learning as developed in the USA and now growing internationally (Annette 2000). Research into the working of the community leadership involved in Single Regeneration Budget partnerships, New Deal for Communities elected boards, 'Local Strategic Partnerships' and now regional empowerment networks in England has highlighted the need for capacity-building programmes for active citizenship and community leadership. This research also recognises the importance of the political context within which these activities take place (Annette 2003; Taylor 2003) The opportunity for lifelong learning for active citizenship through participation in local governance and regeneration partnership working provides for the possible development of a civic republican or participatory democratic conception of citizenship. What is needed is the provision of a lifelong learning for active citizenship that involves participatory experiential learning and an innovative form of 'political' learning.

References

Annette, John (2000), 'Education for citizenship, civic participation and experiential service learning in the community,' in J. Gardner, D. Lawton and J. Cairns. (eds), *Education for Citizenship*, London: Continuum.

Annette, John (2003), 'Community and citizenship education', in Andrew Lockyer, Bernard Crick and John Annette (eds), *Education for Democratic Citizenship*, Aldershot: Ashgate.

Blunkett, David (2003), *Civil Renewal – a New Agenda* (Edith Kahn Memorial Lecture), London: CSV.

Brannan,Tessa, Peter John and Gerry Stoker (2007) (eds), *Re-energising Citizenship: Strategies for Civil Renewal*, Basingstoke: Palgrave.

Coare, Pam and Rennie Johnston (2003), *Adult Learning, Citizenship and Community Voices*, Leicester: National Institute of Adult Education. Available at: http://shop.niace.org.uk/citizenship-community-voices.html.

Cornwall, Andrea (2008), *Democratic Engagement: What the UK can Learn from International Experience*, London: Demos.

Crick, Bernard (2002), *Democracy*, Oxford: Oxford University Press.

Crick, Bernard (2005), *In Defence of Politics*, 5th edn, London: Continuum.

Field, John (2003), *Social Capital*, London: Routledge.

Frazer, Elizabeth (1999), 'Introduction: the idea of political education', *Oxford Review of Education*, 25: 1–2.

Fung, Archon and Erik Olin Wright (2003) (eds), *Deepening Democracy*, London: Verso.

Ginsbourg, Paul (2005), *The Politics of Everyday Life*, New Haven, CT: Yale University Press.

Hall, Peter (2002), 'The role of government and the distribution of social capital', in Robert Putnam (ed.), *Democracies in Flux*, Oxford: Oxford University Press.

Institute for Public Policy Research (2004) *The Lonely Citizens*. Available at: http://www.ippr.org.uk/publicationsandreports/publication.asp?id=225.

Involve (2005), *People and Participation*. Available at: http://www.peopleandparticipation.net/display.

Mayo, Marjorie and Alison Rooke (2008), 'Active learning for active citizenship: participatory approaches to evaluating a programme to promote citizen participation in England', *Community Development Journal*, 43(3): 371–81.

Miller, David (2000), 'Citizenship: what does it mean and why is it important?', in N. Pearce and J. Hallgarten (eds), *Tomorrow's Citizens: Critical Debates in Citizenship and Education*, London: Institute for Public Policy Research.

Newman, Janet (2005), *Remaking Local Governance*, London: Polity Press.

Pattie, Charles, Patrick Seyd and Paul Whitely (2004), *Citizenship in Britain: Values, Participation and Democracy*, Cambridge: Cambridge University Press.

Power Commission (2006), Report of Power inquiry. Available at: http://www. powerinquiry.org/report/index.php.

Putnam, Robert (2000), *Bowling Alone in America*, New York, NY: Simon and Schuster.

Sirianna, Carmen and Lewis Friedland (2004), *Civic Innovation in America: Community Empowerment, Public Policy, and the Movement for Civic Renewal*, Berkeley, CA: University of California Press.

Stoker, Gerry (2006), *Why Politics Matters?: Making Democracy Work*, Basingstoke: Palgrave.

Taylor, Marilyn (2003), *Public Policy in the Community*, Basingstoke: Palgrave.

Woodward, Val (2004), *Active Learning for Active Citizenship*, London: Home Office.

Active Citizenship for Europe and International Understanding

Derek Heater

COMPATIBILITY OF NATIONAL AND TRANSNATIONAL CITIZENSHIP

Twenty years ago, ignoring the precedent (admittedly with a totally different meaning) in the French Revolution, the Home Office claimed to have invented the term 'active citizen'. From 1988 to 1990 the combined words constantly issued forth from the vocal cords of ministers and the pages of the quality press. Douglas Hurd, the Home Secretary, defined its key as the traditions of 'the diffusion of power, civil obligation, and voluntary service' (Heater 1991: 140). Both he and the other contributors to the debate were commending responsibilities for and participation in national, mainly local, social activities. Neither Europe nor international understanding came into it.

Furthermore, traditionally and etymologically, citizenship has meant a status conferred by a city or a state; world citizenship being virtually a metaphor describing a cosmopolitan attitude of mind. Civic activity, accordingly, has related to the former condition. Is active citizenship for Europe and international understanding therefore a paradox, an unacceptable, even meaningless, correlation?

True, because of the terms of the Maastricht Treaty, all citizens of the member-states of the European Union are also citizens of the EU; and thus, uniquely in international law, have a supranational citizenly status. Also, much academic work has been undertaken during the past two decades or so to argue a strong case for a moral and political cosmopolitan identity.

However, definitions are not the only reason to give us pause before accepting the compatibility of the status and feeling of citizenship in the traditionally accepted meaning and an international or transnational meaning: to put the matter in its most common current format – to be able to expect, even require, the citizen to hold multiple loyalties. Indeed, as we shall see below, it is possible to provide manifold examples of modern citizens of states suffering lack of knowledge of world affairs, resenting the powers of supranational institutions, harbouring hatred or suspicion of foreigners and fearing that any advance of cosmopolitan commitment would seriously undermine the solidity of the nation state, dilute national sovereignty.

One vivid example of hostility, from the attempt by several US states to spread and improve the teaching of what has been called 'global education'. Resentment, fear and organised opposition were palpable. One distinguished academic produced in 1979 a plan for school work, which was described as 'the *Mein Kampf* for creating world-centered schools in the U.S.' (Heater 2002: 160). Could such a reaction occur in the UK today? One quite startling illustration relates to the inaugural meeting of the Council for Education in World Citizenship in 1940 and supported by many distinguished educationists. The junior minister dispatched to represent the Board of Education at that gathering, rather than speaking in congratulatory terms, referred to its international understanding objectives as 'humbug and false piety' (Heater 1984: 56).

Yet an investigation into active citizenship in European and international contexts *is* both possible and, more, exceedingly worthwhile. In an essay prompted by the 2006–7 Stevenson Lectures on Citizenship, it is most apt to defend this position by quoting from the opening lecture of the first series, delivered by W. H. Hadow. Sir Henry's starting sentence, expressing the thought of that distinguished educationist at the University of Glasgow, William Boyd, reads: 'Citizenship has been well defined as the right ordering of our several loyalties' (Hadow 1923: 1). Note well the last two words, and the injunction that the plural sentiments be right ordered. So, here is the justification of our task presented in elegant succinctness.

Moreover, the basic idea that the individual, biologically as human being and politically as citizen, has multiple identities and thus loyalties is by no means new. Given Hadow's classical learning it is fit to cite two examples from the ancient world. One is that the Stoics, such as Seneca and the Emperor Marcus Aurelius, declared themselves both citizens of Rome and of the world. The other is the evolution of the idea of concentric relationships, originated by Theophrastus, principal of the Athenian Lyceum. In recent political analysis Henry Shue has written of concentric duties (Shue 1988: 691). He leans heavily in fact on the famous pebble metaphor of Alexander Pope in his *Essay on Man*:

God loves from whole to parts: but human soul
Must rise from individual to the whole.
Self-love but serves the virtuous mind to wake,
As the small pebble stirs the peaceful lake;
The centre moved, a circle straight succeeds,
Another still, and still another spreads,
Friend, parent, neighbour first it will embrace,
His country next; and next all human race . . .

Viewing our problem today, we must recognise: (1) the distinction between citizenship as status, feeling and competence; (2) the need to resolve felt and expressed tensions between national and supranational citizenships/identities/commitments; (3) that understanding means both comprehension and empathy; (4) the distinction, strictly speaking though often confused, between world citizenship and international understanding. Keeping these requirements in mind, we may proceed.

Leaving aside the original, and sustained, meaning of citizen as a denizen of a city, citizenship is a legal and political status accorded by a state and recognised in international law. But in international law it is deemed synonymous with nationality. This is unfortunate for our purpose of studying international understanding because nationality has been hardened by the sentiment of national*ism*, an ideology antipathetic to international harmony. And since citizenship and nationalism emerged in their modern connotations together as political siblings in the late eighteenth century, loosening their bonding after two centuries is not easy. Civic empathy is thus directed towards fellow nationals – in both the political and cultural senses – and away from foreign nationals.

The terms 'world citizenship', 'global citizenship' and 'cosmopolitan citizenship' can all be found, particularly in publications in the field of Education – 'education for . . .'. However, not without some disquiet. After all, if citizenship is a status conferred by a state, it is not possible to be a world citizen because no world state exists to perform that conferring role. It is noticeable, therefore, when, in the 1960s and 1970s, considerable effort was made to enhance this element in and style of teaching, UNESCO and the English Department of Education and Science used the weaker term 'education for international understanding'.

Of weightier bearing for us here is to consider that, if individuals think of themselves as active citizens solely because they are national citizens and have a responsibility just in that context, will their sense of commitment to transnational matters be deleteriously affected? Be diluted at best, at worst be rejected as a hostile competitor for action.

Now, to be an active citizen requires the existence of institutions through which to channel one's activity. Thus the question arises whether operating as a European or world citizen via one's national institutions alone is sufficient. Or, to be as effective as possible, one needs to behave as an active European or world citizen (despite the semantic worries) through supranational institutions. If the latter, then, one must accept that citizenship is not a singular condition in the present world. We exist in an environment of multiple citizenships. In a number of tiers this is already a social, legal and political reality. In terms of identity, rights and duties in the UK an individual can be simultaneously a citizen of, say, Edinburgh, Scotland, the United Kingdom and the European Union.

DISTINCTION: EUROPE AND INTERNATIONAL UNDERSTANDING

This brings us to the specific issue of active citizenship with regard to Europe, a matter which, because of its institutional structures, requires separate treatment from international understanding generally.

It can be said that we are European citizens because we are affected by that status and can participate in that capacity through three main institutional systems.

One is the Council of Europe. The citizens of its member-states have access to its Commission and Court of Human Rights, to its Parliamentary Assembly via their national representatives and can benefit from the work of its education programme, mainly on HRE (Human Rights Education).

Secondly, we are able to express our opinions about the policies and legislation of the European Union via our MPs and, especially, our MEPs.

Thirdly, and most significantly, since 1993, when the Treaty of European Union (Maastricht Treaty) came into effect, our status as European citizens has been notably strengthened. One may say this despite the sound judgment of an American academic that, 'given the ambiguity surrounding the term European Citizenship, it is perhaps best defined ex negativo, i.e., by what it is not . . . "it does not establish a nationality of the Union, but rather a complementary citizenship" to that of a member state' (Sobisch 1997: 82). A matter of relativity.

But, listing a few features of the citizenship of the European Union instead positively will indicate the various ways in which citizens can be active within the EU. Most notably Article 8 of the Treaty establishes the legal status of citizenship of the Union and includes the extension of associative rights thus:

> Every citizen of the Union residing in a Member State of which he is not a
> national shall have the right to vote and to stand as a candidate at municipal
> elections in the Member State in which he resides, under the same conditions
> as nationals of that State. (Art. 8b)

Furthermore, Art. 138e arranges for the European Parliament to appoint
an Ombudsman empowered to receive complaints from any citizen of the
Union.

Since 1979 Members of the European Parliament have been directly
elected by national citizens. The significance of this constitutional
arrangement for our analysis is stressed in Art. 138a:

> Political parties at European level are important as a factor for integration
> within the Union. They contribute to forming a European awareness and to
> expressing the political will of the citizens of the Union.

Even more telling is a statement made by the European Court of Justice
(ECJ) in 1963 to this effect:

> Community law . . . not only imposes obligations upon individuals but is also
> intended to confer upon them rights which become part of the legal heritage
> . . . The vigilance of individuals concerned to protect their rights amounts
> to an effective supervision entrusted by [the Treaty] to the diligence of the
> Commission and the Member States. (Oliver and Heater 1994: 145)

The British constitutional lawyer Professor Dawn Oliver has commented
on this quotation: 'Thus we have the idea of "the citizen as enforcer" or
guardian of the rule of law in the Community' (i.e. the EC, as the EU then
was) (Oliver and Heater 1994: 145).

Yet, a quarter of a century later, complaints were loudly voiced that the
Community was a 'technocrats' Europe', not, in the French term, a *'Europe
des citoyens'*; despite the reforms introduced by the Maastricht Treaty,
including the strengthening of the Parliament's powers (Arts. 138b, 138c,
189b). Another term has been the need to repair the 'democratic deficit'.

Nevertheless, even equivalent, albeit faulty, structures for active citizenship are almost totally absent at the global level. And this, in spite
of occasional arguments historically for mankind to engage in consultative groups about the world's problems. Most famously, Tennyson, in his
poem, 'Locksley Hall', dared foresee in the distant future 'the Parliament
of man, the Federation of the world'; though he did not foretell the suffrage! More remarkable, but much less familiar, was the plan devised by
the seventeenth-century Moravian theologian, Comenius, who, in his
Panegersia, argued that, 'Because the matter [of handling international
tasks] is of common concern, no one should therefore be excluded from

this consultation about human affairs, no one should be allowed to exclude himself.' Indeed, his motto was, '*nihil de vobis, sine vobis*' (Heyberger (translated) 1928: 196, 191).

A devoted reader of Tennyson's lines was Harry S. Truman, US President at the time of the inauguration of the United Nations Organisation, the closest the world has today to a 'parliament of man', yet notably lacking in facilities for the display of active world citizenship.

Faute de mieux, one can point out that the UN specialised agencies and non-governmental organisations (NGOs) provide plentiful and varied opportunities to be active *social* citizens. For we must not forget, as T. H. Marshall taught us, that citizenship is not confined to its legal and political dimensions. Accordingly, we must take into account the possibilities of being employed by the international organs just mentioned. Also, outside these official bodies, there must be included, to cite very few examples, working voluntarily for Oxfam, supporting Amnesty International, contributing to Christian Aid, campaigning for Greenpeace, because participation in any of these numerous activities can surely be valued as behaving as world citizens, including gaining understanding, in both senses. Particularly attractive for some of the increasingly globally conscious younger generation are the opportunities provided by Voluntary Service Overseas (VSO).

Having already written the above judgments on the paucity of official channels for popular political participation at both the European and global levels, I came across a confirmatory echo in a reference to the report of the US National Intelligence Council's (NIC), *Global Trends 2025: a World Transformed*, published in November 2008. Its pessimism about the future is based, inter alia, on its verdict that there is currently a 'democratic gap' separating Brussels from voters and that international institutions are 'ramshackle' (*Guardian* 2008a).

We need now face three fundamental questions. First, insofar as active citizenship for Europe and international understanding is weak in Britain, what are the reasons? Second, does this weakness matter and, if so, why? And third, what ways are there for combating this weakness?

REASONS FOR WEAK TRANSNATIONAL ACTIVE CITIZENSHIP

Lest any reader should doubt the fragility even of interest let alone popular participation in international affairs in Britain, the following example may be pondered. It is drawn from the splendidly thorough analysis of their survey directed by Geraint Parry and colleagues in 1984–5 (Parry *et al.* 1992). They classified 'agendas and political action' into eleven topics (including 'other'), one of which was 'defence and foreign affairs'. One feature of their work was to test six different localities. In that part of the survey, defence and foreign affairs aroused so little interest that the responses had to be classified under 'other'. And in the full national survey it ranked ninth in importance (Parry *et al.* 1992: 357, 248).

A number of reasons can be identified for this comparative lack of commitment to the international scene over the ages as well as currently. We may begin by the resentment of 'Johnny foreigner'. Dislike of 'the Other' is certainly evident as the common use of the Greek suffix *-phobia* reveals: xenophobia, Francophobia, Europhobia, Islamophobia. Perhaps it is endemic in the English character? John Hale described a Frenchman complaining in 1558 that Englishmen 'called him and his fellows knaves, dogs and sons of whores' (Hale 1993: 63).

Ever since the movement for European Union got under way, the issue of Britain's relationship with the continent has been contentious. Pride, vanity and belief in the country's true international interests caused it to cling on to Churchill's 'three circles' definition of our foreign relations: the Commonwealth, the USA and Europe. To plunge too wholeheartedly into the last of these would impair our special relationships with the other two. This pattern has not completely faded; and has been kept in the nation's mind by both the lay public and politicians. Indeed, what senior British politician apart from Edward Heath has constantly displayed keen enthusiasm for the European project to his fellow countrymen?

In addition, the tripartite interpretation has been kept in the nation's consciousness by positive dislike of the European segment. Hostility to this capitalist-shaped organisation strained the Labour Party in the 1980s when the Marxist wing argued for the country to secede. More recently, especially over the issues of the Maastricht Treaty and the proposed Constitution and Constitutional (Lisbon) Treaty, it has been the Conservative Party that has suffered a political schism. The feeling that a large proportion of the electorate was antipathetic has led to interesting reactions. The Conservative manifesto of 2005 committed the Party to a referendum, while the Labour governments of both Blair and Brown dared not risk holding a referendum on the planned EU Constitution. However, the latter's 2005 manifesto committed them to this policy for the more summary Lisbon Treaty, though with a feeble ministerial backing. Statistics are telling. The European Union Eurobarometer revealed that the EU average public opinion from 1981 to 1998 gauging the EU to be a 'good thing' varied from 50 per cent to 51 per cent and British opinion from 49 per cent to 19 per cent. In the 1999 elections to the European

Parliament the fairly evident Eurosceptic Conservative candidates secured 36 per cent of the votes and the aberrant pro-European Conservatives 1.4 per cent. The latter was less than the 7 per cent scored by the secessionist UK Independence Party.

However, when it comes to both European and broadly international matters, a fair proportion of British citizens are DKs (don't knows). This attitude needs explanation. Or rather explanations, because two approaches to the problem are possible. Borrowing the terminology from International Relations, realist and idealist arguments have been developed. Both, in their own ways, can interpret the causes of apathy, ignorance and failure of expression and action.

First, the realist interpretation. This suggests that international political action by its nature is for the elite. The common man cannot be expected to take an interest in, be bothered to learn about and spend time on these distant and complex matters, except in wartime. (Even the elite Neville Chamberlain thought that about Czechoslovakia!) Apart from anything else, hoi polloi are themselves realistic enough to know that they lack the political power to exert any effective leverage on world conditions and events. Consequently, worrying about and striving to rectify this natural indifference is a futile task. Worse: to adapt Horace, the throng, untutored in the arcane mysteries of international relations, could inflict harm if they meddle.

Those, alternatively, of an idealist frame of mind, who yet recognise the political illiteracy of the multitude, are confirmed that this condition is not irremediable. What are required are the kinds of awakening, elucidating and invigorating processes that will be outlined in our final section.

For now, we must identify a particularly significant, although not necessarily persistent, hindrance to the burgeoning of transnational citizenly activity, namely, the views and policies of politicians. The very notion of any potent civic activity causes some politicians trepidation because the popular mood on any issue might well be hostile to their own doctrines and activities. Loudly broadcast outdoor protests or vivid newspaper campaigns can lead to electoral decline. Only when a popular movement is supportive of government policy is official reaction positive. Hence the eagerness for active local citizenship when launched in the late 1980s.

It is instructive to survey the mind-sets of politicians about popular and personal involvement in international affairs since the end of the Second World War. Initial favour for the United Nations Association (UNA) and membership of the Parliamentary Group for World Government (PGWG), for example, soon waned. Backing for UNESCO through the UK National Commission was always weak. Indeed, unique among all member-states, the educational work of UNESCO was allotted not to the National Commission but to the Council for Education in World Citizenship (CEWC), what we would today call a quango. Moreover, through constant reduction in government funding, CEWC withered.

A more up-to-date example of government apprehension at the public's being prepared for activity in the field of foreign affairs occurred in 1991 with the Secretary of State for Education's statement on the teaching of history and geography. This was before the introduction of citizenship into the English National Curriculum and when these subjects were advised to be two of the main vehicles for this teaching, and so render pupils civically aware and capable of judgment. Yet, in the statement, teachers were required to cut short the history syllabus at around 1945 in order to avoid recent and contemporary controversy; and geography teachers were required to shun 'attitudes and viewpoints'!

Finally in this section, what about the press, closely connected to everyday politics? Politicians, ministers primarily, are constantly alert to and apprehensive about the coverage of their policies, speeches and articles. And with good reason. The wide-circulation tabloid newspapers constantly print stories highly critical of and blatantly biased against politicians, mainly those of a different party from that supported by the journalists. Unsurprisingly, readers of the tabloids have a lower opinion of politicians than even the low national attitude. And so too is their news coverage often slanted against full and balanced reportage and educative columns about European and broader foreign affairs.

There are thus plenty of reasons for readily accepting that the British population is rarely conscious of the existence of the opportunities for active citizenship in the field of international affairs including Europe. The major exception, of course, is at the times of mass demonstrations such as those organised by CND and that occurred after the outbreak of the Iraq war.

But is this feeble picture of active citizenship for Europe and international understanding of any consequence?

DOES WEAK TRANSNATIONAL ACTIVE CITIZENSHIP MATTER?

An American researcher four decades ago provided a most trenchant realist warning: 'the vast majority of citizens hold pictures of the world that at best are sketchy, blurred and without detail or at worst so impoverished as to beggar description' (Blumler 1974: 91). As a consequence, the general populace, if politically active, may engage in operations contrary to the national interest, be swayed by demagoguery, be prone to chauvinist, intolerant attitudes, undermine subtle diplomacy. However, since civic political activity will, sometimes and somehow in any case happen, it should not be ignored, but be educated to behave intelligently and benignly.

Furthermore, governments, particularly in a democratic society and age, can benefit from widely devised championships of their intelligent policies. It may be argued, for example, that a widespread awareness of the crucial need for global commitment to alleviate the north-south gap in standards of living originated with the Brandt Report of 1980. Explaining the conditions that could bring about the implementation of the Commission's report, the recommendations of which they hoped would be fully implemented by the end of the century, namely 2000, the document states that

> this requires an intensive process of education to bring home to public opinion in every country the vital need to defend the values without which there will be no true economic development and, above all, no justice, freedom or peace. (Brandt 1980: 268)

Thus, any advocacy of active citizenship for Europe and international understanding in Britain and assessment of what is feasible to achieve, depends on the following: an analysis of how to counteract the negative forces and to improve and build upon the established and potential strengths that currently exist in both theory and practice.

HOW TO COMBAT WEAK TRANSNATIONAL ACTIVE CITIZENSHIP

Before attempting listed answers to the what and how questions in the sub-title of this book, three general, albeit rather obvious, points need to be pressed, because they are so significant. One is that, because the original purpose of 'inspiring and enlisting the active citizen' (Douglas Hurd) in Britain was to overcome what was seen as a lack of responsibility for and lawlessness in local communities, consequent agendas can provide us here with virtually no assistance. The second general point is that methods for gathering information, broadcasting one's opinions and participating in political activities and movements have expanded in recent years. In the words of Peter Mandelson, spoken a decade ago, 'It may be that the era of pure representative government is being complemented by more direct forms of involvement, from the internet to referenda' (Wright 2000: 155). It is pertinent to notice here that the title of his speech was 'European

Integration and National Sovereignty'. The third point is the recent expansion of the swift processes of globalisation.

If we are to undertake enhancement of transnational active citizenship, what should be our basic objectives? The field is so wide and complex, the question could well attract myriad responses. Let us try four. These are: to produce more and better citizens active on issues beyond their nation state; their prime purpose would be to help improve global conditions; in addition, they should campaign for the greater democratisation of supranational institutions; and they should combine their efforts on both urgent problems and far-sighted plans.

Good active citizens must, of course, have knowledge, understanding, judgment and commitment. However, as cosmopolitan citizens, to use a present common terminology, they need extra qualities compared with 'ordinary' state active citizens. These are as follows. One is to accept that operating in response to European and/or global matters is justified; because the really serious issues such as climate change and dire poverty are of widespread geographical scope; and because one's own country is not insulated from conditions and events elsewhere (the economic crisis starting in 2008 made that transparent). So good *national* citizenship requires a *cosmopolitan* frame of mind. A second quality is to be able to recognise the different political levels at which action is necessary and to assess which is the most likely to be effective. Thirdly, the good cosmopolitan citizen must refrain from being overwhelmed and despairing at the mountainous tasks. On this last characteristic the optimistic comment about 'new progressive politics' in the context of globalisation by the Canadian academic Rob Walker is uplifting:

> People are not as powerless as they are made to feel. The grand structures that seem so distant and so immovable are clearly identifiable and resistible on an everyday basis. Not to act is to act. Everyone can change habits and expectations or refuse to accept that the problems are out there in someone else's backyard. (Held and McGrew 2002: 114)

Clearly, effective European or world active citizens need to be equipped with relevant understanding, especially about the issues on which and/or place where they most wish to operate. A particularly delicate judgment must be made about taking up an issue which, deliberately or as an unforeseen result, brings the individual either in direct conflict with the citizen's own or foreign government or finds a government unsympathetic.

So, how does the British citizen choose to vote on EU policies, for example? Compare the two main parties' 2005 manifestos. The Conservatives: 'People face a clear choice: powers brought back from

Brussels and no euro with the Conservatives, or more powers surrendered to Brussels under Mr Blair . . .' (Conservative Party 2005: 22). Labour: 'We are proud of Britain's EU membership and of the strong position Britain has achieved within Europe. British membership of the EU brings jobs, trade and prosperity . . . and international clout' (Labour Party 2005: 83). But selective and partisan comments are dangerous for the honest active citizen.

In fact, and turning to world scale, since the 1980s, a new term has been needed: 'global civil society', to describe the 'many movements reinforcing a sense of human solidarity, [and which] reflects a large increase in the capacity and will of people to take control of their own lives' (Commission on Global Governance 1995: 335).

In parallel, we, as students of active cosmopolitan citizenship, as well as practising and potential members of that community, must be aware of falling into the trap of naivety. We must all understand that there are pitfalls, as April Carter notably has warned. Two cautions here. One is that enthusiastic support for the EU and strengthening its power may create a 'fortress Europe' antipathetic to non-member peoples and thus counteract the ideals of global citizenship (Carter 2001: 139–41). The other is that not all global civic activity is fully beneficial, mainly because of its huge expansion: 'The possible danger for global organizations is that they will be compromised by close cooperation with international organizations and become increasingly professionalized and hierarchical internally. There are also dangers of voluntary bodies wasting funds and becoming inefficient' (Carter 2001: 98).

With these objectives and caveats in mind, how can those supporting the principle of active citizenship for Europe and international understanding go about achieving their ideals?

In considering the multitude of options, a few basic thoughts need to be noted concerning channels of communication for active participation. One is that, apart from supporting charities – and compassion fatigue has often been exaggerated (one may recall the generous response (81 per cent of the population) to the tsunami tragedy appeal) – opportunities to perform regionally or globally are often only weakly available. Secondly, one of the reasons for this difficulty is the paucity of effective democratic institutions and openings at supranational level. But, thirdly, messages or pressure may be activated indirectly via distinguished or celebrated opinion leaders. Fourthly, it is important to realise that the achievement of goals is a two-way process. For instance, citizens express their political wishes to shape politicians' or other decision-makers' programmes and the recipients of those wishes shape their programmes to secure citizens' support.

It is now time to examine some ways in which active citizens may possibly improve their chances of achieving or at least advancing their worthwhile wishes in the European and other international arenas.

First, is to campaign for the reform and addition of supranational institutions. A number of authorities have recognised that due to globalisation and the widening of the gap between developed and underdeveloped countries the world's international institutions, devised largely after the Second World War, are rapidly becoming obsolete. Present-day problems need holistic treatment; existing institutions are fragmented. Referring to environmental and developmental issues, the Bruntland Commission declared, 'The real world of interlocked and ecological systems will not change, the policies and institutions concerned must' (World Commission on Environment and Development 1987: 310). The failure to engage in such modernisation has meant that progress and accountability remain sterile, citizenly activity frail in achievements (for example, see Bellamy 2008: 24, 51). Active transnational citizenship should, consequently, refocus on changing the worn-out system in addition to struggling to work within it.

The EU system is not so much worn out as a confused compromise, the democratic participative elements as afterthoughts. We need, therefore, to ask: why are there constant complaints about the 'democratic deficit' and what should active citizens target for reform? Modern democracy in most countries depends for its success in honestly putting into effect the wishes of the *demos* through a parliamentary system. Thus, in the case of the EU, the powers and efficiency of the European Parliament (EP) and the national parliaments need to be tested.

The constitutional structure of the EU and the will of the member governments have provided for both parliamentary levels to be weak in relation to the other EU institutions. The EP has only limited powers with regard to legislation, though, admittedly, in some areas it has co-decision authority, giving equal power with the other legislative bodies.

With regard to the British Parliament, it can discuss and legislate for the implementation of EU documents; it cannot negate an EU document. The House of Commons has a Scrutiny Committee, whose function is to hold ministers to account for how they use their judgment in the EU Council of Ministers. But, neither House has the time to undertake EU work thoroughly, in particular, there are few debates on matters emanating from Brussels. The central task of active citizens should, consequently, be to campaign, through their MEPs and MPs and by popular action, for reform of this unsatisfactory state of affairs, including forcing all MEPs and MPs to take this work more seriously.

Much more interest is devoted by politicians and the public to two global matters, though what thought and activity is being undertaken could benefit from wider international citizenly support. One is environmental, the other is political.

It is a truism that the most crucial global worry that is in need of urgent and powerful attention is the forthcoming intensification of the climate crisis. At last, all governments accept the necessity for action. What can British active citizens undertake to help? Joining a national organisation such as Stop Climate Chaos, which already has four million members belonging to its constituent bodies, is one option. Another is a more ambitious approach, namely, to build and develop a vast planetary popular campaign to exert truly effective pressure on the world's leaders. In December 2008, the British Environment Secretary, Ed Miliband, effectively admitted the vital need for massive mobilisation to ensure progress. He said, 'I think back to Make Poverty History . . . and that was a mass movement that was necessary to get agreement. In terms of climate change, it's even more difficult' (*Guardian* 2008c).

This is a fine idea. However, many authorities might consider his parallel slightly unfortunate because, after a splendid start, support for the anti-poverty aims sagged. Perhaps one of the reasons for this waning is lack of efficient global democratic institutions. David Held is notable in arguing for thorough reform along these lines in his *Democracy and the Global Order* (Held 1995). Although his agenda is highly intelligent and comprehensive, it is massive – a very long-term programme.

A less ambitious project and very recently revived is for the addition to the UN organs of a Parliamentary Assembly. The Charter allows for revisions (Art. 109) and Charter Review Conferences have been held, unsuccessfully, since 1955. In 2007 a Campaign for the Establishment of a United Nations Parliamentary Assembly was launched, upheld by the Committee for a Democratic United Nations, advocating citizens' representation at the UN. Active world citizens can support this movement.

Topics like these are quite esoteric and beyond the scope of much of the communications media, increasingly available in electronic form. Moreover, the subject of mass media is beyond the compass of the present essay. But it is worth noting the feeble coverage by the tabloid press of international affairs. And, in any case, as the Media Standards Trust has recently shown, the great majority of the public have no faith in the national newspapers to print reliable information.

What captures the interest of the bulk of the population from the mass media, as the content of the red-top newspapers and viewing figures of television programmes reveal, is not serious news and current affairs items (except at times of great drama), but rather the antics of 'people like ourselves' and, even more so, of 'celebrities'.

It is extraordinary that we should have in recent times been plunged so deeply into obsession with the lives of 'celebrated' pop musicians, footballers, television 'stars' and people who, most strangely, become 'famous for being famous'. Could this psycho-sociological phenomenon not be utilised more? The popularity of the musician Bob Geldof's work for poor countries and the comedian Eddie Izzard's support for Europe are models.

When major supranational crises become known – the threat of nuclear war, dire poverty in the underdeveloped regions of the world, the current financial/economic recession, the looming climate disasters – young people often complain that it was the fault of their parents' generation. Should they not have been more aware, more intelligent, more active in taking preventive measures? Yet, it may be argued, in Britain at least, many of the mature adults of today experienced more teaching about Europe and for international understanding than their offspring. For that older generation and their teachers were serviced by, for example, the then quite lively European Association of Teachers and the CEWC. Though, true, the educational work of Oxfam is still flourishing. And it is to be devoutly hoped that the doughty Association for Citizenship Teaching (ACT) and its journal will be able to sustain their invaluable services, albeit providing more stress on cosmopolitan citizenship.

The rising young generation are being able to learn to become active European and world citizens through school reforms. One may mention, for instance, the English national curriculum citizenship lessons. For the revised curriculum includes these topics: 'actions that citizens can take to influence decisions' and 'challenges facing the global community including inequalities, sustainability and interdependence' (Craft 2007: 14). And in Scotland, current curricular development has the advantage of the tradition of international affairs elements in the Modern Studies syllabuses introduced in 1959. Even so, an increased number of specially trained teachers must enter the secondary schools for these pupils to be so informed, excited and absorbed in order to grow up to fill this kind of civic role. The teachers' tasks are, it is true, by no means easy. To note just one comment by leading authorities in the field, 'Education for European citizenship is . . . hopelessly entangled in the web of EU controversy' (Sobisch and Davies 1997: 307). Threats of accusations of bias, indeed, loom over the teachers of much citizenship subject-matter. Yet, what use is an active citizen unequipped to make educated and intelligent judgments on contentious issues?

But lest we finish on a note of gloom, we may cite the positive evidence from a University of London lecturer calling upon his experience of the country's multiculturalism:

> Teaching students in London's East End, one can already sense a far more global sensibility than among my own generation . . . With kin ties to South Asia, Latin America and the Far East, they are drawn to the media landscapes of Mumbai, the art and architecture springing up in China's mega-cities, the street culture of Rio or the prosperity of the Gulf. (*Guardian* 2008b)

If this attitude of mind can be captured by others of all ethnicities, and for many more to urge on a sense of active citizenship for matters beyond our shores, international understanding could develop a liveliness not so easy to grasp from the printed page and the television screen alone.

References

Bellamy, Richard (2008), *Citizenship: a Very Short Introduction*, Oxford: Oxford University Press.
Blumler, Jay G. (1974), 'Does mass political ignorance matter?' *Teaching Politics*, 3(2): 91–100.
Brandt, Willy (ed.) (1980), *North-South: a Programme for Survival*, London: Pan Books.
Carter, April (2001), *The Political Theory of Global Citizenship*, Abingdon: Routledge.
Commission on Global Governance (1995), *Our Global Neighbourhood*, Oxford: Oxford University Press.
Conservative Party (2005), *The Choice in 2005*, London: Conservative Party.
Craft, Liz (2007), 'A curriculum fit for the future', *Teaching Citizenship*, London: Association for Citizenship Teaching.
Guardian (2008a), 21 November.
Guardian (2008b), 23 November.
Guardian (2008c), 8 December.
Hadow, W. H. (1923), *Citizenship*, Oxford: Clarendon Press.
Hale, John (1993), *The Civilization of Europe in the Renaissance*, London: Fontana Press.
Heater, Derek (1984), *Peace Through Education: the contribution of the Council for Education in World Citizenship*, Lewes: Falmer Press.
Heater, Derek (1991), 'Citizenship: a remarkable case of sudden interest', *Parliamentary Affairs*, 44(2): 140–56.
Heater, Derek (2002), *World Citizenship: Cosmopolitan Thinking and its Opponents*, London: Continuum.
Heater, Derek (2007), 'Does cosmopolitan thinking have a future?', in Michael Cox (ed.), *Twentieth Century International Relations*, London: Sage, vol. VIII, ch. 124, pp. 127–46,

Held, David (1995), *Democracy and the Global Order: From the Modern State to Cosmopolitan Governance*, Cambridge: Polity Press.

Held, David and Anthony McGrew (2002), *Globalization/Anti-Globalization*, Cambridge: Polity Press.

Heyberger, A. (1928), *Jean Amos Comenius*, Paris: Librairie Ancienne Honoré Champion.

Labour Party (2005), *Britain Forward Not Back*, London: Labour Party.

Oliver, Dawn and Derek Heater (1994), *The Foundations of Citizenship*, Hemel Hempstead: Harvester Wheatsheaf.

Parry, Geraint, George Moyser and Neil Day (1992), *Political Participation and Democracy in Britain*, Cambridge: Cambridge University Press.

Shue, Henry (1988), 'Mediating duties', *Ethics*, 98: 687–704.

Sobisch, Andreas (1997), 'The European Union and European citizenship', in Ian Davies and Andreas Sobisch (eds), *Developing European Citizens*, Sheffield: Sheffield Hallam University Press, pp. 73–95.

Sobisch, Andreas and Ian Davies (1997) 'Conclusion: some final thoughts', in Ian Davies and Andreas Sobisch (eds), *Developing European Citizens*, Sheffield: Sheffield Hallam University Press, pp. 307–13.

World Commission on Environment and Development (1987), *Our Common Future*, Oxford: Oxford University Press.

Wright, Tony (ed.) (2000), *The British Political Process: an Introduction*, London: Routledge.

Young People as Active Political Citizens

Andrew Lockyer

INTRODUCTION

In the last decade of the twentieth century there was an increasing rec-ognition of children's rights which both informed the scholarly discourse surrounding children and childhood, and significantly influenced public policy in relation to children and families. The widespread subscription to the UN Convention on the Rights of the Child (UNCRC 1989), adopted with minor reservation by the UK government in 1991, pro-voked substantial re-examination of the status and treatment of young people. This is evidenced for example by the creation of four Children's Commissioners with responsibilities, in the several parts of the UK, to safeguard and promote the rights and interests of children and young people in accordance with the provisions of the UNCRC.

This increased focus on children's rights has coincided with the con-tinually expanding discourse on citizenship that has been a feature of the revival of the republican tradition in social and political theorising. This is linked to the critique of self-seeking individualism as the cornerstone of market-orientated liberal democracy. One of the shortcomings of liberal-ism's putative neutrality between chosen ways of life is the minimal role that it assigns to the public sphere, both as the locus of civic engagement and as an institutional setting for the delivery of social justice. One of the implications of the adoption of the UNCRC is that state-parties have an increasing responsibility either to directly deliver services to children or ensure others do; another is to provide opportunities for young people to participate in decisions which affect them. Central to questions sur-rounding the just treatment of children and young people is their status as citizens.

If citizenship is conceived passively to be a legal status conferring state identity, it can be considered straightforwardly as an issue of state and international law. However, when it is viewed as a substantive set of social, economic and political expectations, conventions and obligations informing the relations between individuals and the communities in which they live, citizenship becomes open to multifaceted and malleable construction. To what extent citizenship is then compatible with childhood depends both on what are taken to be its essential elements, or building blocks (Lister 2008), and on how childhood is understood. There is growing insistence both in the literature on childhood and amongst agencies representing young people, to incorporate them within the ambit of citizenship. But to view them as active citizens rather than merely legal citizens requires closer examination.

There are three ways of viewing the relation between children and citizenship. They may be viewed as citizens of the future (not yet citizens), citizens now (citizens from birth), or becoming citizens (citizens in-the-making). Although these are not necessarily mutually exclusive categories because different senses of citizenship might be entailed, nonetheless, there are diverse grounds for favouring one formulation above another.

FUTURE CITIZENS

The case for regarding children as not yet citizens, but with the potential of becoming citizens in the future, is a position of long standing – it might be characterised as the pre-modern orthodoxy. It has separate roots in both classical republicanism and liberal theory.

For Aristotle citizens are those who have the 'opportunity and the ability to participate in government . . . children are citizens in a limited sense' (Aristotle 1962 bk III: 111). Generally children are incomplete or 'unfinished' human beings, but if they have the capacity for 'authoritative deliberation' (not all have) they have the potential to 'share in rule and in being ruled' (Aristotle 1962 bk III: 115) which is the functional prerequisite of citizenship (in the well-ordered polis). In practice Aristotle recognises citizenship as an inherited status, but both the legal entitlement and the economic opportunity are needed to be able to actually share in the business of the polis.

There was a clear contrast between relationships within the household, based on hierarchy and natural necessity, and on membership of the polis which was a free association of equals. The household provides the human resources of the polis which includes the reproduction of the next generation of citizens. While education of the young begins within the household, it cannot be left in the private sphere (Aristotle 1962 bk VIII). Aristotle insists that children belong to the polis and ultimately it is its business to teach what is needed to sustain its 'constitution' – its principles, its forms of virtue, its conception of justice.

The view that children were essentially under the authority of heads of the household was the standard pre-modern view. As Bodin expressed it 'the sovereign state was an association of households' (Bodin 1962 ch. 1) and this view was inherited and accepted by early liberal theorists. John Locke, the father of modern liberalism writing in the 1680s, distinguished political from paternal authority. He maintained that children were under the rule of their parents until they reached the age of reason. Only when they were able to apprehend 'the laws of nature' for themselves were they at liberty to choose to be members of a particular state (Locke 1960 2nd treatise ch. 2) Although, as Hume pointed out, the notion of being free to emigrate at the age of majority was highly impractical, the idea that individuals attain the rights and responsibilities of citizenship only by freely contracting to do so remained a potent idea in both legitimising and setting limits on the power of the state. From the perspective of Lockean liberalism it is an embarrassment that young people are deemed to be subject to positive laws which they have had no part in making, nor opportunity to legitimately avoid (Haydon 1979).

Finding the proper place for children in liberal democratic theory has been problematic since the time of Locke, because it simultaneously recognises not only the moral status of autonomous individuals, but also seeks to privilege the collective institution of the family, placing it beyond the scope of state. It is a well-directed complaint of feminist writers that liberal theorists presume to exclude considerations of justice from the private sphere.

The sharp separation of the private and public spheres not only leads to a gender-biased conception of citizenship, but fails to recognise the state's demands upon children. Yet the imperative to socialise and instruct the next generation of citizens, an obligation which writers since Locke see falling on parents and state educators alike, places responsibilities on young people that cannot be excluded from considerations of obligation or justness.

CITIZENS NOW

It is famously argued by Philippe Aries that the notion of children as innocents, uninitiated in the ways of the world, requiring separation and protection from premature exposure to adult concerns – sex and paid employment – was a 'modern invention' (Aries 1962; 'modern' for Aries is contrasted with 'medieval' and located vaguely in the seventeenth century with Locke at the turning point). Valuing children for what they are now rather than solely for what they will become, is for some a decisive reason for not treating them as current citizens. It said, they have a right as children to be treated as children. The argument is if children are over exposed to the public world of adults 'the glare of this public world makes their growth to maturity difficult at best' (Conway 2004: 73).

However, the view that children do in fact have both responsibilities and rights before they are considered fully autonomous actors, prompts the conclusion that they must be considered citizens now, even if their differences from adult citizens should not be overlooked. This position is the dominant orthodoxy amongst academics who write on children's issues and among agencies that advocate for children's interests.

In the foreword to a recent edited volume on *Children and Citizenship* the chair of the UN Committee on the Rights of the Child, Jaap Doek, makes the case for children as citizens now: 'The Citizen Child is a citizen of today and the full recognition of this fact is one of the fundamental requirements of the UNCRC' (Invernizzi and Williams 2008: xvi).

His starting point is embedded in the right to have a legal identity which is denied to nine million stateless persons. Citizenship is linked to the human right to be 'registered' at birth (Article 7). This registration includes having a recorded name of at least one birth parent and thereby a nationality which extends 'as far as possible, to the right to know and be cared for by his or her parents'. The child as citizen necessarily involves the right to belong to a family as well as a state.

What seems like a thin conception of citizenship as a formal familial and state identity is presented by Doek as a precondition for the delivery of the range of rights guaranteed under the convention. He suggests that the security of the child's identity is a prerequisite for the 'full and harmonious development of the child's personality' which leads to her or his capacity to 'participate fully as active members of their community' (Invernizzi and Williams 2008: xv).

Doek underlines the goal of the UNCRC to deliver rights of protection and participation to all children at every stage of their development; this includes those with special needs (Article 23) and to those in conflict with the penal law (UNCRC 1989 Article 40).

The general point to note is that the claim that children are citizens from birth fixes their rights associated with their identity and locates the state which has the primary responsibility for ensuring their rights are met. It does not resolve the question of how they should be similarly or differently treated from adults.

CITIZENS IN-THE-MAKING

T. H. Marshall, in his seminal essay on *Citizenship and Social Class* (1950), characterised children as citizens in-the-making. They were not yet fully citizens but in the process of becoming citizens. He defined citizenship as 'a status bestowed on those who are full members of a community. All who possess the status are equal with respect to the rights and duties with which the status is endowed' (Marshall 1950: 28–9). Marshall included 'civil, political and social rights' as those bestowed by citizenship, and while some were entitlements from birth, others were either achieved by degrees with growing capacity, or obtained by reaching an age threshold at which legal competence is presumed.

The case for considering children as citizens now emphasises their social citizenship, but it is their lesser standing with respect to political and civil rights that provides the rationale for regarding them as citizens to be, apprentice citizens, or citizens in-the-making. It cannot be seriously questioned that lack of the right to vote or to stand for political office, as well as the limitation on other civil rights on the basis of age, does carry some real and symbolic weight.

Clearly children do not have the same rights and responsibilities as adult citizens in contemporary democratic states until they cease to be children. Whether or not they have 'equal but different rights' whilst children, is open to argument. But it is not simply that they have some rights and immunities peculiar to their present status as children, they also have other rights and responsibilities in virtue of their future citizenship, such that it makes sense to consider them citizens in-the-making.

Although the UNCRC post-dates Marshall, his view of children as citizens in-the-making does provide a model for conceiving of their rights in a way that is compatible with a developmental conception of children. This idea it may be seen is a major feature in the convention (Lansdown 2005).

CHILDREN'S RIGHTS AND THE UNCRC

As we have noted, to a significant degree the status of children in Britain and elsewhere has been affected, most would agree, influenced for the better, by the impact of signing up to the UNCRC.

The preamble to the UNCRC indicates that other UN declarations of universal rights apply to children – adopting Feinberg, call these 'ac' rights (Feinberg 1980). But it also provides the rationale for rights peculiar to children ('c' rights). Although the convention declares itself to be 'against discrimination of any kind' (it uses the term only pejoratively) it in fact both justifies children being treated differently from adults (it recognises some 'a' rights) and justifies appropriately discriminating among children on the grounds of their 'age and maturity', or their 'evolving capacities'.

In the first place the convention defines children by their lack of shared status with adults. Article 1 says: 'A child means every human being below the age of eighteen years, unless under the law applicable to the child majority is attained earlier'.[1] Since 'majority' appears to be the age at which citizens are entitled to vote in state elections, children are differentiated from adults by their lack of the franchise. Incidentally, it follows from this definition that lowering the voting age, which there may be a good case for doing, would entail lowering the age of childhood – the threshold where 'a' rights replace 'c' rights.

What distinguishes the UNCRC from previous international rights declarations relating to children is that it is the first to recognise their right to act on their own behalves. Article 12, more than any other, makes this explicit. In this respect it breaks new grounds. Article 12 (1) states that

> States Parties shall assure to the child who is capable of forming his or her own views the right to express those views freely *in all matters affecting the child*, the views of the child being given *due weight in accordance with the age and maturity of the child*. [Italics, my emphasis] (UNCRC 1989)

This entitles children to participate in all decisions which affect them without qualification of scope. In theory at least, the right applies whether the matter is private or public, and whether it affects only the child, or them amongst others. There is a strong case for grounding children's active 'citizenship now' on this article. However, the qualifying reference to 'due weight' is a considerable limitation, because it entitles others – public officials, courts, and parents – to judge whether the child is old *and* mature enough to be capable of forming a view (it is hard to see why both tests apply), and if so what weight to attach to their views. Moreover, Article 12 must be viewed alongside Article 3 which states:

> In all actions concerning children, whether undertaken by public or private social welfare institutions, courts of law, administrative authorities or legislative bodies, *the best interests of the child shall be a primary consideration*. [Italics, my emphasis]

It has often been suggested that there is a tension between the participatory rights in the convention and those which protect children; the former suggests competent agency while the latter acknowledges their special vulnerability and dependency. But there is no contradiction,

159

because Article 3 trumps Article 12. That is to say 'the best interests of the child' will determine when their views should be heard and acted upon.

It may be that it is rarely in a child's interests not to have the opportunity to express their views. Some have argued that acting in children's interests always requires their views to be heard, in for instance judicial settings where their welfare is the primary focus (Archard 2004), but acting in their interests will frequently require their views to be overridden, or set aside.

That a person is not entitled to be considered the final judge of their own best interest is the core of the doctrine of paternalism. This is not a factual claim about competence, though it may be grounded in the belief that self harm might ensue, it is a normative one; the implication is that autonomy, or the liberty to choose, is not the greatest good. We might recollect that John Stuart Mill's classic critique of paternalism in *On Liberty* makes an exception of children (Mill 1964: 73).

Article 5 of the UNCRC makes it clear that parents and others, who exercise parental authority, have rights and responsibilities with regard to their children. It says:

> States parties shall respect the responsibilities, rights and duties of parents, or where applicable, the members of extended family or community . . . to provide, *in a manner consistent with the evolving capacities of the child, appropriate direction and guidance* in the exercise by the child of the rights recognised in the present Convention. [Italics, my emphasis]

The parental obligation to provide 'in a manner consistent with the evolving capacities, appropriate direction and guidance' leaves much room for doubt. It implies that children's rights are breached if they receive no such 'direction and guidance', or what they do receive is 'inappropriate'. There seems a significant difference between 'direction and guidance'; we might argue that the one is more or less appropriate at different stages in a child's development. The vagueness of the formula reflects the reality of childhood as a journey of 'evolving capacities' from infancy through adolescence, or we might say from passive to active citizenship.

For children, or young people, to be allowed and assisted to make this journey requires in the first place appropriate action from those in a parenting role, and in the second place appropriate state-sponsored institutional support.

Both Mill and Locke see the family as the primary source of nurture and education to enable children to realise their capacity for rational liberty. Mill says that 'the family, justly constituted, would be the real school of the virtues of freedom' (Mill 1984: 294). But the state must rightly be a partner in providing nurture and education, and has the overriding duty to intervene in the interests of 'justice' when parents, for whatever reason, significantly fail in the exercise of their responsibilities.

We will notice of course that the right to receive state education is one of the most fully specified within the UNCRC (Articles 28 and 29). Although it only requires primary education to be compulsory, the higher standard making secondary education compulsory applies in developed states (Article 41). The grounds set out are classically liberal. Specifically they are directed to delivering 'equality of opportunity' and 'developing the child's personality, talents and physical attributes to their fullest potential' (Article 29 i). This employs the standard paternalist case which justifies loss of liberty now to maximise individual choice in the future. (What Feinberg calls the 'right to an open future'; Feinberg 1980.)

However, maximising future opportunities, and developing individual autonomy, are surely only half the story. The convention also refers to the child being educated as endorsing the set of values embedded in the convention. Not, it seems, allowing them the choice to do so. An education in responsible world citizenship is unequivocally prescribed. Thus compulsory education to develop a child's virtues and talents might equally be characterised as a child's duty, as well as his or her right.

Given that the syllabus of state education is recognisably to prepare students for a life useful to society at large it would be more honest to acknowledge that education is to make citizens of a certain sort. Education cannot be value neutral. It is increasingly recognised that the notion of equipping young people to perform and compete as producers and consumers in the market economy, is at best a partial view of fulfilling their potential and seriously inadequate as a basis for education in citizenship.

POLITICAL LITERACY REVISITED

As it has been observed elsewhere, the text of the Crick Report is ambiguous about the status of school-aged children as citizens. In different places children are taken to be citizens now and in others future citizens (Lockyer 2003). However, since learning to be a citizen requires the practice of citizenship there is little difference between preparing for and acting as a citizen. They are citizens being-made-active.

The classroom discussion of controversial issues is seen as having a central part in promoting values and attitudes consonant with citizenship in a pluralist liberal society. The critical role of the classroom teacher is crucial to the prospect of realising the goals of the Crick Report

(McLaughlin 2003). The citizenship agenda is wholly at odds with didactic teaching and passive learning.

What is learned in the classroom must be supported by what happens beyond it in the school. Learning by engagement in actual decision-making is seen as an essential aspect of citizenship education. The Crick Report urges what it calls 'the whole school approach'. The ethos of the school and organisation of the school must be one which encourages pupil participation:

> Schools should make every effort to engage pupils in discussion and consultation about all aspects of school life on which pupils might reasonably be expected to have a view; and wherever possible to give pupils responsibility and experience in helping to run parts of the school. (Crick Report 1998: 36, para. 6.3.1)

This may be facilitated by the schools having 'informal channels' which make the school responsive to the student's voice and through setting up class and schools councils. These can give 'practical experience of decision-making and democratic processes' (Crick Report 1998: 18, para. 3.19) Although we should note that there has been a significant increase in opportunities for student participation within schools across the UK since the report was adopted, we may still question the realism of Crick. How far can we expect schools to become sites for the practice of democracy?

It may no longer be wholly fair to characterise the management and ethos of schools in the UK with the responsibility of teaching democratic values as themselves being 'models of autocracy' (Hart 1992). But equally state-funded schools remain hierarchical bureaucratic structures which are managed to serve the requirements of external audit. They are judged more by criteria of individual student achievement than in maximising opportunities for student decision-making. Schools might at best give some young people a taste of political engagement, but those who take the opportunity are as likely to be made aware of just how limited are their rights and powers.

Thus, if the transformative aspiration of citizenship education depended upon the opportunity for democratic participation within schools, the aspiration must appear to be a distant ideal. But perhaps the demand to democratise schools goes beyond what is required to create active citizens. Let us look again at what learning to be an active citizen requires.

It remains the case that children are expected to acquire the knowledge, skills and attributes required by all the elements of citizenship, including political literacy, before they possess full legal autonomy, or the right to vote. How problematic is this?

It is my contention that the requirement on schools to facilitate citizens in-the-making is less demanding or unrealistic than might be suggested. If we look again at the concept of political literacy underpinning the Crick Report (and evident in Crick's other writings) the skills and attributes embedded are closer to the concept of liberal education than Crick himself was often inclined to suggest.

The Crick Committee no doubt saw a healthy vibrant democracy requiring citizenship education, a dramatic improvement in knowledge, attitudes and action in public affairs. Community service and moral responsibility and political literacy were linked elements. Learning to be a responsible citizen included public service and 'responsibility is an essential political as well as moral virtue . . . in a parliamentary democracy' (Crick Report 1998: 13, para. 2.12).

Crick himself often complained at the way 'politics' had conventionally been 'boringly' taught in schools, focusing on the formal functions of institutions and avoiding 'controversial issues' (Crick 2000: 119) Teachers, Crick says, should 'give children the low down on how political institutions work and what political conflicts are about, rather than the dry bones of parliamentary procedure or the elevated abstractions of "the constitution"' (Crick 2000: 33). But politics teaching is only a small part of what it is to be politically literate.

A politically literate person needs to have general knowledge about the kind of society he or she lives in – know something about their country's 'people, history and the broad economic and geographical factors that define and limit us' (Crick 2000: 73). But equally important is knowledge of political ideas. The politically literate will be aware of the received values embedded in different political traditions, and they must be able to subject them to criticism (Crick 2000: 68). Most important is that students are equipped with the 'conceptual vocabulary' to analyse received values and beliefs and make up their own minds about which to endorse.

At a foundational level political literacy is conceived as a compulsory form of literacy, alongside other forms of literacy (like language and numeracy), involving knowledge, skills and attributes, essential for an individual to successfully function as a citizen in a liberal democracy.

Much of what is endorsed as political literacy is closely akin to active learning; this includes discussing controversial issues in ways that both enliven the subject and promote values associated with recognising and respecting difference. What Crick and Porter set out in their Hansard Society Report of 1978 – 'Freedom, toleration, fairness, respect for truth, respect for reasoning' (Crick 2000: 62) – comports with the 'basic, political concepts' that they invoke. There is no surprise to find that the language and values of politics are to be found alongside the endorsement of non-authoritarian forms of teaching method. Political vocabulary is that which the responsible citizens will deploy to construct or deconstruct, justify and defend his or her beliefs.

Here we may return to the classical republican tradition from which Crick takes his inspiration. For Aristotle diversity and disagreement are at the heart of political life. Politics is a branch of ethics. It requires practical wisdom (phronesis) and right judgement; knowing how to act well, or for the best, in actual (non-ideal) circumstances. It is not acquired by book learning or doctrinal instruction, but through experience.

Here Crick departs from his classical sources (or at least the standard interpretation of them). Politics is not confined to the 'affairs of the state' and the public sphere ceases to be readily separable from the private. This puts him at odds with his much-admired Hannah Arendt (see 'The public and the private realm', in Arendt 1958).

Importantly, politics is to be found wherever there is room for disagreement about ends, argument and compromise. For ordinary citizens, participation in politics is principally found in the business of everyday life – 'in the family, the locality, educational institutions, clubs and societies and in informal groups of all kinds' (Crick 2000: 65). It occurs wherever there are 'actions and interactions between groups' who recognise a mutual entitlement to influence decisions. Politics encompasses activity within rules of conduct where 'ordinary people' share in decision-making that aims at peacefully resolving disagreement and the pursuit of collective ends.

It might be argued that Crick himself only over time came to recognise that the sharp separation of the public and private spheres, which was a feature of the classical republican tradition, must be set aside. Certainly he acknowledged that it was feminist writers and political activists that reminded him of the importance of civil society (Crick 2000). In any case the neglect of politics outside conventionally public institutions is an all-round liberal and republican failing.

Whether or not we find it in Crick or the republican or liberal traditions, for our purposes it is sufficient to argue that politics is to be found where there are legitimate differences of interest; when peaceful resolving of conflict is to be preferred; where there is no monopoly of truth, or monopoly of legitimate claims to power; but where there is plurality of values and where there is accommodation and compromise without resort to coercion.

On this view the opportunities to engage in the practice of politics need not be reified in the public sphere. And it would appear not to be conditional on possessing the right to vote or to stand for office. The skills of political literacy may be practised and developed in those locales, or relationships, where obedience cannot be instructed or demanded. In this sense political literacy is a necessary life-skill to be exercised in non-authoritarian settings and relationships.

BECOMING POLITICALLY ACTIVE CITIZENS

It is in the context of politics thus understood, that the participatory rights of children specified by the UNCRC should be seen.[2] Attributing to the young the right to have their views listened to and given due weight invests them with some power. Right holders need not be autonomous agents (legally the final judges of their own interests) to be acknowledged as political actors. In a sense the lack of autonomy of young people, whose views can be overruled by others even on matters which only affect them, makes the 'political' skills of persuasion even more important to them than to adults.

Moreover, even if for enfranchised adults the locus of political citizenship remains primarily focused on the formal institutions of the state, this will not be so for young people both because the decisions which affect them are made closer to home and because the public institutions they must immediately experience are not principally those characteristically regarded as sites of political action. (Here the parallel between children and women is evident, as Lister (2008) amongst others has noted.)

There is no space here to fully discuss the justness of the existing voting age – either the merits of having a legally fixed threshold, or the case for changing it. We know that for it to be just it must be grounded on a relevant difference between voters and non-voters, but whatever the criterion (competence, capacity, maturity, experience of the world) and whatever the age threshold (twenty-one, eighteen, sixteen, fourteen?), there will be some above the age for voting not 'fit to vote' and some below it who are. The assumption of fitness to vote to coincide with age will always deliver no more than rough justice. (The principle of equal citizenship holds so long as citizens are considered to be equal in those matters where there is no legitimate ground for discrimination – equality of respect, equality before the law and equal opportunity to achieve advantaged positions. This does not require that relevant differences be set aside, rather it requires they be acknowledged.) But we must remember that more than voting is at stake, when we differentiate entitlement to vote by age.

Since the UNCRC defines the threshold of childhood by the age of majority and this is indicated by the age of voting in state elections, lowering the voting age lowers the age of childhood. This means not only

165

lowering the age at which citizens may exercise full political rights, it entails lowering the age at which we grant the protections that attach to childhood (where 'c' rights are replaced by 'a' rights). There may nonetheless be a good case for lowering the voting age to sixteen. It may very well provide the catalyst needed to refocus political education in the UK at present (Lockyer 2003).

It might still be possible in principle to differentiate amongst voters on the basis of age, as we do at present with respect to holding office, but in practice it may be difficult to justify paternalistic or protective discrimination on the basis of age to some who possess the franchise. Those mature enough to vote on what is good for others, or on what is in the common good, must surely be considered fully competent to judge what is in their own interests. It would be difficult to attribute to those considered fit to vote less than adult responsibilities. It may also be harder to treat young offenders with less than adult culpability. (Although, it is arguable that the age of criminal responsibility in Britain already seriously fails to recognise the relevant difference between adults and children – but this is another matter not to be explored here.)

The key argument here is that voting age is a threshold of some importance but it is not a division between those fit to engage in politics from those who are not – any more than it divides citizens from will-be citizens. The conduct of politics takes place wherever there is room for the exercise of deliberative discussion about ends. (The merits for and against lowering the voting age is just such a subject upon which politically active young people should have a significant voice.) The prerequisite for acquiring political literacy through practice is to be found in non-autocratic settings. Whether or not the home or the school are such settings depends on whether they permit the exercise of participatory rights. If they do, then they have a place for political literacy.

IMPLICATIONS FOR SCHOOLS AND THE PRIVATE SPHERE

The school is an arena in which children act and interact with others, and as such is public space in which politics may be experienced. This does not require classrooms to be models of democratic decision-making, but where teachers permit no discussion or allow no views to be expressed except their own there is no opportunity for the exercise or development of political literacy. Similarly, where parent(s) or guardian(s) take every decision regarding a child's welfare with neither consultation nor explanation of their reasoning, the possibility of politics is excluded from their interactions. However, if Article 12 is taken seriously and children are acknowledged as having a legitimate perspective on matters directly affecting them they are recognised as having rights and capable of influencing decisions through political discourse.

The school as a whole is a form of community and a class within it capable of acting as one (Harber and Meighan 1989). As in any community, certain norms of conduct must be established and followed. This is required for there to be interactive discourse with the potential for political engagement. Making active citizens requires the inculcation of the procedural values associated with public reasonableness (toleration, receptiveness towards interlocutors, respect for argument and the possibility of persuasion). In so far as the classroom instils such values in young people it is delivering an important part of citizenship education (whatever the subject under discussion). The norms of public reasonableness are of value in themselves, in the wider learning environment of the school, and beyond. The norms and procedural values encountered in the discourse in the classroom enable young people to conduct themselves appropriately in other contexts – wherever, in fact, opportunities arise in any community to participate in discourse about ends or purposes. Citizenship education also comes to represent a means of influencing the private sphere through the public, since the tenets of public reasonableness absorbed at school may come to animate discourse in the domestic arena.

Since matters emanating from the domestic sphere frequently affect the public domain engagement with issues which traverse the business of home and school is inevitable. Just as encounters between different primary values or conceptions of the good are bound to occur where young people who are members of diverse cultural communities are brought together. School in effect becomes the site of such inter-subjective encounters which provide learning experiences that promote understanding and accommodation within pluralist civil society.

It is sometimes objected that fundamental values and inherited identities are threatened by the promoting of autonomy in liberal education. But equipping young people to think for, and be themselves, in a context of respect for reasoning, where there is also respect for difference, can validate rather than undermine. Students are equipped to express and defend their inherited views and values in the language appropriate to public discourse. Grounding members of communities in discursive ethics and practice allows them to more effectively represent their own particular conceptions of the good in the formal political sphere. Moreover, the exposure to political discourse does not require rejection of the 'self identity' acquired through familial socialisation; it enables the developing self to negotiate new identities through the interaction with peers and in confronting public issues. Civic virtues which promote justice and service to others make calls upon the familial values of loyalty and care that we might expect to be part of normal parental upbringing. Rather than the 'political' constituting an alien imposition on a hermetically sealed private sphere, it acknowledges the interconnectedness of the personal and the public.

Conclusion

The preceding discussion provides the nub of an answer to the question arising from the Preface – what needs to be done to equip and promote young people to be active citizens, and what difference would it make?

My argument is that we do not need to require schools, or families, to be wholly democratic institutions to foster political engagement. But there is much that needs to change within the existing regimes of schools and domestic life (and the other institutions of civil society) for political literacy to flourish. The minimal requirement is the removal of unjustifiable autocracy. The benefits of replacing authoritarian school regimes with those which are consultative and which promote equality of respect for all citizens – students, teachers and parents – would be a great encouragement to reform of other hierarchically governed (and managed) institutions. Equally, the diminution of dictatorial and oppressive domestic regimes would have immeasurable benefits for the private and public life of citizens, old and young.

The obligation to enable or facilitate young people to be made active citizens goes well beyond the recognised providers of formal education and those with direct responsibility for their upbringing. A change of culture is needed to permeate all the institutions of civil society, including state providers of services, civic and voluntary associations. There is of course more to making 'active' citizens than acquiring political literacy, but it can be the spur to motivate young people to participate responsibly in community life beyond the boundaries of school and home. Acknowledging the rights and responsibilities of citizens in-the-making is only a starting point.

There is a tendency for children and young people to be conceived of either as solely dependents (future citizens), or as entirely autonomous individuals (fully citizens now). For the very young the former may be in order, and for teenagers it will sometimes be right to attribute to them adult rights and responsibilities, yet generally what is required is to treat young people as the UNCRC suggests, with respect to their 'evolving capacities'.

Childhood is a 'journey' not a fixed location, so it ought not to be regarded as a singular status, implying uniform rights and responsibilities.

Treating children and young people 'appropriately' as citizens in-the-making, demands not only giving them rights and responsibilities that accord with their maturity or 'evolved capacities', it also requires that they be assisted in developing or 'evolving' those capacities. The more young people are able to fulfil their potential for active citizenship, the greater the benefit to every other citizen and the community as a whole.

Notes

1. The term 'children' in this essay is used in a quasi technical sense – despite adolescents generally disliking it – because the UNCRC's usage is the nearest there is to a recognised definition.
2. My argument in this section in part replicates, modifies and develops what I have previously argued elsewhere (Lockyer 2008).

References

Archard, David (2004), *Children: Rights and Childhood*, 2nd edn, London: Routledge.

Arendt, Hannah (1958), *The Human Condition*, London: Cambridge University Press.

Aries, Philippe (1962), *Centuries of Childhood* (English trans.), London: Jonathan Cape.

Aristotle (1962), *Politics*, ed. T. A. Sinclair, Harmondsworth: Penguin.

Bodin, Jean (1962), *The Six Books of a Commonweal*, ed. Kenneth. D. McRae, Cambridge, MA: Cambridge University Press.

Conway, James (2004), *Betwixt and Between*, New York, NY: Peter Lang.

Crick, Bernard (2000), *Essays on Citizenship*, London: Continuum.

Crick, Bernard (2002), *Democracy: a Very Short Introduction*, Oxford: Oxford University Press.

Crick Report (1998), *Education for Citizenship and the Teaching of Democracy in Schools* (Final Report of the Advisory Group on Citizenship), London: QCA.

Feinberg, Joel (1980), 'The child's right to an open future', in W. Aiken and H. LaFollette (eds), *Whose Child? Parental Rights, Parental Authority and State Power*, Totowa, NJ: Rowman and Littlefield.

Harber, Clive and Roland Meighan (eds) (1989), *The Democratic School: Educational Management and the Practice of Democracy*, Ticknall: Education Now.

Hart, Roger (1992), *Children's Participation From Tokenism to Citizenship* (Innocenti Essays No. 4), Florence: UNICEF/International Child Development Centre.

Haydon, Graham (1979), 'Political theory and the child: problems of the individualist tradition', *Political Studies*, 17(33): 405–20.

Invernnizzi, Antonella and Jane Williams (eds) (2008), *Children and Citizenship*, London: Sage.

Lansdown, Gerison (2005), *The Evolving Capacities of the Child*, Florence: UNICEF/Innocenti Research Centre.

Lister, R. (2008), 'Unpacking children's citizenship', in Antonella Invernizzi and Jane Williams (eds), *Children and Citizenship*, London: Sage.

Locke, John (1960), *Two Treatises of Government*, ed. P. Laslett, Cambridge: Cambridge University Press.

Lockyer, Andrew (2003), 'The political status of children and young people', in Andrew Lockyer, Bernard Crick and John Annette (eds), *Education for Democratic Citizenship: Issues of Theory and Practice*, Aldershot: Ashgate.

Lockyer, Andrew (2008), 'Education for citizenship: children as citizens and political literacy', in Antonella Invernizzi and Jane Williams (eds), *Children and Citizenship*, London: Sage.

McLaughlin, Terrence (2003), 'Teaching controversial issues in citizenship education', in Andrew Lockyer, Bernard Crick and John Annette (eds), *Education for Democratic Citizenship: Issues of Theory and Practice*, Aldershot: Ashgate.

Marshall, Thomas H. (1950), *Citizenship and Social Class and other essays*, Cambridge: Cambridge University Press.

Mill, John Stuart (1964), *Utilitarianism, On Liberty and Representative Government* ed. A. Lindsay, London: Dent.

Mill, John Stuart (1984), 'The subjection of women', in J. M. Robson (ed.), *Collected Works of John Stuart Mill, vol. XX1: Essays on Equality, Law and Education*, Toronto: Toronto University Press.

UN Convention on the Rights of the Child (UNCRC) (1989), Convention report. Available at: http://www.unhchr.ch/html/menu3/b/k2crc.htm.

Active Citizenship and Sharing Power in Scotland: the Need to Go Beyond Devolution

Kevin Francis

SHARING POWER: THE NEED TO GO BEYOND DEVOLUTION

> Our founding principles are openness, accountability, the sharing of power and equal opportunities. These are at the heart of all our activities . . .
>
> (Scottish Parliament Online)

So the Scottish Parliament announces itself on its website and arguably it has done a good job with respect to three of these four founding principles. The building itself, no matter how controversial its design has been, has a distinctly open and accessible feel to it. Sitting in the visitors' gallery, one is close indeed to proceedings on the floor of the house. Sitting in on committee meetings is a relatively easy matter; and the ambience of the building is one of openness. There is live on-line feed from the floor of the House and from committee meetings via its own media operations. Reports and proceedings are available on line; as too are details of bills and amendments before Parliament.

The Parliament's decision to publish all Members' expenses has given it a moral edge in comparison to its great-uncle Westminster. The diversity of its membership, certainly in terms of gender balance, had been seen as one of the Parliament's successes; however, the 2007 election reduced the ratio of women MSPs from close to half to open third. We cannot, of course, tell whether this is a temporary blip or indicative of a return to male-dominated politics. The 2007 election saw the first MSP from an ethnic minority background to gain a seat at Holyrood. So whilst the story concerning openness and accountability in the Scottish Parliament's first ten years looks good, the story concerning equal opportunities is less clear. The story is even more mixed, I shall argue, when we turn to the fourth principle: that of sharing power with the people of Scotland.

The creation of the Scottish Parliament has seen one major development with respect to the sharing of power: the introduction of the public petitions process. With over one thousand petitions registered during the Parliament's short life this has been, as George Reid the former Presiding Officer proudly claims, a genuine achievement. However, only a small proportion of these have been forwarded by the Petitions Committee to the House for debate and few have subsequently become law.

But the original hopes of the new Scottish Parliament were about a wider civic engagement than this. Indeed, a meeting of the Scottish Civic Forum held at Holyrood in June 2001 began by stating that 'this meeting agrees that full representative democracy requires an engaged civic society and welcomes the progress the Scottish Parliament is making in engaging with Civic Society in Scotland'. But since those heady days, the Scottish Civic Forum, having experienced funding cuts, has faded from the headlines and that hoped-for level of civic engagement has not been evident in that most obvious of indicator: electoral turnout. The turnout for the first post-devolution election (May 1999) was some 58 per cent. This declined to under 50 per cent (49.8 per cent) in May 2003; and recovered only marginally to 51.8 per cent in May 2007. Voter turnout for the Glasgow North-East election in November 2009 declined to a dismal 33 per cent. All of this suggests a crisis rather than a development in civic engagement since devolution. Nor was the matter of advancing civic engagement and the sharing of power a matter for the Calman Commission, reporting in November 2009. Even if the proposals for what has become known as 'Devolution-Max' (proposals in large part centred on tax raising powers) are accepted, it is not easy to see how these will impact on civic engagement. I shall argue that the prospect of independence offers the opportunity to think seriously about not merely sharing power but a radical transferring of power to the people of Scotland.

TAKING INDEPENDENCE SERIOUSLY: MORE THAN A THOUGHT-EXPERIMENT

Bernard Crick and David Millar published their draft proposals to the Scottish Constitutional Convention under the title 'To make the Parliament of Scotland a model for democracy'. The fourth principle of the new Parliament is directed towards sharing power with the people; but under devolution so far this has been at best elusive. In this essay I consider what might be achieved, and through what measures, if we think more radically: how can we reshape our democracy so as to bring active citizenship to the fore? I take seriously the prospect of Scotland becoming independent in the not-too-distant future, giving the opportunity for a radical devolving of power to the people: of developing a new 'model for democracy'.

Scotland is better placed than most to ask questions about active citizenship and to effect the radical devolution of power back to the people. For in Scotland we must take seriously the possibility of independence within the foreseeable future. And if independence comes (let us say, within the next decade) then we have the opportunity to radically reshape our thinking and our practice of democracy. Such reshaping of democracy requires us to reshape our practice of citizenship. Even if independence does not happen this is still an opportunity for us to reflect on how we might reshape our ideas about democracy and citizenship. So, what follows is a thought-experiment, an exercise in speculative political theory; but it is also a proposal about how we might 'do' democracy in the future and how we might instil the virtues of active citizenship.

I want to argue that deliberative democracy, a theory that has emerged over the last twenty years or so and which will be familiar to many through the idea of citizen juries, might be developed so as to give 'popular assent' to proposed legislation. Randomly selected members of the population (a citizen jury) would be asked to vote on behalf of the entire population to approve legislation: that is, to transform Parliament's bills into law. As things stand, that role is given to the monarch. The Queen signs Parliament's bills (Westminster and Holyrood) and thereby enacts them: '*La Reine le veult*' ('The Queen wills it'). A newly independent Scotland would have to decide how its Parliament's bills would be enacted. The bills could go forward for presidential assent: we would then have the same arrangement as now, except it would be an elected head of state and not the monarch approving legislation. A more radical move would be for the bills to go to the people for popular assent.

But why give Parliament's bills to just some of the people and not to all of them, as in a plebiscite? And what has this to do with active citizenship? Would any such proposal really be practicable? In an attempt to answer these questions, let me turn to that great English philosopher of Scots descent: John Stuart Mill.

JOHN STUART MILL AND POPULAR SOVEREIGNTY

John Stuart Mill remains a benchmark in most things for our modern, secular, liberal society. His *On Liberty* is perhaps best known to us. This is the work that gives us the Harm Principle: the argument that the only legitimate grounds for state intervention in our lives is to prevent us harming others – and not from harming ourselves. *On Liberty* also gives us Mill's arguments for freedom of speech and for 'experiments in living' – the need to tolerate, even encourage, eccentricity. And it is Mill who most fully rejects paternalism: that others (such as doctors and teachers) know what is best for us, what is in our best interests. Mill characterises this as self-sovereignty: 'Over himself, over his own body and mind, the individual is sovereign' (Mill [1859] 2008: 14). In all this, Mill is the philosopher we turn to.

And so we might now look again at some of the insights to be gained from his *Considerations on Representative Government*; an insightful if somewhat neglected work, now approaching the 150th anniversary of its publication (1861). Chapter Three of *Considerations* in particular offers a comprehensive set of reflections on what we would recognise as the republican ideal of citizenship. Maximal participation in the public realm brings both internal and external goods: through participation the citizen expands their understanding of their social world and grows in the resulting responsibility and exercise of power; and society benefits from the collective wisdom and expertise – and perhaps just good common sense – of its citizenry. Furthermore, the value of this participation is both intrinsic and instrumental: Mill has it that through participation the citizen develops 'an active, self-helping character' (Mill [1861] 2008: 252) and it is this 'active' character which Mill contrasts throughout *Considerations* with a 'passive' character. These benefits are independent of outcome. Perhaps some wise and good despot could reach 'better' decisions for the nation and probably the people will make mistakes in their decision-taking; but we learn from our mistakes and must be given the chance to make them. Even if mistakes are made, the internal benefit and thus the intrinsic value of a people-led democracy holds. Mill thought that, given certain qualifications, all good things would flow from this active engagement of the citizenry; and in the end the outcome is likely to be better than that resulting from the decision of any benevolent despot or Platonic 'Rule of the Wise'. Given this perfect coincidence of benefits, it follows for Mill that 'nothing less can be ultimately desirable than the admission of all to a share in the sovereign power of the state' (Mill 2008: 256).

But Mill offers a number of reservations to the exercise of this popular sovereignty. In particular, the people should be willing and able to do those things necessary to uphold the form of government, whatever it is. For a democracy, that meant a universal system of education, at least at primary level. Not that Mill thought voting required high levels of education but rather that each voter must have the means to find out for themselves the facts that might influence how they cast their vote. But once equipped for democratic participation, the willingness to participate becomes all. Here Mill's concerns join ours. The general decline in electoral turn-out over the last half-century has formed the ground for a genre of political eco-doom; it is as if the whole political ecology is thought to be collapsing. Foremost in the literature is Robert Putnam's *Bowling Alone* (2001), extending his initial analysis of the decline in political literacy in Italian society to that of the United States of America. Morris Berman's *The Twilight of American Culture* reflects the sense of doom surrounding the 'dumbing down' of political culture and the coming of a new 'Dark Ages' (Berman 2006). To focus solely on UK politics, 2009 has seen a sustained assault on the presumed integrity of Members of Parliament over their expenses. There has been a mass exodus from the Cabinet on a scale not seen since Harold Macmillan's Night of the Long Knives;[1] we have witnessed the defenestration of the Speaker of the House of Commons, Michael Martin (the first Speaker to be publicly forced from office in over 300 years); and the 'innovation' of an open election for a new Speaker has resulted. Indeed, the turmoil at Westminster and the responses to it have drawn talk of a 'revolution' in Westminster politics, albeit a 'quiet' one.[2]

A wide range of proposals have been floated for this quiet revolution, including: open primaries for the selection of parliamentary candidates; codes of conduct for MPs; Proportional Representation of one form or another; election of the second chamber; fixed-term parliaments; a written constitution – and an attempt to escape the domination of parties and whips by encouraging and facilitating the standing of independent MPs. Yet in all this, there is little that suggests that any significant power will be given (back?) to the voter. If this is to be a revolution, then, at this point, it looks like being a very in-House affair. There is no sign yet of a popular uprising.

JOHN STUART MILL AND ACTIVE CITIZENSHIP

Of course, we should be relieved about the absence of revolutionary fervour. After all, we live in a parliamentary democracy. Our concern should be to scrutinise our representatives and to choose between policy agendas, competing parties and political elites, not to actively exercise power ourselves.

But this was not the picture that Mill was painting in the *Considerations*. As we have already noted, Mill argued for a republican form of engaged citizenry. For sure, local democracy would play a crucial part in acquiring the skills and exercising the responsibilities and powers of citizenship; and in *Considerations* Mill devotes a short chapter to this (Mill [1861] 2008: 411–26). Indeed, Mill had pointed out that

> A person must have a very unusual taste for intellectual exercise in and for itself, who will put himself to the trouble of thought when it is to have no outward effect, or qualify himself for functions which he has no chance of being allowed to exercise. (Mill 2008: 239)

So it is the exercise of power and not simply the scrutiny of others' exercise of power that becomes crucial for the Millean active citizen – and this exercise of power goes beyond what we would normally imagine. In Chapter Ten of *Considerations* Mill insists that, unless circumstances really do not allow, the ballot is to be open and public rather than secret because, though there are rights to be protected, voting is an exercise of power and all power is to be open to scrutiny and account. Mill's citizens, voting in the market place, are thus expected to argue their case and defend their position should their vote run counter to popular sentiment. Mill's active citizens need to be made of sterling stuff! This is why Mill thinks that universal suffrage requires a universal system of education: voters need to be literate and numerate in order not just to understand the issues but to be able to communicate their understanding to others. This is all part of using the vote responsibly. So we have in Mill an advocate for maximal participation and engagement of the citizenry in public affairs, in politics.

Except that Mill draws back from this radical proposal. He concludes Chapter Three of *Considerations* by declaring:

> But since all cannot, in a community exceeding a single small town, participate personally in any but some very minor portions of the public business, it follows that the ideal type of a perfect government must be representative. (Mill 2008: 256)

Well, I think the situation is not as clear-cut as Mill would have us believe. Although it is true that the size and complexity of a modern state such as the United Kingdom makes it hard to see how Mill's conception of the active citizen could be realised, we are not left without some response. Mill's retreat from an Athenian-style democracy leads him to place an emphasis on local government and on moments of civic responsibility such as jury service. This is right and proper; but I want to ask if we can draw from the well of Mill's insights and restructure our thinking about how we might further democratic engagement at the national and not just local level, through active – *political* – citizenship such as we might foster in a newly independent Scotland.

DELIBERATIVE DEMOCRACY AND EFFECTIVE POLITICAL POWER

The great move in recent years in democratic theory has been the development of deliberative democracy and the use of the citizen jury. David Held, in the third edition of his *Models of Democracy*, suggests that we might regard deliberative democracy as a 'paradigm shift' (Held 2006: 254) – or at least, that it has 'moved democratic thinking along new paths'. In many respects, deliberative democracy seeks to capture and reinforce those elements we have already seen in Mill and in republican citizenship in general: the responsibility of the citizen, the assumption of competence among the members of the citizen body, of equality and the absence of privileged judgement, and the willingness to achieve a rational, argued judgement. But for Mill this only makes sense with the exercise of power.

Here then is the problem. Citizens' juries, whilst embodying the sort of Millean/deliberative elements outlined above, tend to be used either for local decisions or for consultative input on policy discussions. This is not to be lightly disregarded. Over an evening, a day or a few weeks, a group of citizens hear from expert witnesses, discuss among themselves and make policy recommendations. For the deliberativist, these citizens gain in educational and political terms: they *learn* (about the policy subject) and they develop and exercise *political literacy* (they discover what is and what is not viable, what the policy constraints are, what their fellow jurors think and how they approach the matter). These are largely transferable skills thus making these citizen-jurors, in Millean terms, independent and active citizens. But it is only in the most distant sense that we could regard this as an exercise of *power*.

Mill drew rather startling conclusions from his analysis of voting as an exercise of power: like all questions concerning the exercise of power, it introduces questions of who is fit to vote and indeed, whether some might qualify for additional votes. Mill insists that this is not about land ownership, income or class; but rather, it concerns the ability to exercise power responsibly. So, literacy and numeracy must be established (thus the need for universal education) to qualify for the vote, and those with university education and/or positions of responsibility at work would qualify for additional votes. This idea of plural voting (of some having more votes than others) is quite outrageous to us today; though we might note that the university vote was not finally abandoned in the United Kingdom until the election of 1950. The General Election of 1945 was the last in which graduates had a second vote in their university constituency.

Mill's insistence on plural voting was grounded in his fear that exten-sion of the suffrage would bring class war, that governance would pass from one extreme to another: from a land-based and mercantile elite to a new 'tyranny of the majority' (i.e. the working class); and thus the need for a group of MPs that would hold the balance of power in Parliament.

But in all this, Mill falls into a fundamental error: the confusion of what is merely *nominal* political power with what constitutes *effective* political power. For whilst it is clearly true that en masse, Mill's newly enfranchised workers had considerable power, as individual citizens that power was and remains mostly symbolic. It is vitally important that power is there to be exercised; but it doesn't justify Mill's prescriptions regarding fitness to vote. Mill says:

> no person can have a right (except in the purely legal sense) to power over others: every such power, which he is allowed to possess, is morally, in the fullest force of the term, a trust. But the exercise of any political function, either as an elector or as a representative, is power over others. (Mill 2008: 353–4)

The vote is an 'exercise . . . of power over others'. This insight is one we should hold on to. But as we've seen, it does not do the work Mill wants of it. The power exercised over others at the ballot by the individual in their role as citizen is minimal: it does not carry enough burden, enough weight of consequences to justify considerations of fitness to exercise that power. The power is nominal and in this sense, citizenship as politi-cally considered is also nominal: its power is in its name, not in what it can bring about. I want to ask how we might go about transforming that power into something more than a nominal identity, however important that is. How can we transform it into *effective* political power? How can the citizen, simply as citizen and not as party member, or local official, or elected representative . . . how can the citizen come to exercise effective political power?

Citizen juries and popular assent

Despite the introduction of non-plurality (i.e. non first-past-the-post) voting in Scotland for Holyrood elections and despite the pressure to introduce it for Westminster elections, it is hard to see how electoral reform itself can bring about this desired restructuring of the citizen's power, from nominal to effective power. Yet at the local level the citizen may be called upon to act in precisely this way: in jury service the citizen is asked to exercise a power that carries just such a distinctive burden of responsibility. Although no longer literally a matter of life and death in the United Kingdom, the impact of the juror's deliberations may still carry a life-determining responsibility.

Notwithstanding the increasing hesitations over the way juries reach their verdicts we hold on to the image of 'twelve good persons and true' as emblematic of public service; of public service carrying the highest burden of responsibility. We ask our jury of twelve persons (fifteen in Scotland for criminal trials), chosen at random, to put aside their own background and personal history, their prejudices and preferences, and even any specific knowledge they may have so as to hear the case and 'faithfully try the defendant and give a true verdict according to the evidence'.[3] It is hard to imagine how the weight of responsibility might be greater. This is what we might call the 'existential burden'. The juror, with her/his fellow jurors may be condemning an innocent person to life imprisonment or finding a guilty person, one who might quickly re-offend, innocent. Lives are at stake.

So we trust our fellow citizens to exercise power in a Millean mode, at least at an immediate and local level. Could we not do so at a national level? And not on individual cases in law as they are heard in the courts, but on the very law itself? In this respect, we in Scotland are in a particularly privileged position. While independence remains on the agenda we are not merely permitted but are actively called upon to reflect on what Scotland under a new constitution might be like. It may not quite be that we have a blank canvas – but we do have a full palette with which to paint the picture of what the constitution for a new and independent Scottish polity might be like.

So here is the question: assuming independence happens, how in this newly independent Scottish polity might laws be approved? Let us assume that the parliamentary process remains in place: that bills are introduced to the Holyrood Parliament, debated and then approved or rejected in Parliament. But whereas bills having been approved now require the royal assent before being declared Acts of Parliament, how would this be done in an independent Scotland? Assuming Scotland does not decide to retain the monarchy, the process would be for an elected President to fulfil the role of assenting to (or vetoing) Parliament's bills. But given our freedom to re-imagine the constitutional settlement, the bolder move would be for Parliament's bills to go to the people for *popular*, as opposed to *royal* or *presidential* assent. Given the people's decision, the President could then sign or withhold her/his signature from the bill on behalf of the people.

We can refine this picture a little further. Other than emergency legislation, popular voting on bills (and it is worth repeating that this would be on only such bills as had completed their passage through Parliament and had been approved there) could be once a quarter. Assuming increased legislation resulting from independence, this might be as many as eight or ten bills each quarter. Voting could be over the weekend, say from 5 p.m. on Friday to midnight on Sunday and rather than open polling stations, voting could be electronic: either on-line, using a log-in and password; or at public terminals in libraries, or in supermarkets, where a citizen swipe-card might be used. And we can refine this one further stage: amendments to the constitution might require a majority of 50 per cent plus one for popular approval, and perhaps a minimum turnout of, say, two-thirds of the registered electorate. Non-constitutional legislation would have lower tariffs: perhaps a minimum turnout of 50 per cent and a simple majority within that.

I wonder if we would be confident of achieving this level of popular approval? Even once a quarter, would we confidently expect at least half the population to vote? We could say that the role of the popular vote is simply to exercise the right of veto: thus the presumption lay with Parliament and bills would proceed into law *unless* the popular vote expressed a veto. Low turnout would thus be taken as registering either support for, or indifference to, the proposed legislation.

But that would offer unfortunate consequences in terms of our goal of active citizenship; although it may represent some element of effective political power this would be cast in a largely negative light. The popular vote as veto invites an oppositional construction of participation. On this model, participation in terms of the quarterly exercise of the popular vote is required only to defeat proposed legislation; or, for supporters of the bill, to fend off its possible defeat. And whilst some bills may provoke widespread political engagement by the citizenry, other bills may pass unnoticed. So for instance, the bill to ban smoking in public places (the Smoking, Health and Social Care (Scotland) Bill) was the subject of sustained popular debate far beyond Holyrood. Had this gone to the popular vote one would have expected a large turnout; everyone seemed to have an opinion. However, the Charities and Trustee Investment (Scotland) Bill, introduced just one month earlier, passed with little notice. Who, other than those directly concerned with the contents of the bill, would have voted on it?

Well, suppose we made voting on bills compulsory, as they do in Australia and many other countries? Here we encounter a central problem with plebiscitary democracy, one that is fatal to our project of attaching an existential burden to the exercise of effective political power. This is the opportunity for what is known as 'random voting', but which we might better term 'maverick voting'. Of course, this can occur at any time in any electoral process; but where voting is made compulsory and sanctions are in place for those who do not vote, we can expect a higher incidence of votes cast against no background of thought or candidate/party/manifesto identification. Worse, given compulsory voting, would be for voting to be available at home on-line or by telephone. In this case we would invite a situation whereby a vote might turn on nothing more than the spin of a coin or the cut of the cards.

So, let us put aside the idea of plebiscitary democracy. In addition to the considerations above, in terms of the existential burden it undercuts itself: instead of being one of say 80,000 voters (the approximate size of the average UK constituency in 2009) the voter in a Scottish plebiscite becomes one of some 4 million voters.[4] Straightforward plebiscitary democracy may satisfy some concerns about legitimacy and the binding of every citizen into an obligation to the laws of the state, but as well as inviting maverick voting it dilutes the existential burden to the point of disappearance.

Yet we need not lose sight of the idea that parliamentary bills might require popular assent rather than royal or presidential assent in order to be enacted and so become law. If we take seriously the prospect of exercising effective political power then we might properly see this as a form of ruling. It was Aristotle in *The Politics* (Aristotle 1996: 186) who argued that among equals (that is, among citizens) each governs and is governed in turn. So perhaps we should not think of *everyone* voting on *every* bill, but of a randomly selected jury voting on behalf of the whole nation, what I have elsewhere called *qualified popular assent* (Francis 2000).

Let us suppose that something like the following were to be agreed by a constitutional convention for a new independent Scotland (we might imagine this taking place as from the year 2020 – a perfect time for such utopian-democratic imagining!).

On the day a bill is introduced into Parliament, the Social Security numbers of, say, 10,000 citizens are drawn at random and ascribed to the bill. These citizens then receive notification that they have been empanelled to scrutinise the debate on the bill (the debate in Parliament and in wider society), so that, should the bill be approved by Parliament, they will then be asked to vote on it on behalf of their fellow citizens.

All the proceedings of the bill – in the chamber, in committee and report stage – would be shown live on national television and be available on-line; as would downloads and podcasts. Should the bill be passed all the members of this citizen-jury would receive a CD of the complete proceedings as well as the written parliamentary record.

On the due weekend for voting on the bill our citizen-jurors would be asked to vote either on-line or using a citizen swipe card (at libraries or perhaps supermarkets). Voting would be compulsory; though an option to abstain would be offered. If 5,001 or more citizens vote for the bill it goes to the President for popular assent to be registered and thereby enacted into law.

Should the bill fail to secure a simple majority Parliament would be asked to consider whether it wished the bill to be re-presented. Where support for the bill in the popular vote was low then we might assume this would be unlikely. Even so, but especially where the bill was narrowly defeated, Parliament could ask for a double jury (i.e. of 20,000 citizens) to be empanelled. Any given jury might, on the basis of random selection, contain particular biases. A second jury would be unlikely to mirror precisely the same bias. Doubling the jury would give greater assurance of avoiding particular bias.

A second defeat for the bill would mean that it could not be reintroduced during that parliament. A failure to secure popular support would not be treated as a matter of confidence in the government. Finance bills (budgets) would not normally be subject to popular support but be a reserved matter for Parliament alone.

If legislation runs at twenty bills a year then 200,000 citizens would be directly involved in the legislative process each year; each citizen (given current population figures) could thus expect to serve on average once every twenty years. Every citizen could expect to serve as a citizen-juror two or three times over their adult lifespan.

But there is also a wider engagement on offer here. The assumption is that the citizen-jurors selected will want to discuss the bill and the issues involved with friends and family and workplace colleagues. We might conjecture as many as a further five or ten citizens being engaged in this informal deliberative process; and so the total engaged each year in the legislative deliberations may be as many as half the entire electorate. Now that would be an active and engaged citizenry!

So, here we seem to have an example of Aristotle's 'rule and be ruled in turn' as the distinctive mark of the citizen. Aristotle was describing the duties of the citizen in classical Athens. We usually think of the Assembly as the great hallmark of Athenian democracy; but it was in the operations of the Council, the *Boulē*, that we can best see in action this principle of ruling and being ruled in turn. Five hundred citizens, fifty from each of the ten tribes of Athens, would serve for a year and constitute the Council, the formal administrative body of Athens. The following year another 500 citizens would be chosen; and so on. These citizens were neither appointed nor elected but chosen at random by lot, a process formally known as sortition. Although estimates vary, a not unreasonable figure for the citizen population of Athens is about 20,000. (Only male Athenians could be citizens.) Thus, on average most if not all citizens would be asked to serve as a member of the Council at least once during their lifetime (Aristotle 1996: 244–7).

If this was good enough for Athens and the *Boulē* then why should it not be good enough for Scotland and the citizen-juror now? In the sketch of a new citizenship above, citizens are to be drawn at random to exercise their office. This means there can be no assumption of pre-given expertise among the citizen-jurors: some may have expert knowledge, most won't. This in turn directs our attention to three key features. First, it puts an emphasis on education. Mill, we recall, argued that 'universal education' was a pre-condition for universal suffrage; that education, at least at the level of basic literacy and numeracy, was necessary for the responsible exercise of power. Whilst it is hard to attach this to the merely nominal power of the vote in a general election, we can see how it readily attaches to the effective power of the citizen-juror. We may not want to say that any given level of educational achievement is a pre-requirement for selection by lot as a citizen-juror; but we can see how we would want it to be the case that our citizens were in general well-educated. We would want to think that most of those chosen at random for the citizen-jury would cope with the information and the ideas presented to them. For us, the emphasis would be on the quality of the education offered to all, not on the educational attainment of any given individual. Education matters; but if we are going to ask citizens to be directly implicated in the act of legislation then it *really* matters for *all* citizens.

Second, the role of Parliament would be transformed. Although its principal legislative role would remain that of debating, amending and passing or rejecting bills, it would also have a clear educative role. Members of the Scottish Parliament would now be engaged in a project going beyond those in the chamber: of reaching out and explaining to and arguing with the wider population; including but not confined to, the citizen-jurors selected for that bill. The MSPs will not know who their 10,000 citizen-jurors are for any given bill. Their task in Parliament will be to speak to the nation and not to any given section of it. Each bill will demand justification in national and not sectional or regional terms; its content explained so as to be clear to all and not solely to party members, sectional or geographic interests, and so on.

Third: trust. This has been the subject of much discussion in recent years, but typically with a focus on the decline of trust in our public services, both institutions and professionals.[5] But it is trust between fellow citizens that must concern us here. To what extent would we trust our fellow citizens, each and any one of them, to act responsibly when it comes to legislating for us all? There is no simple answer to this and we can determine grounds for exclusion for many groups of citizens: the homeless, those in prison and those with unspent convictions . . . we might even feel tempted to go down Mill's line and insist on some level of educational attainment (five standard grades, perhaps?). Or we can argue that trust repays trust more often than not; and that in putting people in this sort of position of responsibility we create the conditions for citizens to become trustworthy. Not all will. We need not be perfectionist about this. But we do need to feel confident that the vast majority will repay that confidence and exercise their power in a trustworthy way.

But why use randomly selected as opposed to representative citizen-juries (carefully chosen to represent communities directly involved with any given bill)? The answer is challenging but simple: it is because we are asking citizens to act on behalf of their fellow citizens and not on their own behalf. To be empanelled as a citizen-juror precisely because one is, say, a university teacher or a police officer or home-carer for bills directly affecting universities or legal matters or lifelong care arrangements is to ask citizens to consider only their narrow self-interest. The assumption that lies beyond this proposal for the radical transformation of citizenship into the exercise of effective political power, involving the development of political literacy and the practice of active citizenship, is that ordinary citizens be asked to act in the interests of the political community as a whole.

Conclusion: active citizenship in the twenty-first century

John Stuart Mill thought that '. . . since all cannot, in a community exceeding a single small town, participate personally in any but some very minor portions of the public business, it follows that the ideal type of a perfect government must be representative' (Mill 2008: 256). For the nineteenth and twentieth centuries Mill's assumptions held and active citizenship in its political form meant engagement in local democracy and making sure one was informed and ready to argue about politics. One could choose to augment that engagement by standing for office, joining political parties, signing up for campaigns, and so on. All of this represented, and still does, good modes of active citizenship. But simply as a citizen, one's power was limited to the point where it was barely recognisable as *power*. We had either to organise ourselves by joining associations or to hand over our power to our representatives. But we need no longer be so hamstrung. Technological developments mean that twenty-first-century citizens can reclaim to themselves, simply as citizens, some of that power.

I have been deliberately provocative in much that I have offered here. For some, this will make it easy to dismiss as impractical, utopian. But there is also a very real, hard edge to these thoughts. If we are to take democracy seriously and to take active citizenship seriously, then we must talk about power and the power of the citizen. Bernard Crick was committed to a republican view of politics: one of argument and controversy; but also one of civic and citizen virtue. How else is that virtue to be developed fully other than through the exercise of power, the exercise of effective political power? The prospect of an independent Scotland offers us the opportunity for some speculative political thought; but it also offers us the opportunity to move forward in our thinking about, and practice of, democracy and active political citizenship.

Notes

1. Macmillan sacked seven members of his Cabinet on 13 July 1962. The term was used of Gordon Brown's Cabinet reshuffle by, among others, Martin Ivens, *The Sunday Times*, 7 June 2009.
2. See, for instance, 'A quiet revolution', *The Spectator*, 5 August 2009.
3. From the UK affirmation for jurors: http://www.hmcourts-service.gov.uk/infoabout/jury_service/oath_taking.htm.
4. The electoral roll for Scotland as of 2009 is 3,930,244 (General Register Office for Scotland: http://www.gro-scotland.gov.uk/statistics).
5. Thus, for instance, the Reith Lectures of 2002 given by Onora O'Neill, *A Question of Trust* (Cambridge; Cambridge University Press; see also: http://www.bbc.co.uk/radio4/reith2002/).

References

Aristotle (1996), *The Politics and the Constitution of Athens*, ed. S. Everson, trans. J. Barnes, Cambridge: Cambridge University Press.

Berman, Morris (2006), *The Twilight of American Culture*, London: Duckworth.

Francis, Kevin (2000), *Democracy as Qualified Popular Assent*, Glasgow: University of Strathclyde Papers in Government no. 115.

Held, David (2006), *Models of Democracy*, 3rd edn, Cambridge: Polity Press.

Horsburgh, H. J. N. (1960), 'The ethics of trust', *Philosophical Quarterly*, 10: 343–54.

Mill, John Stuart [1861] (2008), *Considerations on Representative Government*, in J. Gray (ed.), *John Stuart Mill: On Liberty and Other Essays*, Oxford: Oxford University Press.

Mill, John Stuart [1859] (2008), *On Liberty* in J. Gray (ed.) *John Stuart Mill: On Liberty and Other Essays*, Oxford: Oxford University Press.

Putnam, Robert (2001), *Bowling Alone: the Collapse and Revival of American Community*, London: Simon and Schuster.

Scottish Parliament Online (date unknown), 'About the Parliament'. Available at: http//www.scottish.parliament.UK/corporate/index.htm.

Identity Politics: Multiculturalism, Britishness and Europe

Bernard Crick

That every nation *should* constitute a state was an idea and an ideal of nineteenth-century European nationalism, arising from the French Revolution that spread throughout the world. Here in Britain we used to remember vividly the struggles of the Poles, the Hungarian's and Garibaldi's Italians against dynastic oppression. And at the end of the nineteenth century feudal Japan in the Mejii restoration adopted Western-style nationalism as well as Western science and industrial and military technology.

But in fact not every nation does constitute a state, and many states in Africa, South America and South East Asia have proved highly unstable as state and party bureaucracies try to create an artificial nation out of often highly diverse groups within externally fortuitously imposed colonial boundaries.

England was a state for almost 800 years before 1707 when a negotiated union with the slightly less ancient state of Scotland created the United Kingdom, which after 1800 (the Act of Union with Ireland, in fact the suppression of the Irish Parliament) became the United Kingdom of Great Britain and Ireland. And in 1922, with the secession of the Republic of Ireland, my country became the United Kingdom of Great Britain and Northern Ireland. But the English majority did not try to make the other three nations English. Anglicisation was not pursued in the French manner. So the United Kingdom is an example not only of a multinational state, consisting of four self-consciously diverse nations, but since 1707 a multicultural society. Scotland when it gave up its parliament for the sake of peace and to share in England's external trade and internal economy did not lose its intense national consciousness. Today of the 60 million or so inhabitants of the United Kingdom, the Scots constitute only a tenth and the Welsh half that. Northern Ireland has a mere million and a half inhabitants, smaller, for all its troubles to itself and others, than each of the six major cities of the mainland.

The Industrial Revolution gradually brought appreciable numbers of Scots immigrants into England, large numbers of poor Irish peasants migrated to Scotland and England, and in the late nineteenth and early twentieth century, Jews fleeing persecution in Russia, Poland and the Ukraine entered the United Kingdom, as Protestant Huguenots had entered from France a century and a half before. They are all now well enough integrated, and integrated through gradual social change more than by government policies. But originally they stirred quite as much prejudice and worry as did post-war immigrants from the 'third world'.

In the nineteenth century Great Britain was seen, all over the world, as the very model of a centralised sovereign state with representative government (well, more or less representative), and with, it was falsely believed, by the English as well, a high degree of cultural and religious homogeneity. Until quite recently statistical tables either did not differentiate Scotland and Wales or simply gave figures for England. The English tended to believe that these little local differences would soon iron themselves out and Scots and Welsh would inevitably become more or less English. Perhaps the English never felt the need to impose Englishness. The governing elite was happy enough amongst themselves and cried patriotism in time of war but were suspicious that nationalism, Englishness, was something popular, radical, even democratic, a myth of 'the people'. Ireland, of course was a different question.

But how many times did I hear twenty and thirty years ago the cry from Scottish orators 'we will lose our very identity if we do not regain our parliament'. But it seemed to me plain as a pikestaff that Scots had not lost their identity. In fact national consciousness is far less dependent on political institutions then most historians and political scientists have believed.

My passport calls me a 'citizen of the United Kingdom of Great Britain and Northern Ireland', but I notice that hotel registers demand 'nationality?' (a nationalist assumption, for the bureaucrat's question plainly means of what country am I a legal citizen). Most of my fellow citizens, I notice, write 'English' rather than 'British'. This is not merely because most of them are English, but because they ordinarily think that 'English' is the adjective corresponding to 'citizen of the United Kingdom of Great Britain and Northern Ireland'. Most English do not use the word British very much. Please reflect on the oddity that we compete in football as four separate nations not as the United Kingdom.

That the English confuse English with British angers me personally because my children are half Welsh, I came to live in Edinburgh, the capital of Scotland, with a Scottish partner – herself a signatory of 'The

Claim of Right'[1] – and Edinburgh is now the seat of a devolved Parliament with considerable powers. After the Act of Union Scotland retained its own legal, ecclesiastical and educational system, there was a kind of administrative federalism but not a political or legal federalism. And confusion of English and British irritates me intellectually precisely because I think it all too clear that the United Kingdom state is a union of different nations with significantly different cultures and histories.

The older generations of gentlemanly Conservative politicians, who were nicknamed Tories, knew this well. They knew that the main business of politics for almost three centuries had been holding the United Kingdom together. But the new breed of Thatcherite men on the make had none of the historical sense that the old gentry had possessed. Margaret Thatcher in speeches north of the border twice inadvertently referred to a strange country called 'England-oh-I-am-so-sorry-I-mean-Scotland-of-course'. English Labour leaders are more careful; a lot of their votes depend upon it. Scots are disproportionately well represented in Parliament and in the present Cabinet.

So some questions of national identity are not simple. Many of us in the United Kingdom have a strong sense of dual identity. I am obviously British and English, and as I have lived in Scotland for nearly twenty-five years and have been a prominent devolutionist, indeed while sceptical that a majority of Scots, even of SNP voters, want separation, I believe that a majority should have the right to separate if so they clearly wish. When I say that sincerely some people begin to think of me as Scottish and British, at least I hope so – despite my accent. Indeed all questions of identity are not simple. National identity exists alongside many other meanings of identity (Smout 2002). It does not always override them all, or not in every circumstance. Consider personal identity philosophically or psychologically. Three questions can be asked: how do each of you perceive yourselves, how do you want to be perceived by others, and how do others actually perceive you? These three questions are obviously related, but do not always give the same answer.

Then there are social identities, some more important than others, but all real: family, occupation, religion, neighbourhood, region, ethnicity; and clan was once as important in the Highlands and on the borders of Scotland as in pre-modern Japan. These identities can be cross-cut and complicated by class, religion and also by political and intellectual ideologies. Transnational or even international political identities have been obvious enough, such as commitment to types of socialism or convictions like democracy, civility or citizenship. Some of us in Britain think of ourselves as European in part, culturally and politically I mean not just ethnically; and this part-identity is stronger in the political classes in Scotland than in England. None of these identities are necessarily exclusive, all can overlap and have different intensities of affiliation and allegiance at different times; some by force of circumstance, some by individual choice. In the old pre-industrial world there was far less individual choice of identities, for many no real choice at all. When most people never left their locality, neighbourhood and region certainly counted for more than nation. But in the modern capitalist world of individualism, many fortunate or favoured individuals believe that they can choose and change identities almost at will, certainly to some significant extent – senior employees of international companies, for instance, especially oil-men and arms dealers.

We are in a capitalist world and global communications systems have created, for some professional or simply wealthy elites, choice of where to live, not just neighbourhood and region but country and continent. But not to forget that even in the old world many nobles dressed and spoke one way at court but another way in their own rural territories, sometimes a different language even. The Gaelic Scottish and Irish clan chieftains often, like some Slavic aristocrats, went to the expense of being painted twice, once in court dress and once in country cloth and wolf skins.

National identities have come to dominate the modern world more than ideological identities, but not always more, as we have been surprised to learn of late, than religious identities. The old feudal divisions of loyalty, even of languages, suited neither the needs of the new economies and market relationships, nor the bureaucratic and impersonal rather than the older dynastic ethos of the state – the state itself a modern political institution. There is no putting the clock back, even when ethnic nationalists turn racialist and persecute and purge minorities. But it is worth reminding ourselves of what is both a sociological and a moral proposition when we live in societies larger than ethnically defined tribes, specifically in a modern world of diverse values and interests: *that loyalties can never be exclusive*. Therefore even the claims of a national state cannot be exclusive, except by excessive force; and nor are national characteristics any longer, if they ever were, sufficient explanations and justifications of behaviour.

Academics take a long time to come to the point, especially old professors. Before I say what I think Britishness means, let me give just one historical example to show that national consciousness, the consciousness of being a nation, and nationalism, the belief that a nation should be a state, are different things.

When the great Queen Elizabeth died in 1602 without a direct heir, she was succeeded on a clear hereditary connection by the king of the great rival kingdom, James the Sixth of Scotland, who became James the First of England as well. Scots were then generally disliked by the English. But national feeling was not so strong in England that two other beliefs proved more important: first, the belief that family inheritance of property was part of the natural order – 'the great chain of being' – and that if a king's right to inherit even a kingdom as personal property was denied, everyone's right to inherit could be denied; but another belief was one so obvious in politics but so often ignored by political theorists and ideologists, even though Thomas Hobbes had written a masterpiece justifying it – his *Leviathan*: utility, usefulness, prudence, pragmatism we now say, and rational fear – that power should go to whoever can maintain and enforce law and peace and maximise our chances of dying in bed rather than on the battlefield with our boots on. Strong feelings of national identity were not in doubt in 1602, but this was not nationalism in the nineteenth-century separatist sense.

James the First and Sixth was a thoughtful man, for a king, and he would have liked to unify his two kingdoms as one government and one British people. But he was thwarted without great difficulty by both parliaments in each country acting quite independently of the other. For them he was king of two countries with different laws and law-making, not one. Multiple monarchies were not uncommon at that time in Europe. James styled himself 'King of Great Britain' but neither parliament endorsed that title.

Even after the negotiated Act of Union of 1707 between England and Scotland, which many Scots still call 'The Treaty of Union', Scottish consciousness remained strong; indeed in the eighteenth century famously it flourished, the Scottish Enlightenment, the envy of intellectual Europe. The act or treaty was a toughly negotiated political bargain, not a complete defeat or betrayal as legend was to make it seem. Modern Scottish nationalists lament the 'surrender of our parliament', but it was an unpopular medieval parliament, even more unrepresentative and corrupt than the English parliament of the time.

To this day older members of the Scottish National Party polemicise that unless Scotland regains her independence, her identity and way of life will wither away. They seem to assert the primacy of political institutions. But cool heads among Scottish historians and intellectuals point out that a distinctive, if changing, national way of life has survived almost 300 years without a parliament: the church, the law, the schools and literature have seen to that. Lindsay Paterson was the first among strongly national-minded intellectuals to argue this clearly and in convincing historical and sociological detail (Paterson 1994).

And much the same could be said for Wales. The Welsh Nationalist Party does not now press for independence but to maintain and enhance the privileged position of the Welsh language that they have won by peaceful political action. To them culture is more important than political independence.

The younger and middle generations of Scottish nationalist intellectuals recognised that the retention of the culture, a changing culture indeed, but with continuity and continued distinctiveness, is not dependent on a national political institution. They based their arguments for a parliament on democratic demand today and dual identities, not on a historically minded nationalism (see the exchanges between Stephen Maxwell and the late John Mackintosh; Drucker 1982). Indeed the Scottish National Party, now the second largest party in the Scottish Parliament, perhaps to be the largest after the May elections, now states its goal as 'independence in Europe', no longer independence as such. However, a majority of Scots want or are content with what they have now got, a subsidiary or quasi-federal parliament within the United Kingdom.

So the United Kingdom is not only a multinational state practicing, contrary to what was in all the old textbooks, a kind of quasi-federalism, but a state in which many people have a real sense of dual nationality. Most Scots see themselves, clearly enough, as Scottish and British.

In Northern Ireland nearly all Protestants and, it is often forgotten, about 20 per cent of Catholics, favour the Union. The conceptual difficulty among the majority in Northern Ireland is not in having a dual sense of identity and calling themselves British, but in agreeing what to call, how to conceptualise, their other local half: Ulstermen, Northern Irish, just Irish sometimes, or 'the Protestant people' – if they are Protestant. And their uncertainty is not helped by the undoubted fact that to the majority on the mainland they appear more foreign, certainly more obviously strangers, more obviously 'others' than do the Irish of the modern Republic of Ireland, or certainly than the large immigrant Catholic Irish population in England and Scotland, which is almost as large as the population of the Republic of Ireland.

The English are the most confused about national identity, confusing as they do 'English' with 'British'. And this has left them uncertain, sometimes angry, sometimes xenophobic, when faced with new circumstances. Among these circumstances was the post-war influx of immigrants from the 'new Commonwealth' which has certainly resulted in discrimination and revealed racial prejudice. How badly? Comparisons are difficult and circumstances differ so much. Unlike in Germany, there was no legal obstacle to full citizenship (though increasing legal obstacles to immigration itself), and unlike in France, the idea of an official campaign to 'nationalise' or 'naturalise' the immigrants has neither been debated nor attempted. The American public-school system emerged in the late nineteenth century specifically 'to Americanise the immigrants', and Americanism then, let it not be forgotten, was taught as a universal secular civic religion. But equally in Britain the theory of multicultural education, an admission of, acceptance of, even sometimes a positive welcoming of cultural diversity, has become only a half-hearted and somewhat confused policy, if national policy it ever has been at all.

But it is the new immigrants who have the clearest view as to the distinction between British and English. I have never heard anyone call themselves 'Black English' or 'Black Scottish'. They say 'Black British', or more and more they would say 'Asian British' or 'Afro-British', although there is now much anecdotal evidence that many Asians in Scotland call them themselves Scottish-Asians (but that does not at all put them in separatist ranks; they are plainly also British in their allegiance). I think that immigrants see instinctively that the adjective 'English' refers to a culture, as does Scottish and Welsh; but that British refers to an allegiance. The immigrant gives his or her allegiance to the state, in Britain symbolically the Crown. The immigrant rarely tries to become English: enough for legal citizenship to speak English. So 'British' is either not a cultural term at all, as we speak of Scottish, Welsh and English novels, poetry, music and folk song, but never of British novels, poetry, music and folk song. But if British is a cultural term at all, then it refers to a narrow if strong and important political and legal culture: the Union itself, the rule of law, the Crown and Parliament, perhaps the practice of a common political citizenship. But there's a lot of society and human life beyond these pillars of the state, the political and legal culture. And never forget that within the umbrella of Britishness there are three thriving national cultures, interactive indeed and also with Ireland. Is there any other state in the world that FIFA allows to field four national football teams?

Precisely because in days gone by the main business of English politics was holding the multinational United Kingdom together, the majority English to a large extent suppressed an explicitly English nationalism not to provoke the others. Indeed they actually encouraged and patronised Irish, Welsh and Scottish culture – so long as it did not take a politically separatist form. Imperialism, of course, could become a good substitute for a comprehensive nationalism. In Ireland the tactic of cultural tolerance failed, but in Wales and Scotland it succeeded. But this has left, paradoxically, English self-consciousness the most uncertain. Conservatives often feel that England has been neglected in the interests of Scots, the Welsh and of integrating the new immigrants; and liberals and social democrats often feel that to be nationally conscious, which they should be, is to be aggressively nationalistic, which none of us should be. To be patriotic, to love one's country is one thing; but to be nationalistic, to believe in its superiority, is quite another. I end this part of the argument by endorsing a growing paradox, a paradox to Scottish and Welsh nationalists: that the English should no longer suppress their Englishness and should see what it means to be both English and British, not to swallow the one in the other.

This takes us to Mr Gordon Brown and his recent spate of speeches on Britishness. It could also take us to Mr Blair and Mr Blunkett, but time and life are too short. When he characterises Britishness, it is in terms of a civic culture. I quote:

> The values and qualities I describe are of course to be found in many other cultures and countries. But when taken together, and as they shape the institutions of our country these values and qualities – being creative, adaptable and outward looking, our belief in liberty, duty and fair play – add up to a distinctive Britishness that has been manifest throughout our history, and shaped it. (Brown 2004; see also Brown 2006; Lee 2006)

Now I find these quite acceptable as generalities – as usual the devil will be in the detail, how such values appear in practice and policy, or sometimes disappear in practice. But I will not be going into that now. As I have said, these are indeed strong values of Britishness, if more narrow, less comprehensive, than many commonly think. Britishness needs rounding out, however, with a narrative of three nations, at least, and Northern Ireland and Islam need more empathy than exhortation to abide by a common civic culture. But this is precisely what Brown does not do. Not merely is there this understatement of the exact nature of the Union, but the examples he gives of our long British tradition, he says, of civic values are all English. The myth of the importance of Magna Carta is once again disinterred and ne'er a word on the Declaration of Arbroath. The Bill of Rights is fundamental to Britishness, which would have surprised the English legislators of 1689. And he invokes Milton, Wordsworth, Edmund Burke and Orwell as British rather than, it seems to me, typically English voices. Significantly, Walter Scott and Robert Burns are, for once ignored, though both are unionists, powerful voices for a dual not a single identity.

Continuity is also a Brownite theme of Britishness. For, he tells us, we have never had a revolution or a foreign conquest since 1066. This does rather ignore the interlocking civil wars in the three kingdoms of the mid-seventeenth century and also a Dutch fleet and army in 1688.

Brown clearly wants us to believe that a heightened Britishness is necessary to hold the Union together rather than simply a rational calculation of mutual advantage and – as David Hume would have said – habit. So he is attacking the SNP in Scotland with the wrong weapon. He plays into their hands by confusing nationalism as tradition and as national consciousness with nationalism as separatism. Identity politics may come a poor second to pragmatic worries about disruption and scepticism about the economic benefits of separation. Also he ignores the comforting fact that about a third of SNP voters favour the Union and are uncomfortable that many SNP voters are old Labour voters most unhappy with New Labour. Politically, of course, he walks a tightrope: British Brown for Middle England is neither music to Scottish ears nor faces squarely the task of persuading English voters to distinguish Englishness from Britishness and to be both.

Brown's disappointing mixture of rhetoric, bad history and perhaps a wee poke of political opportunism comes out clearly in the mission statement or *sloaghan* he had drafted for a conference hosted by HM Treasury in November 2005.

> How 'British' do we feel? What do we mean by 'Britishness'?
> These questions are increasingly important in defining a shared purpose across all of our society. The strength of our communities, the way we understand diversity, the vigour of our public services and our commercial competitiveness all rest on a sense of what 'Britishness' is and how it sets shared goals.

So Britishness must express 'a shared purpose' and 'shared goals'? And he wants this to be taught in 'the new citizenship curriculum', forgetting that it only applies to schools in England. (As former chair of the committee whose report brought in the schools' citizenship curriculum for England, based on learning for active participation, I have protested strongly against the sudden proposals of ministers, including Brown, to include 'the values of Britishness as shown in social and cultural history'.)

Such language is like that of the old-fashioned nationalism of central Europe between the two world wars. But is that really how states hold together, especially in the modern world of, whether we like it or not, a global economy and of all notions of national sovereignty needing to be so qualified as to be almost useless in understanding actual politics? (See my 'The sovereignty of Parliament and the Irish question' and 'On devolution, decentralism and the constitution', Crick 1990.)

This idea of national purpose is what Goethe called 'a blue rose'. And the search for it could prove damaging as well as frustrating. Both Thatcher and Blair openly speak of restoring our sense of national importance, a hangover from the days of Empire and the Second World War – which, of course, we won, with a little help from the USA and the USSR.

The only way to box above our declining weight, fatally assuming that we need to box above our weight, has been, of course, to tie ourselves to the coat-tails of the United States, no matter whether Clinton or Bush was President both embodying very different rival national identities. Indeed if one must talk about British national identity, there has been at least different conservative and radical versions.

Perhaps it is thinking that the United Kingdom lacks a unified national culture and purpose that makes so many English (more so than Scots) nervous of European Union, prone to fear mythic monsters like 'a federal superstate' (if it was federal it could not be a superstate at all). Belief in the sovereignty of Parliament lingers on: federal implies Parliament being restrained by constitutional law, a terrible thought to many of the English political elite from Blackstone to Blair. All this is strengthened by Blair's presidential populist style. All demagogues appeal to an unthinking patriotism. A thinking patriotism can appreciate, value and respect complexity.

However many times have we all heard pundits quote the words of that former American Secretary of State Dean Acherson: 'Great Britain had lost an Empire and has not yet found a role'? But ten years ago I became curious to see the context of that sentence. Curiosity was rewarded by the archivist at West Point Military Academy. For the Anglophile but wise and shrewd Acherson went on to say:

> The attempt to play a separate role – that is, a role apart from Europe, a role based on a 'special relationship' with the United States, a role based on being head of a 'Commonwealth' which has no political structure, or unity, or strength and enjoys a fragile precarious economic relationship by means of the Sterling area and preferences in the British market – this role is about played out. Great Britain, attempting to work alone and to be a broker between the United States and Russia, has seemed to conduct policy as weak as its military power. HMG is now attempting – wisely, in my opinion, to re-enter Europe, from which it was banished at the time of the Plantagenets, and the battle seems about as hard fought as those of an earlier day. (Speech of 5 December, 1962 at the United States Military Academy, West Point. The full text is in their library)

I rest my case. I leave you to consider either that our rulers have been playing the wrong kind of game of national purpose and identity politics or whether that game is itself mistaken. Certainly Blair's conceit that he could be a bridge between Europe and the United States is blown. And perhaps rather than a world role under a pretend world leader, we would be left with ourselves and our partners in Europe. Is that too bad? I think not.

NOTE

1. This is a document of 1988 written by a diverse group of Scottish notables asserting both the right to a devolved parliament and, should a majority of the people in Scotland wish, independence (Edwards 1989).

REFERENCES

Brown, Gordon (2004), 'Britishness', Speech of 8 July, the British Council Annual Lecture.

Brown, Gordon (2006), 'The future of Britishness', Speech of 14 January, Fabian Society's Conference.

Crick, Bernard (1990), *Political Thoughts and Polemics*, Edinburgh: Edinburgh University Press.

Drucker, Henry (ed.) (1982), *John P. Mackintosh on Scotland*, London: Longman.

Edwards, Owen Dudley (ed.) (1989), 'For my fellow English', in O. D. Edwards, *A Claim of Right for Scotland*, Edinburgh: Polygon.

Lee, Simon (2006), 'Gordon Brown and the "British Way"', *Political Quarterly*, July–September.

Paterson, Lindsay (1994), *The Autonomy of Modern Scotland*, Edinburgh: Edinburgh University Press.

Smout, Thomas C. (2002), his entry in Tom Devine and Paddy Logue (eds), *Being Scottish*, Edinburgh: Edinburgh University Press, pp. 245–7.

Index